The Judge Is the Savior

To Ruth
With very much love

mum

X

march 2015

The Judge Is the Savior

Towards a Universalist Understanding of Salvation

By Jean Wyatt

Foreword by
Rod Garner

RESOURCE *Publications* · Eugene, Oregon

Resource Publications
An Imprint of Wipf and Stock Publishers
199 W. 8th Ave., Suite 3
Eugene, OR 97401

www.wipfandstock.com

ISBN 13: 978-1-62564-817-4

Manufactured in the U.S.A.   02/16/2015

Permission to use the diagram on p.142 courtesy of MacDonald, Gregory. *The Evangelical Universalist.* London: SPCK, 2008.

Dedicated to those who want to explore "How wide and long and high and deep is the love of Christ, and to know this love that surpasses knowledge" (Eph 3:18–19).

You are worthy O Christ,
for you were slain
and with your blood
you redeemed the human race for God;
and have chosen us to be a holy priesthood
from every people and nation.

—*METHODIST SERVICE BOOK*

Contents

Foreword

THE POET WILLIAM BUTLER Yeats once described his poetry in terms of "the quarrel with ourselves."[1] It represented his wrestling with personal experience, conscience and the challenges posed by an ambiguous world that can seem indifferent to our deepest hopes or expectations. Yeats' quote came naturally to me as I read this moving, thoughtful, and deeply personal book, which attempts to grapple with a major stumbling block for Christian truth claims: the doctrine of everlasting punishment for unbelievers. Jean Wyatt has been troubled by this hard teaching for many years. Her varied life and vocation as a medical practitioner has compelled her to question and reformulate some basic scriptural teachings in a way that aligns the implications of divine judgment with tutored moral sense. It is an urgent read, informed by a searching acquaintance with the Bible and some of the key elements of Christianity, most notably the nature of the Christian hope. To this task she brings personal testimony and an evident love of the rich and varied Christian tradition that has shaped her faith and understanding. She works on a wide canvas, drawing on an impressive range of reading material that illuminates her concerns. The result is an accessible and well-constructed testimony. Step by step, we are led down familiar and sometimes unexpected paths (with interesting asides on the way) but always with the aim of moving the reader to a deeper awareness of why this implacable theological difficulty still matters and how it might be resolved without jettisoning one set of dogmatic beliefs for another. The "middle way" that she has chosen is brave and will be of help to conscientious believers or seekers troubled by the notion of a savage God or the promise of a heaven that is available only to relatively few. I commend her work and the persistence that has brought it to birth. I hope that many will profit from its wisdom and moral clarity.

Canon Dr. Rod Garner
Theologian to the Diocese of Liverpool

1. Yeats, "Anima Hominis" in *Essays* (1924), quoted in Ratcliffe, *Oxford Dictionary of Quotations*, 367.

Acknowledgments

THIS IS AN UNDERTAKING that has taken me about forty years of thinking, praying, and reading. My thanks go to those friends who have taken an interest in the project; several of you have read chapters and made suggestions or have otherwise encouraged me.

My particular thanks go to Michael Tunnicliffe, whose excellent teaching has given me some understanding of church history to act as a backdrop to the work; he has also carefully read several chapters, and I am grateful for his endorsement of the book.

My deepest thanks go to Rev. Rod Garner, an inspiring and thought-provoking teacher, who always invites his students to think through challenging issues. He kindly read my manuscript at a preliminary stage, encouraged me to continue the project, and has read later versions as the book has developed. He has continued to encourage me, and has kindly written the foreword to this book. I am most grateful for all his support.

Finally, my thanks go to my husband, who has patiently suffered being something of a computer-widower for the many years that it has taken me to research and write this book.

Introduction

Why This Book Was Written

"I can indeed hardly see how anyone ought to wish Christianity to be true; for if so the plain language of the text seems to show that the men who do not believe, and this would include my father, brother and almost all of my friends, will be everlastingly punished. And this is a damnable doctrine."

—CHARLES DARWIN, *AUTOBIOGRAPHY*[1]

1. Quoted in McGrath, *Dawkins' God*, 75. McGrath comments that in October 1882, six months after Darwin's death, his widow wrote in the margins of her husband's manuscript at this point: "I should dislike the passage in brackets to be published . . . Nothing can be said too severe upon the doctrine of everlasting punishment for disbelief—but very few now would call that 'Christianity.'" Perhaps that is why the biography of Darwin I read did not contain this passage, though it showed that Darwin had other problems with Christianity and that he moved from considering entering the priesthood to a position of agnosticism.

Many Victorians rejected the doctrine of "everlasting punishment for unbelievers," including my great uncle, Dr. Basil Morley, who in 1870 wrote to a friend: "It seems very strange that an inexperienced and raw youth like myself should object on conscientious grounds from accepting a religion received by such a number of good and clever men . . . I can only say, 'I would if I could . . . as without doubt Christianity is at present the salt of the earth . . . yet I cannot believe that a God all-good and all-powerful would make a revelation to his creation on the acceptance of which depended their eternal happiness—and yet a great number of them never knew whether it was a revelation from him or not" (collection of the author). I do not know how Uncle Basil solved the issue, but a window is erected in his honor in Saint Aubin Methodist Church, Jersey, UK.

IN 1974 MY FAMILY was worshipping in a friendly Baptist church. The worship and preaching were dynamic and the fellowship warm, but there was one drawback: the church had a formidable doctrinal basis to which members should assent. It was the last statement that I found so difficult:

> We believe in the judgment by the Lord Jesus Christ at His coming again, of all men; of believers to eternal blessedness, of unbelievers to eternal condemnation.[2]

Starkly and brutally, it stated the way that God would judge.

We either have eternal blessedness, or eternal condemnation. And we can know where we stand. We can know that we are saved . . . and perhaps that our friends are not . . . in fact it looks as if most people will be under "eternal condemnation,"[3] because most people do not believe in the Lord Jesus Christ.

I came across other devastating comments:

In 1981 Martin Goldsworth challenged the Christian Union members at the Scottish UCCF conference: "Do you really care that 98% of the students in your university are going to hell?"[4] and similarly, Dick Dowsett states that "98% of Asia is a write-off."[5]

Of course, such statistics are only a guess, proclaimed to shock Christians into spreading the gospel (and thus hopefully keeping a few more from eternal condemnation)—but a guess that is based on doctrine similar to our church statement. That is, orthodox evangelical doctrine based on some well-known passages of the bible.

For example, John writes, "Whoever believes in him is not condemned, but whoever does not believe stands condemned already because he has not believed in the name of God's one and only son."[6]

2. "Constitution: Doctrinal Point 6," Boroko Baptist Church, Port Moresby, Papua New Guinea, 1974. See also http://borokobaptistchurch.weebly.com/what-we-believe.html.

3. When nearing the completion of this book, I came across William Barclay's very helpful book *The Apostle's Creed*. He interprets *kolasis aionion*, or "eternal punishment" (Matt 25:46), as "a disciplinary, curative punishment, and it certainly describes the punishment which only God can inflict" (Barclay, *Apostles' Creed*, 190) See p.172–173. This makes it easier to accept the above doctrinal statement. But at the time—some forty years ago—I felt that I could not do so, and this book is the result of my long struggle with the issues involved. I am grateful for the fact that the statement motivated me to think things through to some sort of conclusion.

4. A talk by Martin Goldsworth, quoted in *Share* (Summer 1982).

5. Dowsett, *God, That's Not Fair!* 2.

6. John 3:18. See John 3:16–20. See also John 3:36; 5:24; 9:41, and Rom 10:9–11.

And in Matthew we find: "Wide is the gate and broad is the road that leads to destruction, and many enter through it. But small is the gate and narrow the road that leads to life, and only a few find it."[7]

We are taught that the few who find the road to life (and are therefore destined for heaven) are those who have been born again, or who have believed in Jesus and so entered into his grace. But the rest, "the many" who have not believed, are eternally condemned (whatever that means).[8] And even if, aided by our earnest prayers and by laying down our lives for others, God saves a few more . . . still so many will *not* be saved . . .

The teaching seems to be undeniably orthodox—the flip-side of the glorious gospel of grace—and many lovely, kind Christian people seem to live quite happily with a belief system that includes this doctrine in all its starkness. Have they really allowed the impact of what they say they believe to sink into their hearts? Or have I misunderstood?

How can we call our gospel "good news" if such statements encapsulate the ultimate summary of the judgment of God? And how can we speak of the "unconditional love of God" when we go on to hedge that love with conditions ("You have to accept it and believe, or you will be condemned") that may mean anything from annihilation to eternal torment?

And how can we sing of the "Amazing grace . . . that saved a wretch like me"[9] if we believe that the majority of mankind—including many people we know, love, admire, and know to be honorable and caring—are not under grace because they do not believe in Jesus, and so are apparently heading for "eternal condemnation"? Or, to put it bluntly, the majority of mankind are heading for hell or destruction . . . if this doctrine is right.

In the crucible of real life as a doctor (now retired), how can I speak authentically with a person who is facing death without faith if I am supposed to believe that he or she is heading for hell because of unbelief? How can I speak of a God of love (or believe in him myself) when ministering to one whom I presume to be dangling over the pit?

Or should I be striving to persuade such a person to a deathbed repentance in order to "flee from the wrath that is to come,"[10] which would

7. Matt 7:13–14.

8. Based on Jesus' teaching to Nicodemus in John 3:3–8.

9. John Newton wrote the hymn "Amazing Grace" in 1772. Two hundred years later, in 1972 an instrumental version of this hymn by the Scots Dragoon Guards spent five weeks as "Top of the Pops."

10. Matt 3:7; Luke 3:7. This phrase was used by John Bunyan in *Pilgrim's Progress*.

force me into a "bible-bashing" role out of step with those who work empathically with the terminally ill.[11]

Sometimes such a belief can hit home with disturbing effect.

I recall a woman who wept for years after her husband's death, not so much because he had died, but because he had died an "unrepentant sinner." Her faith was of no comfort to her, for though she herself could continue to love and forgive her husband, she believed that God would only forgive him if he had repented and believed. So she wept, but dared not pray for him, because protestant orthodoxy leaves no room for prayer for the dead. She believed he faced eternal condemnation and hell. Friends seeking to comfort her suggested that he might have repented in his dying moments, but she had been present when he died and seen no discernible sign of a deathbed repentance, so according to her belief system, there was no chance of redemption after death.

This scenario could lead to the unlikely conclusion that a grieving widow could be more merciful than God.

It may be thought that the fear of hell can lead sinners to repentance and that the desire to rescue others from such a fate should motivate Christians to evangelize. But what kind of love is it that has to use such fear as its motivation? It is just as likely to turn people away, as it seems to have done for Darwin, as seen in the quotation that opens this introductory chapter, and my uncle Basil (see n.1 p. xiii) and surely many others.

I once experienced a very negative reaction to the gospel when, in a fit of evangelical zeal, I gave a little booklet about salvation to a needy patient. It included a fairly strong statement about the danger of hell for unbelievers. The booklet was almost thrown back at me at his next visit with the dismissive words: "Well, I'm going to hell then. But I don't believe it!"[12]

It may have been about that time that I wrote this little poem:

11. It occurs to me that Jesus himself made no recorded appeal to the "unrepentant thief" to turn to him as he was dying on the cross (Luke 23:39).

12. I have learned to be extremely circumspect in my use of evangelistic pamphlets and tracts. A brief tract is necessarily an abstraction of a huge body of thought— but what is abstracted and what is left out, as well as the overall tone of the thing, can vary enormously. It is indeed difficult to pitch it right.

Have we not, O Lord, missed the point,

as we hem your death with our theology?

For you died for all men.

Your cross towers over the world for sinner and saint.

You died between two thieves:

in the place of Barabbas, and me.

For the sin of the world you shed your blood.

But we narrow it to believers, the born again;

and believe that lost mankind will go to hell . . .

To them we should show your light.

Is this poem a pious hope, a sign that I have not comprehended the exceeding sinfulness of sin? Or is it an insight into the meaning of the gospel and the compassionate heart of God? That is the burden of this inquiry, and my prayer is that what I write will be in line with what God wills to say to the church in this twenty-first century.

In the end, it has to rest with God himself.

The task I have set myself is an awesome one indeed, perhaps one that only a fool would undertake. Yet a certain foolish doggedness seems to compel me to persist—mainly by exploring the biblical witness (which is many-layered and composite), though I will also take a few relevant glimpses at church history.

I do not want to replace one dogma (which I find distasteful) with another (that I find more palatable), but I am personally convinced that in the end, God's love—revealed to us in the crucifixion of Christ—will ultimately triumph over his wrath, and his saving grace will triumph over his condemnation of sinful mankind. Love Wins.[13]

I know that many good Christian people will disagree with me, but I hope that there will be others who will welcome this book. Not all Christians share the belief crystalized in the doctrinal statement above, and thankfully the historic creeds that state that Christ will judge do not presume to state how he will judge.[14]

---

13. *Love Wins* is the apt title of a recent book by Rob Bell. He quotes various church's doctrinal statements (Bell, *Love Wins*, 95–97) similar to the one which started the inquiry that has, after many years, led to this book. He seems to feel much the same as I do about such statements of faith.

14. The Apostle's Creed simply states that "Jesus Christ . . . shall come to judge the living and the dead."

I find encouragement and great hope in the fact that the Judge will be the Savior: "the lamb slain from the creation of the world;"[15] "the lamb of God, who takes away the sin of the world."[16]

The Format of the Book

The book has developed into an exploration of some of the major themes of the Christian faith, with each chapter looking at an aspect of that faith through the lens of one of the sentences of the Lord's Prayer and a possible universalist viewpoint, but it does not aim to be a commentary on that most profound of all prayers. I am acutely aware that I am not a trained theologian, and the book is certainly not an exhaustive exposition of Christian doctrine, but if it prompts some debate on these important issues, it will have served its purpose.

15. Rev 13:8. See also Rev 5:6; 14:1.
16. John 1:29.

1

Father, Hallowed Be Your Name

When did He begin to love you? When He began to be God, and that was never, for He ever was, without beginning and without end. Even so, He always loved you from eternity.

—SAINT FRANCIS DE SALES, SIXTEENTH CENTURY

What does the Lord require of you?
To act justly and to love mercy, and to walk humbly with your God.

—MIC 6:8

WHEN WE PRAY, AS Jesus taught us: "Father, hallowed be your name,"[1] we hold together the intimacy and the otherness of God, his love and his holiness: two fundamental (and apparently opposite) faces of our God.

God loves us with the compassion of a parent, even from before the beginning of time, and like any earthly parent, he cares—enormously—how we treat each other, and how we treat him.

It matters to him because he loves us and is opposed to our sinfulness, injustice, and rebellion.

So he is our loving, holy and just judge, whose name is to be revered, honored, and *hallowed*.

---

1. Luke 11:2.

1

But as we read our Bibles, there often seems to be an extraordinary tension between the love and the holy wrath of God. Passages of frightening wrath and judgment are juxtaposed with passages of poignant tenderness and wonderful promises of restoration. Vengeance and redemption seem to go hand in hand. There are passages that (if taken literally) might imply that God has punishments in reserve that make the death-camps of Ravensbrück and Auschwitz look merciful.[2] However, other passages give inspiring vistas of the salvation of all peoples[3] and the restoration of all things[4] (which we will explore in chapter 7.) Paradoxes abound, especially in the areas of the justice and mercy of God and the eternal destiny of human beings.

There are plentiful accounts of God's anger with men, and his severe judgment, even his curses on his sinful people.

Adam and Eve are rejected from the garden of Eden;[5] there is the devastation of the flood, the scattering of proud mankind at Babel, and the wandering of the disobedient people of God in the wilderness. Deuteronomy 28 lists wonderful blessings in store for the Israelites if they obey God, followed by a much longer section of terrible curses if they disobey him. The "historical books" (which the Jews regard as prophetic books) seem to be based on the criteria laid out in Deut 28 and usually imply that when Israel prevailed, it was because the king did "that which was good in the eyes of the Lord," while when things went wrong, it was a punishment against the king or the people for doing "that which was evil in the eyes of the Lord."[6]

Long sections of the prophets deal with God's threats not only to his disobedient "chosen people," but even more catastrophically, to the surrounding nations, who are often seen as wicked and deserving of punishment. God is portrayed as a God of both wrath *and* salvation.

Recently, in a group studying Isaiah, we found the oscillation between prophesies of devastating judgment and wonderful promises of restoration to be mind-blowing and even confusing at times. For example,

2. See Mark 9:48 (also vv. 44 and 46, omitted in some MSS) quoting Isa 66:24; 2 Thess 1:9; 2 Pet 3:7; Rev 14:9–11; 20:9–15, etc.

3. See John 1:29; Phil 2:10–11 (which is resonant with Isa 45:22–23); Col 1:20; 1 Tim 2:3–6, to cite but a few.

4. See Col 1:20; Phil. 2:10–11, and the "Apokatastasis" (Acts 3:21). See also chapter 7.

5. Gen 3:16–19, 23–24.

6. Jer 52:2–3.

one realizes with an almost physical shock that the vengeance of God appears to be the very agent of salvation in this joyous hymn about return from exile and the ultimate restoration of both people and nature:

> Here is your God. He will come with vengeance, with terrible recompense. He will come and save you. Then the eyes of the blind shall be opened, and the ears of the deaf unstopped; then the lame shall leap like a deer, and the tongue of the speechless sing for joy. For waters shall break forth in the wilderness, and streams in the desert.[7]

God's vengeance is sometimes directed against his chosen people, the Jews. The prophets saw their defeats and the exile into Babylon as a punishment for idolatry and apostasy, and perhaps even more for injustice and the oppression of the poor by the rich. The vengeance is later directed against the oppressors themselves, as Babylon falls to the Persians. God's wrath is against sin (which he hates), not against his people (whom he loves). The book of Isaiah closes with a final devastating apposition of what looks like universal salvation with the destruction and apparently endless torture of those who rebelled against the Lord—which could be part of a classic picture of hell:

> "From one New Moon to another and from one Sabbath to another, all mankind will come and bow down before me," says the Lord. "And they will go out and look upon the dead bodies of those who rebelled against me; their worm will not die, nor will their fire be quenched, and they will be loathsome to all mankind."[8]

However, we need to remind ourselves that Isaiah is not thinking here of the fire of an everlasting hell, but the physical valley of Gehenna where dead bodies were thrown (see chapter 6, p. 150–151).

The Lord's final coming is often visualized as a cleansing fire. So it is that Malachi prophecies, "Who can stand when he appears? For he will be like a refiner's fire or a launderer's soap. He will sit as a refiner and purifier of silver."[9]

Perhaps restoration and salvation are possible *only through* the destruction and elimination of evil—often portrayed as the destruction and

7. Isa 35: 4–6.
8. Isa 66:23–24.
9. Mal 3:2.

elimination of *evil people*. We will look in more depth at concepts surrounding the final elimination of evil in chapters 5, 6, and 7.

Turning to the New Testament, we find that although its main thrust is the good news of salvation through Christ, this is set against the shadow of God's wrath against sin. Jesus warns that those who allow even their imagination, their eye, or their hand to offend will be in danger of hell;[10] Ananias and Sapphira are struck dead for lying to the early church, and thus to God;[11] the letters and the book of Revelation also contain many dire threats and warnings of judgment to come . . . I could go on, and fill this entire book with the warnings, the dooms, the woes, and the threats of judgment that we find in the pages of our Bibles, but I have made the point. Anyone who reads the Bible will soon come across such passages. They permeate every book.

The Coming of Jesus Christ Reveals How God Deals with Sin and Its Results

The tension between God's love and his wrath erupts in the crucifixion of Jesus such that in the very midst of heaven, John sees a vision of "a lamb slain before the foundation of the world."[12] Similarly, the author of the second letter to Timothy writes:

> This grace was given to us in Christ Jesus before the beginning of time, but it has now been revealed through the appearing of our Savior, Christ Jesus, who has destroyed death and has brought life and immortality to light through the gospel.[13]

Jesus' death revealed what has always been true since before the beginning of time—since before the "Big Bang" (if the widely accepted theory of the "how" of creation is correct).[14] When we look at the cross, it is as if we see the cross-section of a tree that has been sawn across, revealing a

---

10. Matt 5:21–30.

11. Acts 5:1–10.

12. Rev 5:6; 13:8.

13. 2 Tim 1:9b–10. See also 1 Pet 1:18–20: "It was not with perishable things such as silver or gold that you were redeemed . . . but with the precious blood of Christ, a lamb without blemish or defect. He was chosen before the creation of the world, but was revealed in these last times for your sake," and Eph 1:4 "He chose us in him before the creation of the world to be holy and blameless in his sight."

14. See also Eph 1:4; 2 Thess 2:13.

darker ring. We only see a ring, but we know that there is in fact a cylinder of darker wood that goes up and down the whole length of the tree.[15]

After the resurrection, Peter—who had been confused and totally bereft by the crucifixion of his master but had come to realize that this was part of God's plan—inspired by the Holy Spirit, boldly proclaimed: "Men of Israel . . . This man [Jesus of Nazareth] was handed over to you *by God's set purpose and foreknowledge*; and you, with the help of wicked men, put him to death by nailing him to the cross."[16] A little later, Peter again said to the Jewish leaders, "Now brothers, I know that you acted in ignorance, as did your leaders, but this is how God fulfilled what he had foretold through all the prophets, saying that his Christ would suffer."[17] Later, the believers prayed to God: "They did what your power and will had decided beforehand should happen."[18] It is clear that the Christians soon realized that what had happened was part of God's plan. The victory was God's—not the evil powers who had crucified Jesus.

So let us explore what the life and death of Jesus signifies in God's great scheme of things.

Jesus Was Fully Human and Fully Divine

Christians believe that Jesus of Nazareth, who was born about the year 4 BC[19] and crucified by the Romans as a would-be revolutionary in about AD 30, was both fully human and fully God.

Jesus' humanity is everywhere evident in the gospels, and he delights to call himself "the Son of Man"[20] or "the Human One," to use the

15. This analogy is credited to Peter Abelard.

16. Acts 2:22–23, emphasis mine.

17. Acts 3:17.

18. Acts 4:28.

19. I am using the traditional BC (Before Christ) and AD (Anno Domini) dating convention, rather than the more modern BCE (Before the Common Era) and CE (Common Era) because it expresses an idea which is fundamental to this book: Jesus is Lord. If that is not true, this book is waste of time, a tale told by an idiot.

20. See Mark 14:62; Matt 8:20; 9:6, 10:23, etc. This phrase also echoes Daniel's vision in Dan 7:13–14, where "one like the Son of Man" was given dominion over all peoples, nations and languages. It may be that Jesus was appropriating this image of a cosmic figure rather than emphasizing his humanity when he used the phrase. Wright deals with this in his *Jesus and the Victory*, especially 512–19. By describing himself as the "Son of Man," Jesus may also have seen himself as fulfilling the role that Israel should have fulfilled, including the role of the servant as foreseen in the various

evocative phrase used in the Common English Bible. The phrase appeals to me not only because it is gender-neutral, but also because it captures the idea of Jesus as a fully human being.

The gospels portray Jesus as a wandering Jewish teacher, prophet, preacher, and teacher, as a healer and worker of miracles, and as an extraordinary, unconventional, and charismatic figure untrammeled by the religious constrictions of his time, but undoubtedly as a human being.

He ate and drank, became exhausted and slept, felt anger and sorrow.

But after his resurrection, his disciples came to believe that although he was indeed a fully human being (perhaps *the most* fully human being of all time), he was also God. He was God revealing himself to humanity by becoming one of us; he was God *incarnate*.[21]

Glimpses of this understanding are seen in such passages as the beautifully poetic prologue to John's Gospel:

> In the beginning was the Word, and the Word was with God, and the Word was God. He was with God in the beginning. Through him all things were made; without him nothing was made that has been made."[22]

Several of Paul's letters also imply that Jesus Christ is the fully divine creator of all things, who will one day judge all things and restore all things[23]—both actions that were expected of God himself—despite the fact that such ideas would have been a quantum leap for a good, monotheistic Jew like Paul to have made. Before Paul's radical experience of the risen Christ, which totally transformed his worldview, he (like any other pious Jew) would have reacted rather like the first-century Jewish philosopher and historian Philo, who expressed absolute horror that the Romans deified their leaders. For Philo, the change from man to god "was no small one but an absolutely fundamental one, namely the apparent transformation of the created, destructible nature of man into the uncreated, indestructible nature of God, which the Jewish nation judged to be the most horrible of blasphemies; for God would change into man sooner than man into God."[24]

"servant prophecies," especially in Isaiah.

21. "Incarnate" comes from the Latin, and literally means "into flesh."

22. John 1:1–3.

23. See Eph 1:10,22; Col 1:15–20; Phil 2:6–11.

24. Philo of Alexandria, quoted in O'Grady, *And Man Created God*, 35.

The concept that Jesus Christ was God *incarnate* became a philosophical minefield in the early church, and it took more than three hundred years of thinking, debating, arguing, and fighting to work out in detail just how this could be. Many early Christian theologians[25] were educated in Greek philosophy, and perhaps they argued for too much precision as they tried to comprehend the incomprehensible: Did God have twins, Jesus and the Holy Spirit? Did Jesus have one nature or two? Did he have one will or two?[26] And how, if Jesus was God, did he relate to the Father to whom he taught his disciples to pray? It is beyond the scope of this book to say more than that the New Testament portrays Jesus as *both* fully human and fully divine, without attempting to work out in philosophical terms how both statements could be true. I shall follow the New Testament and leave it to theologians to debate how this can be so! This is not to imply that the debates about the nature of Christ and his relationship with the Father were trivial; they were vital, but are beyond the purview of this book. The Christian understanding of our salvation is based in the fact that he is both human and divine. He suffers wrath as a representative human being—in our place; and as God, who carries our sin and sorrow himself, he bears it away, and deals with it.

Sadly (from a Christian point of view), but perhaps not surprisingly, most Jews do not accept the claims Christians make about Jesus. To the strictly monotheistic Jews, Jesus was perhaps a prophet, maybe a

25. Including Saint Paul, who probably had some understanding of Greek philosophy (see Acts 17:22–31) He was also learned in Jewish theology (see Acts 22:3; Phil 3:4–6).

26. Maximus the Confessor (AD 580–662) is an important theologian in the Eastern Orthodox Church who argued strongly that it is necessary to understand that Jesus Christ was *fully human, and this meant that he had a human will.* At that time, arguments were raging between Christian factions that held that Christ had only one nature (the Monophysite position) and those who held that he had two natures (the Dyophysite position). A compromise idea, that Christ had two natures but only one, divine will (Monothelitism), was also suggested. Maximus strongly argued that if Christ had only a divine will, then the work of salvation would be rendered meaningless—the actions of a mere puppet. Human nature without a human will is an unreal abstraction: if Christ does not have a human will as well as a divine will, he is not truly man, and if he is not truly man, then the Christian message of salvation is rendered void. Christ's human will was free to conform to (or reject) God's will. He was truly tempted by Satan to take easier ways, and at Gethsemane he was truly tempted to avoid the cross. He submitted his fear of death, by an act of human will, to the Father, and so was able to overcome his natural repulsion to death in order to say to the Father, "Not my will but yours be done" (Matt 26:39). "Thus Christ in his two natures, wills and operates our salvation."

messianic pretender, whose crucifixion showed that he had failed in his attempts to save his people from their Gentile oppressors.

The resurrection, which Christians understand as a vindication of their faith that Jesus was indeed the longed-for Messiah, or Christ (which is Greek for "Messiah," both words meaning "the anointed one"), seems to most Jews to be at best a figment of the imagination and at worst a fabricated tale, something which, in any case, they cannot understand. And if he was the Messiah, that would not prove his divinity because the Messiah they awaited was expected to be *human*, not divine.

Rabbi David Rosen may be typical of many puzzled Jews when he comments in an exchange of letters with a Christian:

> The idea that God is somehow exclusively incarnate in one human being is totally beyond my comprehension. The idea of the Trinity[27] leaves me baffled. The concept of vicarious atonement defies my moral comprehension.[28]

Saint Paul encountered similar incredulity when he was trying to explain the meaning of Jesus' death a few years after it happened. He wrote to Christians in Corinth, "We preach Christ crucified: a stumbling block to Jews and foolishness to Gentiles, but to those whom God has called, both Jews and Greeks, Christ the power of God, and the wisdom of God."[29]

His death was and is central to the Christian message; all four Gospels deal with the events surrounding his trial, crucifixion, and resurrection in great detail, and the fact that he was crucified and then raised from the dead is central to the whole of the New Testament.

Why, then, did Jesus die?

God Allowed History to Take Its Unjust Course

Even the most skeptical scholars have difficulty evading the evidence that a man called Jesus of Nazareth was crucified under Pontius Pilate. The Hellenistic Jewish historian Josephus comments, "Pilate condemned him

---

27. The word "Trinity" does not appear in the Bible or even in the creeds, though the creeds spell out the belief that the one God exists in three persons and one substance. The word was first used in its Greek form, *trias*, by Theophilus of Antioch in about AD 180.

28. Kendall and Rosen, *Christian and the Pharisee*, 83.

29. 1 Cor 1:23–24.

[Jesus] to the cross, the leading men among us having accused him."[30] The Roman historian Tacitus, writing about Christians early in the second century, comments, "Christus, the author of their name, had suffered the death penalty during the reign of Tiberius, by sentence of the procurator Pontius Pilate."[31] So we need not doubt that Jesus was indeed "crucified under Pontius Pilate," as the Apostles' Creed declares.

According to Mark's Gospel, people said that Jesus "has done everything well."[32] Why, then, should a *good* Jew be crucified?

The gospels portray a man who went about healing those who were blind, lame, ill, and demonized. He violated some of the religious taboos of strict Jews by touching "untouchable" people (lepers, a woman with an issue of blood, and at least two dead bodies), he ate with those who the strict religious leaders considered to be sinners, and he broke the Sabbath by healing people during it. But these were not offenses that deserved death, even in the eyes of the strictest Jews.

Yet it was the Jewish leaders who instigated his death. Why should this be so?

In his monumental *Jesus and the Victory of God*, Wright sees that Israel was facing a climactic moment in its history and was threatened with imminent judgment: a judgment that came about in the Jewish war and the destruction of the temple in AD 70. Many of Jesus' prophetic warnings, which Christians have often thought referred to "the end times," were warnings of these imminent events. "Jesus is not merely . . . one in a continuing line of prophets. His warnings include the warning that he is the last in the line. This is, I think, what Jesus' eschatology is all about. Israel's history is drawing to its climax."[33]

When Jesus threw over the tables in the temple,[34] he was acting out a prophetic parable, demonstrating that the authority he had from God the Father was greater than the authority of the temple authorities. The Jewish leaders felt that their authority as interpreters of Judaism was under threat. This was the final straw that led to Jesus being arrested and handed to the Romans to be crucified.

---

30. Josephus, *Antiquities*, 18:3.3, para. 63–64. Some critics consider this statement to be a Christian gloss.

31. Tacitus, *Annals*, 15:44.

32. Mark 7:37.

33. Wright, *Jesus and the Victory*, 97.

34. Matt 21:12–13; Mark 15:11–18; Luke 19:45–48; John 2:13–22.

The Romans crucified people they considered to be a threat to their authority. So did Pilate think that Jesus posed a threat to the Pax Romana it was his duty to keep?

Almost certainly not—Pilate's past fraught relationship with the Jews explains why he acted as he did.

Josephus and Philo record three earlier incidents that made Pilate wary of crossing the Jewish leaders. Early in his office, Pilate had removed his army headquarters from Caesarea to Jerusalem. He had wanted to plant the troops' standards, with their metal images of the reigning emperor, Tiberius, in the holy city. To the Jews, the standards counted as graven images, and their presence in the holy city was an outrage. The Jews pleaded with Pilate to remove the offending images, but he initially refused, only to capitulate when he realized that the Jews were willing to die rather than have the offending images in their city: "Pilate was defeated and the standards were removed, for it is hardly possible to slaughter a nation."[35]

The second incident was when Pilate hung in his palace a series of gilt shields bearing the names of the Roman gods—also graven images in the eyes of the Jews. Again the Jews protested, and this time they took their protest to Emperor Tiberius, who ordered Pilate to remove the shields.[36]

The third showdown between Pilate and the Jews came when Pilate planned to build a new and improved water supply to Jerusalem—financed by the temple treasury funds! Riots broke out immediately, but were savagely suppressed by troops who had gotten out of control.[37] In Luke 13:1 we read of the Galileans, whose blood Pilate mingled with their sacrifices, a glimpse of another incident not recorded elsewhere. So Pilate's relationship with the volatile and fanatical Jews was fragile to say the least, and on at least one occasion, the emperor himself had sided with the Jewish people.

When the Jews shouted, "If you let this man go, you are no friend of Caesar,"[38] they were in effect threatening to report him to Emperor Tiberius again, "and Pilate could not afford another such report. If it had gone in, dismissal would have been certain. The plain fact is that Pilate's past gave the Jewish leaders their opportunity to blackmail him . . . he had to choose between principle and his own career—and he chose his career. Pilate

---

35. Josephus, *Antiquities*, 18.31–2; ibid., *Wars of the Jews*, 2.9.2–4, quoted in Barclay, *Apostles' Creed*, 71.

36. Philo, *Ad Caium*, 38, quoted in Barclay, *Apostles' Creed*, 71.

37. Josephus, *Wars of the Jews*, 2.9.4, quoted in Barclay, *Apostles' Creed*, 71.

38. John 19:12.

ordered the crucifixion of Jesus Christ, the Son of God, for no other reason than that he could see no other way to remain procurator of Judaea."[39]

There are some who suggest that Jesus was in fact a revolutionary, and that the early church played down his revolutionary message and "transformed Christ from Jewish prophet into a Hellenistic savior-god."[40] However, these speculations are not supported by the gospels. Jesus *opposed* the national resistance movements. His aim was to renew Israel to function as she should, as a light to the Gentiles—even as a light to the occupying Romans. With this interpretation in mind, parts of the Sermon on the Mount[41] can be understood as a blueprint of passive resistance: "Do not resist one who is evil . . . turn the other cheek . . . if anyone forces you to go one mile (i.e., any Roman soldier, who were allowed to compel subjects to go one mile,) go with him for two miles . . . pray for your enemies,"[42] even the hated Romans. That is, win them by showing grace and love. Jesus may of course have been *tempted* to raise an armed band of warriors (though if so, rejected the idea). In the garden of Gethsemane, "he could have chosen to call for twelve legions of angels, or more likely their earthly equivalent; there would have been plenty of people in Jerusalem ready to rally to him."[43] Plenty of Zealots wanted a war and would have been ready to follow a Messiah-figure in rebellion against the Romans.

But this was not Jesus' mission.

Jesus told his disciples, "The reason my Father loves me is that I lay down my life—only to take it up again. No one takes it from me, but I lay it down of my own accord. I have authority to lay it down and authority to take it up again. This command I received from my Father."[44] It may be that Jesus in his humanity was tempted (perhaps during the temptations in the desert after his baptism, perhaps during the years of his ministry, and surely even more so in Gethsemane) to choose the path of military resistance, but he knew that this would not serve the salvation plan of God. So he *allowed* the Sanhedrin's religious fanaticism to take its course; he *allowed* Pilate to command an unjust crucifixion for the sake of political expediency; and he submitted to one of the cruelest death penalties the world

39. Barclay, *Apostles' Creed*, 72.

40. Faulkner, *Apocalypse*, 97–98. Faulkner writes from a Marxist perspective.

41. Matt 5–7.

42. Matt 5:39–45.

43. Wright, *Jesus and the Victory*, 606.

44. John 10:17–18.

has ever known because this horrific death was, astonishingly, part of the purpose of God. "We see in the Cross . . . the inevitable climax, under the conditions which confronted him, to a consistent life-practice of meeting evil not by violence, not even by invoking law, but by the way of forgiving and reconciling love. Jesus died rather than betray that love method."[45]

God in Jesus *submitted* to the effects of man's sin and identified with it, and by so doing, overcame it. John understood this, and as he wrote in one of his letters, "This is how we know what love is: Jesus Christ laid down his life for us."[46]

The Cross Reveals a God Who Suffers with Us

A few years ago, I was sitting in a little Catholic chapel looking at the simple crucifix in front of me—an unusual exercise for a Protestant Christian like myself.

I was taking part in an Ecumenical Quiet Day, and we had been invited to pick a text from a given selection and think about it for about forty minutes. Almost at random, I had chosen Isa 9:6–7:

> And the government will be on his shoulders.
> And he will be called
> Wonderful counsellor, Mighty God,
> Everlasting Father, Prince of Peace.
> Of the increase of his government and peace
> there will be no end.
> He will reign on David's throne
> and over his kingdom,
> establishing and upholding it
> with justice and righteousness
> from that time on and forever.

Christians often read this passage during the run-up to Christmas, understanding it to be a prophecy of the Messiah who had been awaited for centuries by the Jews, and believing that Jesus *was* that expected Messiah who fulfilled this and many other prophecies.

---

45. Macgregor, *New Testament Basis*, 103.

46. 1 John 3:16.

But most Jews are still awaiting their Messiah because, despite the fact that he seems to Christian believers to fulfill many prophecies, Jesus was not what they expected.

They expected a charismatic warrior-king in the mold of David—someone who would save them from their earthly enemies. When Jesus came, the earthly enemies of the Jews were of course the Romans, so they expected someone who would at the very least liberate them from Rome,[47] which Jesus failed to do. Instead, the Romans crucified him.

Was that not defeat and failure?

And here I was, contemplating one of the many thousands (or perhaps millions) of depictions of that crucifixion since it happened nearly two thousand years ago—how strange that we love to paint pictures, wear emblems, or gaze at depictions of a scene that is so shameful and so horrifying.

But we do, because we believe it changed everything.

However, on this Quiet Day, my mind balked at the comforting ideas that we Christians usually derive from this passage, and I seemed to be siding with the skeptical Jews.

Jesus may be a wonderful counselor, I thought (when and if people really allow him into their hearts), but as a Prince of Peace or a reigning king (which was what the Messiah was expected to be) who *rescues* his people from their real, earthly enemies (such as the Romans), he is a failure.

His coming has made no difference. There has been no peace on earth, and Christians have been involved in just as many wars as anyone else. And if he is "Mighty God . . . reigning over the world and establishing and upholding his kingdom of justice and righteousness," then he is not making a very good job of it. The lovely sentiments of Isaiah—if applied to Jesus—seemed like wishful platitudes with no more substance than the false promises made by a desperate politician just before an election.

I continued to contemplate the passage from Isaiah while gazing at the gaunt and anguished figure on the cross, which was beautiful in its simplicity. The shoulders were dragged down and almost dislocated by the weight of the body so that the arms formed an arc, and I began to imagine the whole world—in all its beauty and confusion, its violence and its greed—resting on the shoulders and wrenched arms of the crucified Christ. I thought of people in their fear and uncertainty at this time

47. Wright points out that there "was no single monolithic and uniform 'messianic expectation' among first century Jews . . . we cannot say what, if anything, the average Jew-in-the-market-place believed about a coming Messiah" (Wright, *People of God*, 307–308).

when capitalism looks to be collapsing (and communism has already collapsed). I thought of the gross materialism, the greed, and crass over-sexualization of Western "developed" society and of the rampant poverty and disease in the "under-developed" or "developing" nations. I thought about the inequalities and the lack of justice or righteousness. I thought about the many areas where there is still conflict and war, especially as I write this in the spring of 2011 in countries affected by the so-called Arab Spring (chiefly Libya and Syria—at the moment). I thought about the recent earthquakes in Japan and New Zealand, the flooding in New Orleans and Bangladesh, the tsunamis, and so much more.

The crucified Christ formed a unity in my mind with all that pain, suffering, and conflict. And I began to realize once more that he reigns in weakness, not in strength. He is "a man of sorrows and acquainted with grief"[48] not a conquering hero. He identifies with the pain and sorrow in this sinful and broken world. He suffers with and for humanity and prevents our total destruction and collapse into chaos. He himself bears our wounds, and by bearing them (when we understand and allow him to), he also carries them away from us and heals them: "The gospels . . . tell the story of the creator God taking responsibility for what has happened to creation, bearing the weight of its problems on his own shoulders."[49] God in Jesus *knows* what it is like to be rejected, let down, unjustly abused, and racked with pain. He has been there himself.

And, in the Father, God has felt the pain of fathers and mothers the world over whose children have suffered or died, or who have been rejected or misunderstood. He has seen his beloved and only Son die a hideous death. Many of the Old Testament pictures of God reveal a God of deep compassion, a covenant keeping God, a husband who loves his unfaithful wife, a loving father, and a good shepherd, not the immutable, passionless deity of the Greek philosophers (see p. 53–60.)

The life and death of Jesus deepen these pictures.

There is a remarkable verse in the letter to the Hebrews: "Although he was a son, he learned obedience from what he suffered and, once made perfect, he became the source of eternal salvation for all who obey him."[50]

48. Isa 53:3.

49. Wright, *Evil and the Justice*, 58.

50. Heb 5:8–9.

Was Jesus not perfect from the beginning? Yes, but the meaning seems to be that the incarnation was not an optional extra, but was *necessary* for salvation to be effective. It was *necessary* for Jesus to learn:

> what it means to be his father's obedient son; and that will mean suffering, not because God is a sadist who simply wants to see his dear son having a rough time of it, but because the world which God made and loves is a dark and wicked place and the son must suffer its sorrow and pain in order to rescue it . . . he needed to attain the full stature of sonship through experiencing the pain and grief of the father himself over his world gone wrong. He became truly and fully what in his nature he already was.[51]

When we are in the midst of suffering, it is hard to believe that God knows or cares about us. When I was practicing as a doctor, people would often ask, "Why did God let this happen to me?" There is no answer to such a cry from the heart. The nearest I could get to an "answer" was something like: "I don't know, but he did not spare his own Son."

And when my own son, who had suffered from schizophrenia for about nine years, took his own life at the age of twenty-four, the same thought was of some comfort. The compassionate, *involved* love of our triune God is most profoundly revealed by the cross of Christ.

I was once given a card with these thoughts by Dorothy Sayers, which beautifully sums up what I am trying to say:

> For whatever reason God chose to make man as he is—limited and suffering and subject to sorrows and death—He had the honesty and courage to take His own medicine. Whatever game He is playing with His creation, He has kept His own rules and played fair. He himself has gone through the whole of human experience, from the trivial irritations of family life and lack of money to the worst horrors, pain, humiliation, defeat, despair and death.[52]

What could be more humiliating than being strung up naked (surely without the loincloth with which he is modestly clad in Christian art)? At some point during his long, harrowing death he would undoubtedly have soiled himself, and perhaps those nearest the cross. He had no option.

How could this weakened, humiliated, overpowered, dying figure be God incarnate?

51. Wright, *Hebrews for Everyone*, 49.
52. Sayers, *Christian Letters*, 14.

I recently came across the moving story of Elie Wiesel, a deeply spiritual young Jew who believed his life to be a spark from the Shekinah of God and had longed to learn the mystic secrets of Kabbalah when he was only thirteen and considered too young to do so. As a teenager he had been told, "Man asks and God replies. But we don't understand His replies. We cannot understand them,"[53] a remark that seems almost prophetic in view of subsequent events.

Wiesel poignantly describes his awful experiences in Nazi concentration camps, which he survived, although the rest of his family did not. Wiesel's faith finally died within him when two men and a young boy were hanged in front of him. The two men died quickly, but the young boy lingered horribly.

> "Where is merciful God, where is He?" someone behind me was asking . . . the child, too light . . . remained for more than half an hour, lingering between life and death, writhing before our eyes . . . He was still alive when I passed him. His tongue was still red, his eyes not yet extinguished. Behind me, I heard the same man asking: "For God's sake, where is God?" And from within me, I heard a voice answer: "Where is He? This is where—hanging from this gallows."[54]

After that, Wiesel could no longer bless the name of God.

> Why would I bless Him? Every fiber in me rebelled. Because He caused thousands of children to burn in His mass graves? Because He kept six crematoria working day and night, including Sabbath and the Holy Days? Because in His great might, He had created Auschwitz, Birkenau, Buna, and so many other factories of death? How could I say to Him: Blessed be Thou, Almighty, Master of the Universe, who chose us among all nations to be tortured day and night, to watch as our fathers, our mothers, our brothers end up in the furnaces? Praised be Thy Holy Name, for having chosen us to be slaughtered on Thine alter?[55]

Wiesel's cry seemed to be met by silence, and he felt terribly alone in a world that was apparently without God. Would it have helped him to know that Jesus, the Son of God—even God incarnate—did indeed hang

---

53. Wiesel, *Night*, 5.
54. Ibid., 64–65.
55. Ibid., 67.

from a gallows, and also experienced anguish and forsakenness, and also cried out, "My God, My God, why have you forsaken me?"[56]

The Reverend Edward Shillito was a Free Church minister serving the forces in the terrible brutality of the First World War. As he watched wave after wave of wounded and dead young men returning from the front lines, his faith—and the faith of the men he served—was profoundly challenged.

He wrote a moving poem entitled "Jesus of the Scars." Here is the last verse:

> The other gods were strong; but Thou wast weak;
> They rode, but Thou didst stumble to a throne;
> But to our wounds only God's wounds speak;
> And not a god has wounds, but Thou alone.[57]

Jews and Muslims (and many others) may not accept that God would allow his incarnate Son to suffer, but for Christians it is a precious and profoundly moving truth, absolutely central to our faith.

The Cross Deals with Our Sinfulness—It Is the Means of Atonement between God and Humankind

The death of Jesus Christ not only reveals the depth of God's love and identifies with our pain, it has even deeper effects. In some profound way beyond our comprehension—and which we can only begin to understand through analogy—his death deals with the deep-rooted effects of our sinfulness and imperfections: spiritual death and alienation from God.[58] Because Jesus was both fully God and fully human, he took upon himself all the wrath of God against the sinfulness of mankind, which would otherwise have separated the human race from God.[59] So Paul could say, "God was reconciling the world to himself in Christ, not counting men's sins against them."[60]

Christians down the centuries have a terrible record of vilifying and persecuting the Jews because of the part they played in the crucifixion

56. Ps 22:1, quoted in Mark 15:34 and parallels.

57. Shillito, "Jesus of the Scars," 199.

58. "For the wages of sin is death, but the gift of God is eternal life in (or through) Christ Jesus our Lord" (Rom 6:23).

59. See Rom 5:12; 6:23.

60. 2 Cor 5:19.

of Jesus. Yes, the Jewish leaders arranged his death, and yes, his disciples (who were Jews) forsook him and fled, but it was Pontius Pilate who unjustly commanded that he be crucified, and it was *Roman* soldiers who carried out the deed. He died not only because of the sin of the Jewish leaders, not only because of the duplicity and weakness of his own disciples, not only because Pontius Pilate had him crucified for expediency when he knew it was unjust to do so—he carried the sins of the *whole world* on the cross.

And when I realize that Jesus was crucified for *my* sins, then I realize my solidarity with the guilt of the Jews and the Romans. There are no grounds for vilifying the Jews.

The good news is that *I* (and anybody who believes, and receives God's grace) can be released from my guilt, because "there is now no condemnation for those who are in Christ Jesus."[61] The author of the letter to the Hebrews explains to his Jewish readers that the death of Jesus Christ destroys the power the devil holds over us by *making atonement* for sin:

> Since the children have flesh and blood, he too shared in their humanity so that by his death he might destroy him who holds the power of death—that is, the devil—and free those who all their lives were held in slavery by their fear of death . . . he had to be made like his brothers in every way, in order that he might become a merciful and faithful high priest in service to God, and that he might *make atonement* for the sins of the people. Because he himself suffered when he was tempted, he is able to help those who are being tempted.[62]

Although "atonement" is a straightforward Anglo-Saxon word, it is rarely used except in theology. It simply means what it says: *at-one-ment*: "making one those who are separated or estranged." The NIV uses it here to translate the Greek *ilaskesthai*, which comes from a root meaning "to appease, to expiate, make atonement for, be gracious, show mercy, or pardon." The N.I.V. footnote explains it as: "and that he might turn aside God's wrath, taking away the sins of the people."

So we can say with confidence: Jesus died for our sins; he died that we might be forgiven.

He died to reconcile us to God, to make it possible for us to be one with God.

---

61. Rom 8:1.

62. Heb 2:14–17, emphasis mine.

One would have expected Rabbi David Rosen, (see p. 8) to understand the meaning of atonement, even if he finds that "the concept of *vicarious* atonement defies my moral comprehension."[63] In the Old Testament, the Hebrew word *kippur* or *kaphar*[64] is regularly translated as "atonement," and Yom Kippur, the "Day of Atonement," is one of the holiest days of the Jewish year, when the events described in Leviticus chapter 16 are remembered.

This is a chapter ripe with descriptions of the sacrificial offerings of innocent animal life on behalf of guilty human beings. First a bull was slaughtered and sacrificed for the sin of Aaron the priest and his family, and then two goats were brought to Aaron: one was chosen by lot to be slaughtered and sacrificed for the sins of the people, the other was to be a living "scapegoat." Aaron "is to lay both hands on the head of the live goat and confess over it all the wickedness and rebellion of the Israelites—all their sins—and put them on the goat's head. He shall send the goat away into the desert . . . the goat will carry on itself all their sins to a solitary place."[65]

The psychiatrist Paul Tournier comments:

> The removal of evil and guilt has two interdependent aspects: its obliteration from before God, and its expulsion and return to the devil to whom it belongs . . . under earthly conditions the exorcism of evil is forever an uncertain affair. The scapegoat continually roams the desert in company with the evil spirits, ready to reappear on the horizon.[66]

There is a haunting picture by William Holman Hunt[67] portraying this banished animal, gashed with purple to show its anguish. But just as even the most realistic pictures of the crucifixion show the pain but not the victory of Christ's cross—which is revealed by his resurrection—this anguished portrayal of a hopeless and helpless animal, which seems to be crying out and near to death, does not show the hope or the release from the guilt of sin that this cruel ritual was designed to achieve for the Jewish people. That would need another picture.

63. Kendall and Rosen, *Christian and the Pharisee*, 83, emphasis mine.

64. See also the discussion of the "Mercy Seat" in chapter 5 p. 132–134.

65. Lev 16:21–22.

66. Tournier, *Guilt and Grace*, 178.

67. William Holman Hunt, *The Scapegoat*, Lady Lever Art Gallery, National Museums Liverpool, Port Sunlight, England, http://www.liverpoolmuseums.org.uk/about/collections/pre-raphaelites/scapegoat/.

The sacrifices of the Day of Atonement were designed to deal with guilt and sin—but they did so only partially. Christians believe that Jesus has achieved a removal of sin far more effective than the combination of sacrificed animals and the banished scapegoat; indeed, the rituals were a pointer to the sacrifice of Jesus, planned from the beginning of time: (see p. 4–5.) "The ministry Jesus has received is as superior to theirs as the covenant of which he is mediator is superior to the old one."[68]

He is not only "the lamb of God, who takes away the sin of the world"[69]; he is the priest as well as the victim. He is "a merciful and faithful high priest in service to God, that he might make atonement for the sins of the people,"[70] and even more explicitly: "He sacrificed for their sins once for all when he offered himself."[71]

Perhaps Rabbi David can accept the concept of the vicarious sacrifice of an animal for the atonement of the Jewish people in ancient times—though Rabbinic Judaism has not practiced animal sacrifices since the destruction of the temple in AD 70, so he, like us, can only read his Tanakh and ponder the meaning of passages like Lev 16. Perhaps what "defies his moral comprehension" is the conception of the sacrifice of a *human being*, and—even more shocking for a Jew—the Son of God, and—more shocking still—God himself, in his humanity, and on behalf of all humanity, carrying our burden of guilt.

Many Christians, too, feel a sense of distaste at this understanding of the cross. Sometimes the idea of vicarious atonement is thought of as if Jesus was in some way appeasing a wrathful Father, but this is a parody of the Biblical concept. God the Father did not sit unmoved in heaven while his Son suffered: "God was *in Christ*, reconciling the world unto himself."[72]

The whole Godhead suffered in the crucifixion. This is brought out beautifully in a sketch of the trinity by William Blake. In this picture, the Father holds the Son, who is stretched out as on a cross, but the figures of the Father and the Son are so entwined that it is difficult to make out which head is which, and the Spirit hovers over both with outstretched wings. "The doctrine of eternal punishment has been decisively

68. Heb 8:6.

69. John 1:29.

70. Heb 2:17.

71. Heb 7:17.

72. 2 Cor 5:19 (AKJV). I have quoted from the Authorized Version because the translation brings out more strongly than most modern translations the identification of God with Christ. God the Father suffered with the Son.

answered within the trinity . . . we do not know of a God who dispenses eternal judgment who is not also the God who has taken this judgment upon himself in Christ."[73]

But "vicarious atonement" is only one way of explaining the cross; there are many others

Ransom and Redemption

An analogy that we in the twenty-first century may understand more easily than atonement is the concept of ransom. In biblical times, slavery was universally practiced, and the idea of ransoming was well understood. When a slave was set free, a ransom price was paid for that freedom.

This was similar to what happens when an item is pawned. The pawnshop keeps the item as surety for a loan of money, and the item is later redeemed (or bought back) when the borrowed money is repaid—usually with a hefty interest! If the money is not paid back, the pawnshop keeps the item.

In the Old Testament, the Israelites are often called the ransomed of the Lord or the redeemed of the Lord; Isaiah pictures the "ransomed of the Lord" returning to Zion with singing and everlasting joy.[74] Jesus picks up this idea when it is said he came to "give his life as a ransom for many."[75] And Paul writes in his first letter to Timothy, "There is one God and one mediator between God and men, the man Christ Jesus, who gave himself as a ransom for all men."[76]

The Judge Is the Savior

We can picture God, who is our judge, passing a sentence of "guilty" on mankind in general and on each of us as individuals, for all are guilty to a greater or lesser degree. Then he steps down from the judgment seat, and in the crucifixion of Jesus, he fulfills the sentence himself on behalf of each one of us—on behalf of sinful humanity.

The Judge is the Savior. He carries our sentence himself.

---

73. Anderson, *Theology, Death and Dying*, 77–78.

74. Isa 35:10.

75. Matt 20:28; Mark 10:45.

76. 1 Tim 2: 5–6.

Perhaps that is why throughout the Bible the judgment of God is often coupled with salvation and redemption and proclaimed as a cause for joy:

> Let the sea resound, and everything in it,
>
> the world, and all who live it.
>
> Let the rivers clap their hands,
>
> let the mountains sing together for joy;
>
> let them sing before the lord,
>
> for he comes to judge the earth.
>
> He will judge the world in righteousness
>
> And the peoples with equity.[77]

Recently I was praying with a young Christian man who had lost his way in life for many years and was trying to get his life straight with the help of his newly found faith in Jesus. He was profoundly repentant for many things that he knew he had done wrong and was confessing to God with deep sincerity. As he prayed, he saw Jesus bowed down by a heavy cross that he was carrying, but the young man was upset because Jesus was walking away from him. I was able (with awe in my heart) to say, "Jesus is carrying your sins away."

Because Jesus carries our sins, we do not have to.

David Pawson summarizes the cosmic effects of the cross: "Only at the cross do justice and mercy meet. Sins are both punished and pardoned at the same place and at the same time—Jesus takes the punishment and we get the pardon."[78]

Above All, the Cross Shows Us
the Extent of God's Love

It can be difficult for us to grasp ideas of atonement that relate to the Old Testament system of animal sacrifices; we can misunderstand the images used, and explanations can seem to imply that an angry god must be appeased by this most terrible sacrifice—the sacrifice of his Son.

But this is a horrible distortion of the truth.

Jesus *gave himself willingly*; he was not unwillingly slaughtered, as a sacrificial animal would have been. He gave himself *for us*.[79] The

---

77. Ps 98:7–9.

78. Pawson, *Unlocking the Bible*, 441.

79. Gal 1:4; 2:20; Eph 5:2, 25; 1 Tim 2:6; Titus 2:14; 1 John 3:16; John 15:13.

Greek word used is usually *huper*, which means "for the sake of" or "on behalf of."[80]

Barclay makes the point beautifully:

> To us the sacrifice of animals is quite alien and quite strange; but what we can clearly and unequivocally say is that *it cost the life and death of Jesus Christ to restore the lost relationship between God and man.* But how? If God does not need to be pacified, if God is not outraged justice at all, if at the back of all this, there stands the wondrous love of God, wherein the necessity of the death of Christ? . . . Before Jesus came, no man knew what God was like; men thought of God as king and judge, as justice and holiness, as wrath and vengeance, but they never conceived the supreme wonder of the love of God. So in Jesus Christ God comes to men, and he says: "I love you like that." When we see Jesus healing the sick feeding the hungry being the friend of outcasts and sinners, this is God saying: "I love you like that." When we see Jesus still refusing to do anything but love even when men betray and insult and revile him, this is God saying: "I love you like that." And if Jesus had stopped before the cross, it would have meant that there was some point beyond which the love of God would not go, but because Jesus, having loved men, loved them to the end, it means that there is nothing which can alter the love of God. It means that God in Christ says: "You can betray me; you can hate me; you can misjudge me; you can scourge me; you can crucify me, and nothing can alter my love." . . . Jesus came not to persuade God to forgive us, but to tell us that God in his love has forgiven us, and that all we can do is in wondering gratitude to accept the forgiveness of sins, which it cost the cross to make known to us.[81]

80. Barclay, *Apostle's Creed*, 276. The Greek word *anti* is translated "for" when the English meaning is "instead of" and is used only in Matt 20:28 and par. Mark 10:45: "The Son of Man did not come to be served, but to serve and to give his life as a ransom for many". He paid the price instead of us because we could never pay it for ourselves.

81. Barclay, *Apostles' Creed*, 278–79.

The Resurrection Reveals That the
Cross Is a Victory, Not a Failure

It is highly significant that at the moment when Jesus died, there was an earthquake, and "the curtain of the temple was torn in two from top to bottom."[82]

We read in Exod 26:31–33 that this curtain divided the holy place from the most holy place in the Jewish tabernacle, so it symbolized to the Jews their need for the atonement sacrifices discussed above. Because of the death of Jesus, these sacrifices are no longer necessary.[83] The atonement had been achieved once for all. In and through his awful crucifixion, Christ was overcoming Satan, sin, and death.

The cross looked like a defeat. Several would-be Jewish Messiahs were put down and killed by the Romans in the century surrounding Jesus' crucifixion, and Jesus looked like another failed would-be Messiah. If he had not risen from the dead, Christianity would never have developed, and few people would have heard of Jesus Christ. But the New Testament unequivocally proclaims that Jesus *did* rise from the dead, and the resurrection became the focus of the preaching of the early church.

Tom Wright emphasizes the absolute centrality of the resurrection to all Christian understanding and way of life: "Jesus is risen, therefore Israel and the world have been redeemed. Jesus is risen, therefore his followers have a new job to do . . . to bring the life of heaven to birth in actual, physical, earthly reality . . . Jesus' resurrection is the beginning of God's new project . . . to colonize earth with the life of heaven. That, after all, is what the Lord's Prayer is about."[84]

Because of the resurrection, Paul can describe the cross as a victory over evil, using language that might be used to describe a Roman military victory parade:

> Christ . . . forgave all our sins, having cancelled the written code, with its regulation that was against us and that stood opposed to us; he took it away, nailing it to the cross. And having disarmed the powers and authorities, he made a public spectacle of them triumphing over them by the cross.[85]

82. Matt 27:51; Mark15:38; Luke 23:45.

83. See Heb 9.

84. Wright, *Surprised by Hope*, 305.

85. Col 2:13–15.

This victory theme is reflected in early hymns and liturgies. The Homily of Melito of Sardis (probably written in the second century) contains what might have already been an ancient hymn in which Christ identifies himself as the doer of heroic deeds in the underworld:

> I am he who put down death,
> and triumphed over the enemy,
> and trod upon Hades,
> and bound the Strong One
> and brought man safely home to the heights of the heavens.[86]

From our viewpoint in the here and now on earth, where the ravages of sin and evil are all too evidently still with us, this victory is clearly incomplete, but the Bible offers us hope that in the end the kingdom of God will come in its fullness, and the victory over evil will ultimately be completed (see chapters 6 and 7).

Meanwhile, we have a foretaste of what is to come, and we are commissioned to live and work for God's kingdom to come and for his will to be done "on earth as it is in heaven." Or, we could say, to work for that victory to be completed. This will be explored further in the next chapter.

Pointers to Redemption in Unexpected Places

Don Richardson's *The Peace Child* is one of those rare books that changed the way I view the world.

It tells the story of the author's pioneer missionary work during the 1960s among the Sawi tribe in the highlands of Netherlands New Guinea (now West Papua). I first read the book in the 1970s while living with my family in Papua New Guinea. We visited the highlands, which shares a border with West Papua, and because the peoples of these neighboring countries have much in common, it was easy for me to visualize the society that Richardson describes. Until the mid-twentieth century, the highlanders of both countries were head-hunting, cannibalistic societies living in a stone-age culture, but now, through missionary and government efforts to provide education and basic medical care, and of course the all-pervasive cash economy, Western culture is rapidly influencing the traditional way of life—and not always for the better.

---

86. Quoted in Bernstein, *Formation of Hell*, 273.

Richardson was the first white person to live amongst the remote and warlike Sawi people, and he could well have been killed and eaten. However, he was able to win their friendship and trust, and his wife and children soon joined him.

Richardson was invited to the men's house to tell them why he had come and to tell them about his God, so he told the story of Jesus' life and death. His listeners were filled with admiration for the cleverness of the hero—who they took to be Judas!

Richardson soon learned that in many of the Sawi legends, the heroes formed "friendships" with the purpose of betraying the "befriended one" to be killed and eaten! They called this practice "to fatten with friendship for the slaughter."[87] How could Richardson explain the gospel in this culture?

It was two years before he found a key to explain the gospel in a way that the Sawi people could understand.

There had been continual, vicious fighting between two neighboring tribes, the Haenam and Kamur, which Richardson had tried to defuse. Eventually the tribal leaders listened to his pleas to stop fighting, but their route to peace amazed him.

To forge a peace deal, one of the leaders of Haenum gave his infant son to the opposing Kamur tribe to look after as a "Peace Child." In return, Haenum adopted the son of one of the leaders of Kamur. As long as the children lived, there would be peace between the two tribes, but if one child died, fighting was likely to erupt again. Richardson movingly describes the unfolding of this contract, enacted with great anguish and sacrificial love by stone-age warring tribes, and ponders:

> If I had known my call for peace would provoke fathers to give up their sons, plunge mothers into grief, and cast babies into strangeness, what would I have chosen? To let the mothers continue suckling what their own wombs have borne, or to let violent men go ahead and kill each other? I had no answer.
>
> But three hundred Sawi had lain hands on a peace child. And they were singing. And laughing. And inside me, the little bell was ringing a little louder.[88]

Here was an analogy that he could use to explain the good news of the love of God to these people: *Jesus is God's "Peace Child" given for the whole world!* Moreover, although Jesus died, he overcame death, and rose

---

87. Richardson, *Peace Child*, ch. 2.

88. Ibid., 203.

again, and will now never die. Thus, the peace he brokers between God and sinful human beings, and potentially also *between* human beings themselves—even those who would otherwise be locked in enmity—is for all people, forever. This explanation of salvation made sense to the Sawi, and many who had previously been indifferent or hostile to the gospel became Christians.

The Sawi also had a myth that, many ages ago, people were able to be renewed after death, like a caterpillar becoming a moth or a snake renewing its skin, and when someone died they mourned and wailed because this ancient ability of renewal had been lost. Here was a myth that opened their understanding. The resurrection of Jesus—and one day of themselves too—was like a caterpillar becoming a moth or a snake renewing its skin. Because the people believed that the ancients of old had had this ability, they were able to see how faith in Jesus could restore an ability that had been lost. Richardson had found what he calls "redemptive analogies" that the people understood.

He writes:

> Redemptive analogies, God's keys to man's cultures, are the New Testament-approved approach to cross-cultural evangelism . . . Some redemptive analogies stand out in the legends and records of the past: Olenos the Sinbearer: Balder the Innocent, hounded to his death, yet destined to rule the new world; Socrates' *Righteous Man*; the unknown god of the Athenians, an analogy appropriated by the apostle Paul; The Logos, appropriated by the apostle John; the sacrificial lamb of the Hebrews, appropriated by both John the Baptist and Paul . . . How many more are yet waiting to be found, waiting to be appropriated for the deliverance of the people who believe them, waiting to be supplanted by Christ, that they may then fade from sight behind the brilliance of His glory, having fulfilled their God-ordained purpose? Only those who go and search will find them.[89]

As Alison Morgan explains,

> The Gospel is the word of God, spoken before time but spoken also into time . . . spoken therefore in a particular language and into a particular culture, and yet containing universal truth which can be carried by any language and be understood in any culture. If it is to be successfully appropriated by anyone other than a first-century Jew, it therefore has to be translated . . . not just verbally,

89. Ibid., 288.

from Aramaic to English or Bemba or Punjabi, but conceptually, so that it speaks to the needs and values of a given people."[90]

To aid in that translation of concepts, we need to seek out and find the "redemptive analogies" that sustain a particular culture. Let us briefly look at one or two others:

In his "First Apology" in the early second century, Justin Martyr saw analogies in Greek philosophy that could be used to explain Christianity to puzzled pagans: "Justin argued that traces of Christian truth were to be found in the great pagan writers. His doctrine of the *logos spermaticus* ('seed-bearing word') allowed him to affirm that God had prepared the way for his final revelation in Jesus Christ through hints of its truth in classical philosophy."[91] And many of the early Church Fathers continued the tradition of explaining the Christian faith through Greek philosophical concepts.

Recently, I heard a lecture on the basic philosophy of Laozi (who possibly lived in the sixth century BC). The lecturer was not a Christian, but he pointed out that there are similarities between Tao (which is "the Way") and Jesus, "The Way, the Truth and the Life." He summarized the Tao with this quote from Laozi: "Tao/Way is the creator and determinant of all things in the world . . . Tao is eternal and has no name though its simplicity seems insignificant, none in the world can master it."[92]

The concept of Tao is of course debated and explained in many different ways, but this definition reminds me of the personification of Wisdom in Prov 8, and of the Word or Logos of John 1:1–3. Here was a "creation analogy" rather than a "redemptive analogy," but I was reminded that our Lord God has many witnesses, even beyond the pages of the Bible.

We are surrounded by metaphors of death and renewal in the cycle of nature. Leaves fall in autumn, and trees and many plants look dead only to reawaken and come to life in the miracle of spring. The caterpillar is entombed in its chrysalis, later to emerge, changed beyond recognition, as a glorious butterfly or moth.

Whatever "redemptive analogy" makes most sense to us, we must always admit that the full meaning of the life, death, and resurrection of the incarnate Son of God is beyond our human understanding. The

90. Morgan, *Wild Gospel*, 30.

91. McGrath, *Historical Theology*, 25.

92. Lecture given by Professor Zixin Hu, co-director of the Liverpool Confucius Institute, University of Central Lancashire, in 2012.

analogies that we have been considering act as pointers to the reality beyond them, as Wright comments:

> Theories of atonement are all, in themselves, *abstractions* . . .
> the flesh-and-blood, time-and-space happenings, are the reality
> which the theories are trying to understand but cannot replace
> . . . it is through the narratives [in the gospels] that we are brought
> in touch with the events which are the real thing, the thing that
> matters. And it is through other events in the present time that
> we are brought still closer: both the Eucharist, which repeats the
> meal Jesus gave as his own interpretation of his death, and the
> actions of healing, love and forgiveness through which Jesus'
> death becomes a fresh reality within the still-broken world.[93]

Through the gospel accounts of the life and death of Jesus, we realize that God is *for* us—he has always been for us. In the person of Christ, he reaches out to us. For our sake he humbled himself and took upon himself the role of a servant and became obedient to death, even death on a cross,[94] because He *loves* us. We are left exclaiming with Saint Paul: Oh, the depth of the riches of the wisdom and knowledge of God! How unsearchable his judgments, and his paths beyond tracing out![95]

The Cross Reveals How We Should Live

The cross not only reveals the fact that God is involved in our suffering and deals with our sin, it is also an *example* that those of us who seek to follow Christ are asked to emulate.

As John writes, "This is how we know what love is: Jesus Christ laid down his life for us. And we ought to lay down our lives for our brothers."[96]

The task of the church is to show Christ to the world through lives that reflect his life, as well as by words that try to explain it, even if our words or actions lead to suffering or even death.

Those Christians who follow Christ's example to the extreme of dying for their faith are often recognized as heroes, saints, or martyrs.

I could give many examples, but Martin Luther King Jr. springs to mind. Twenty centuries after Jesus' death, King was assassinated for

---

93. Wright, *Evil and the Justice*, 59.
94. Phil 2:7–8.
95. Rom 11:33.
96. 1 John 3:16.

speaking out about the injustice with which he and his colored brothers and sisters were treated in the US, a country whose founding principle was theoretically equality before God!

King wrote, spoke about, and practiced redemptive love. He challenged institutionalized racial discrimination, especially in Georgia, deep in the American "Bible Belt." Christianity shaped his ideals, but he had learned his methods of nonviolent protest from Gandhi, who, though he deeply respected Jesus of Nazareth and especially his "Sermon on the Mount,"[97] never became a Christian and was highly critical of what he saw of Christianity in practice.

In the 1960s King became a leader of the movement for equal civil rights for all races in America, and he wrote many articles and five books. In *Strength to Love* he wrote:

> We shall match your capacity to inflict suffering by our capacity to endure suffering . . . Do to us what you will, and we shall continue to love you. Throw us in jail, and we shall still love you. Bomb our homes and threaten our children, and we shall still love you. Send your hooded perpetrators of violence into our community at the midnight hour and beat us and leave us half dead, and we shall still love you. But be assured that we will wear you down by our capacity to suffer. One day we shall win freedom, but not only for ourselves. We shall so appeal to your heart and conscience that we shall win you in the process, and our victory will be a double victory.[98]

King had many admirers, but like Jesus Christ, his master, King also had many enemies who hated his ideals and were opposed to the integration the campaigns promoted. King was imprisoned more than twenty times and assaulted at least four times. On the April 4, 1968, on the eve of a protest march, he was assassinated on the balcony of his motel in Memphis, Tennessee. He was thirty-nine years of age.

We are inspired by the life and death of the human Jesus, who was opposed and killed because of his ideals. We are inspired too by those who, like Martin Luther King, follow Jesus' example to the uttermost and "lay down their lives for their brothers," as well as by others who, like Gandhi, would not claim to be Christians but whose lives show similar ideals: compassion for those rejected and overlooked by society's

---

97. Matt 5–7.

98. King, *Strength to Love*, 56.

"important people," a passion for justice and equality of everyone, and (where necessary) nonviolent action to bring about change.

But most human beings do not believe in Jesus and do not follow his Way.

We Have Choice, and All Have Chosen (at Least Sometimes) to Rebel

We all need salvation.

From the very beginning, the Bible makes it clear that we have choice as to how we live our lives. We are not puppets, because love can never be forced.

Knowing that we would misuse our freedom, knowing that we would go our own way and cause the fractured and imperfect world with which we are all familiar, God in his love still chose to allow us to *choose* whether to love and serve him and each other—or not.

The Old Testament opens with two accounts of God's creation of the world.

The first account affirms God's good pleasure with his creation: "God saw all that he had made, and it was very good,"[99] but in the second account we are told how the first man and woman, Adam and Eve, rebelled against the commandment of God, and were therefore rejected from the idyllic garden of Eden.[100] This account is commonly referred to as "the fall."

Since Augustine in the fourth century, many Christian theologians, particularly in the West, have taught that sin and evil entered the world *because* Adam and Eve disobeyed God by eating the forbidden fruit, which would give knowledge of good and evil.[101] "The imagery of 'The Fall' . . . expresses the idea that human nature has 'fallen' from its original pristine state . . . The created order no longer directly corresponds to the 'goodness' of its original integrity. It has lapsed. It has been spoiled and ruined—but not irredeemably as the doctrines of salvation and justification affirm."[102] But the story of Gen 3 has also been read as an account of developing sexual awareness. In the second century, Irenaeus wrote, "Be-

99. Gen 1:31.
100. Gen 3:16–19, 23–24.
101. Gen 3:4.
102. McGrath, *Historical Theology*, 35.

ing but recently made, they had no knowledge of procreation of children; they had to grow up first then in this way to propagate themselves."[103] And following this interpretation, Clare Amos comments, "The play and dynamics of the relationship of male and female is undoubtedly a theme in the story . . . it is not a 'fall' that human beings experience . . . but an over-abrupt rise, a too hasty transition from naivety and innocence to maturity. Human beings are children who grew up too quickly."[104]

In this first book of the Bible, we immediately read other stories of a humanity prone to discord and unease. Perhaps Karl Barth is right when he argues that "there never was a golden age. There is no point in looking back to one. The first man was immediately the first sinner."[105] So we read that Adam and Eve's first-born son, Cain, was a murderer who killed his brother Abel.[106] Then there is the strange account of the "sons of God marrying the daughters of men,"[107] a story that some rabbis have taken as the primal account of how the good creation was spoiled:

> Jewish writings from around the New Testament period tended to prefer to use stories based on Gen 6:1–4 rather than Gen 3 to explain the origin of evil in the world—it is perhaps more comforting to suggest that evil originates from outside human beings rather than from within.[108]

The rabbis' theory is perhaps supported by the fact that it is *after this* that God laments,

> The LORD saw that the wickedness of humankind was great in the earth, and that every inclination of the thoughts of their hearts was only evil continually. And the LORD was sorry that he had made humankind on the earth, and it grieved him to his heart. So the LORD said, "I will blot out from the earth the human beings I have created—people together with animals."[109]

This leads into the story of the flood and the rescue of righteous Noah, who "found favor in the eyes of the Lord."[110] Carefully obeying

---

103. Irenaeus, *Against Heresies*, 3:32.

104. Amos, *Book of Genesis*, 41–43.

105. Barth, *Church Dogmatics*, 4:509.

106. Gen 4.

107. Gen 6:1–7.

108. Amos, *Book of Genesis*, 36.

109. Gen 6:5–7.

110. Gen 6:8.

God's instructions, Noah built a huge boat, the ark that housed all his family and representatives of the animals, and safely rode out the flood.

The early chapters of Genesis—and indeed the whole Bible, as well as the experience of every one of us—show again and again that humans, who have the privilege and responsibility of free will, inevitably make wrong choices. Since the first man and the first woman lived on earth, this is the way things have always been. The name Adam is very close to the Hebrew *Adamah*, meaning "from the earth," and physiologically, humans are highly intelligent animals. There are only minute differences between the genetic structure of humans and chimpanzees; we retain animal instincts and often their ruthless drives. It is entirely appropriate to interpret Gen 3 as a myth showing how "everyman" and "everywoman" make wrong choices. Adam is mankind; he is humanity—akin to the animals, but more than an animal. I like Terry Pratchett's picturesque description of humanity as "the place where the falling angel meets the rising ape."[111] Despite the fact that he declares himself to be an atheist, Pratchett's catchy comment resonates with the biblical teaching that humans are made in the image of God,[112] but that the image is marred in each one of us.[113]

Because of the wrong choices we all make, we are all out of fellowship with God and all too often in conflict with each other. It has often been observed that original sin is the only verifiable doctrine.

We all need salvation.

Even "righteous Noah" soon fell into disgrace.[114] He was not perfect, but he was saved from the flood because he believed God and obeyed him (despite the fact that the instructions to make a huge boat must have seemed mind-bogglingly foolish before the rain started). This obedience is, of course, in stark contrast to Adam and Eve, who disobeyed what must have also seemed a foolish command not to eat the fruit of a certain tree.

God ever looks for faith and obedience, but he has created humankind with a capacity to reason and question—to *choose* whether or not to believe in God, and whether or not to take what seems to be the right way with the evidence before us. And all too often, we choose *not* to believe, *not* to obey . . .

---

111. Pratchett, *Hogfather.*

112. Gen 1:26–27; 5:1; 9:6; Wis 2:23; Col 3:10; Jas 3:9.

113. Rom 3:23; Isa 64:6. Hence Calvin speaks of the "total depravity" of humankind.

114. Gen 9:20–25.

After the horror of flood, a beautiful rainbow appears in the sky, and God makes a covenant with creation itself never again to destroy it.[115] This is the first of several covenants in the Bible, but it is unique because it is without conditions. It is a one-sided promise that despite man's continuing sinfulness, God will not destroy humanity or nature again. It is a promise of pure grace—unconditional, universal, and eternal. God knows that human beings will always be sinful,[116] but he will care for them anyway.

Since that time, there have been many massive floods. In recent years, there have been terrible tsunamis and major floods. As I write this, New York is recovering from a massive hurricane and the worst flooding for over one hundred years.[117] But terrible as these floods have been, they have not been worldwide. There seem to be some limits (arguably set by God) to the destructive power of nature.

The awful judgment of the flood was perhaps not the end of the story for those who were drowned. The New Testament tells us that between his death and resurrection, Jesus descended to hell and preached specifically (but not only) to those "who disobeyed long ago" while Noah was building the ark.[118] I take this as one pointer among many towards the hope that God's love extends even beyond the grave, seeking and saving the lost. (See chapter 6.)

And a few generations after Noah, we read the beginnings of a salvation plan.

Abraham becomes the father and founder of God's chosen nation, the Jews—chosen not because they were the only nation loved by God, but "to be a kingdom of priests and a holy nation"—the ultimate aim is to reveal God to the nations.[119] God had promised Abraham that "all peoples on earth will be blessed through you,"[120] and throughout the Old Testament we glimpse prophetic pictures of the nations coming to worship the God of Israel. Christians believe that these prophecies will in the end be fulfilled through Jesus, who is the Savior of humanity, and ultimately of all creation. More on this will be discussed in chapter 7.

---

115. Gen 9:8–17.

116. Gen 8:21.

117. Hurricane Sandy in October 2012.

118. 1 Pet 3:19–21.

119. Exod 19:6.

120. Gen 12:3.

The Jewish Scriptures (our Old Testament) unsparingly recount humanity's sinfulness right from the start, and not only the apostasy of "the nations" (nations other than Israel), but also of Israel herself—yet Judaism has no doctrine of the fall.

The primacy that Christian theology usually gives to Adam and Eve's sin by calling it the fall, or the root of original sin, is based on the writings of Saint Paul in the New Testament. However, this was not emphasized until Augustine in the fourth century—and the Western church has largely followed Augustine in this.

Paul probably accepted the historical fact of Adam as a person, though he may have seen this as mythical representation rather than a historical reality.[121]

In his closely argued letter to the Romans, Paul writes,

> Just as sin entered into the world through one man, and death through sin, and in this way death came to all men because all have sinned . . . just as the result of one trespass was condemnation for all men, so also the result of one act of righteousness was justification that brings life for all men. For just as through the disobedience of the one man the many were made sinners, so also through the obedience of the one man the many will be made righteous.[122]

And to the Corinthians he writes in similar vein:

> As all die in Adam, so in Christ all will be made alive . . . The first man, Adam became a living being; the last Adam, a life-giving spirit . . . just as we have borne the likeness of the earthly man, so shall we bear the likeness of the man from heaven.[123]

Paul's aim in these passages is to stress that we *all* need salvation "because all have sinned," just as Adam did. Or, taking evolution into the picture, we are all "earthly," like Adam—we are human animals. Elsewhere, Paul speaks about "the old man" in us.[124]

Christ reverses that sinfulness by carrying sin on the cross—both actual sins and our innately sinful animal nature. And this is for *all men*. A straightforward reading of these passages is unequivocally universalist—both as regards the damning effects of human sinfulness, *and* the

121. He would, of course, have no concept of evolution to weave into his theology.
122. Rom 5:12, 18–19.
123. 1 Cor 15:22, 45, 49.
124. Rom 6:6, Eph 4:22, Col 3:9.

redeeming effect of Christ's death. However, many Christians who accept the concept of universal condemnation apply the effects of Christ's
death only to those who are "in Christ" (that is, only to believers). I was
therefore heartened to read Gregory MacDonald's endorsement of the
more straightforward and obvious interpretation of Paul's argument in
Romans. He writes:

> Christ's redemption is as wide as sin's corruption in that it reach-
> es everyone . . . Christ's act of righteous obedience on the cross
> totally reverses the results of Adam's act of disobedience in Eden
> . . . Adam's sin brought condemnation and death to *all* people
> (compare 3:23). Christ's righteous act brings justification and
> eternal life to *all* people. Indeed Paul is at pains to make clear
> that the 'all people' who were 'made sinners' and 'condemned'
> are the *very same* 'all people' who will be 'made righteous'; and
> who, in Christ, are justified and have life. This is clear from the
> way he uses parallelism in v. 18 and 19.[125]

Because, like Adam, we are made of dust, our human or animal
nature is sinful, and we will die. But death is overturned by Christ's resurrection, and because of our solidarity with the incarnate, crucified, and
resurrected Christ, we too are promised resurrection.

The New Testament reveals again and again that Jesus Christ lived
and died *for us* (that is, for all humankind) and *for our salvation.* Because
he loves us, God longs for our responding love and faith, and those who
respond in faith can *know* that they are saved and rejoice with Paul.

Christ's death was for all people and all times—even for those who
do not know about him or believe in him yet:

> God our Savior . . . wants all men to be saved and to come to a
> knowledge of the truth. For there is one God and one mediator
> between God and men, the man Christ Jesus, who gave himself
> as a ransom for all men—the testimony given in its proper time
> . . . we have put our hope in the living God, who is the Savior of
> all men, and especially of those who believe.[126]

But the salvation, offered for all, faces us with a crisis of choice: we
in the twenty-first century must choose whether to follow him, or not, no
less than his contemporaries in the first century.

In his gospel, John writes,

125. MacDonald, *Evangelical Universalist*, 80.

126. 1 Tim 2:3–6; 4:10.

> God so loved the world that he gave his one and only Son, that whoever believes in him shall not perish but have eternal life. For God did not send his Son into the world to condemn the world, but to save the world though him. Whoever believes in him is not condemned, but whoever does not believe stands condemned already because he has not believed in the name of God's one and only Son. This is the verdict: Light has come into the world, but men loved darkness instead of light because their deeds were evil. Everyone who does evil hates the light, and will not come into the light for fear that his deeds will be exposed.[127]

The purpose of Jesus' coming is to save the world. His desire is that men and women might turn to him and receive "eternal life"—*aionios*, which could be expressed as "the life of God himself," or the life of the age to come—beginning now.[128] Those who stumble in the darkness, like Nicodemus (to whom these words were spoken), may come to Christ, who is the light; and when they come, they will find love and acceptance and will be transformed in a transformation that is as radical as being born again or made new.[129]

The Greek word *krinein*, translated in the passage above as "condemn," means to judge *or* to condemn and is the root of the English words "crisis" and "critic." As a person comes to realize the meaning of Jesus' life and death, he or she faces a critical moment of judgment and decision. Jesus does not come as judge *with the purpose of* condemning the world. The situation is that those who do not believe are *already lost and in danger of perishing* in their darkness and evil deeds,[130] because, as we have seen, we all have what I have called an animal or sinful nature. So it is that John says, "they stand condemned already."[131] Here, and in many other passages,[132] John faces his readers with a stark choice: to perish without God, or to receive his gift of eternal life—*the life of God himself* —which is the very reason that God sent his Son into the world.

Similarly, in Matthew's gospel Jesus says, "Enter through the narrow gate. For wide is the gate and broad is the road that leads to destruction,

---

127. John 3:16–20.

128. We will look at the meaning of *aionios* in more detail in chapter 6 (p. 170–171).

129. John 1:12–13, 3:3–8.

130. vv. 18–19.

131. v. 18.

132. See John 1:10–13; 5:25–29; 6:33–40; 6:53–54; 7:37–39; 8:39–47; 10:26–28; 12:47–48.

and many enter through it. But small is the gate and narrow the road that leads to life, and only a few find it."[133]

This leads me to the central dilemma this book explores.

What Happens to Those Who Make the Wrong Choice?

What happens to those who do not hear about the good news about Jesus, or who hear but do not believe? Or, to pose the question in biblical terms: What happens to those who do not "come to the light" or "take the 'broad road that leads to destruction"?[134]

The New Testament reveals Jesus as the one who brings light and life to a world that is in darkness and to people who are perishing without him. Not everyone who heard Jesus when he was alive responded to him, and we know only too well that the majority of the population of our globe does not respond to the Christian message now, in the twenty-first century.

Many have never heard or understood the gospel. Many hold to other faiths or ideologies. Many are just too busy or too traumatized to believe in a God of love, and many are simply indifferent, cynical, skeptical, or wrapped up in self, and the list could go on . . .

And we may well ask: What happens to those who die in infancy (or even those who are aborted before birth) before they can properly choose between right and wrong or respond to the gospel? What happens to those who do not hear the message of the gospel? Or who hear but do not understand? Or those who hear a distorted message? "What if the missionary [who might have shared the good news] has a flat tire?"[135] What happens to those who cannot see the light because the darkness in which they are enveloped is too great? To many people, the idea of a God of love seems to be nonsense because they have never known love, or the burden of the world's pain is so great that they cannot comprehend the gospel of a God of love. None of us sees God clearly. To a greater or lesser extent, the sin of the world and our own spiritual blindness hides his face, and the church often gives a distorted or feeble message. As Paul writes,

133. Matt 7:13–14.

134. John 3:20; Matt 7:13.

135. Bell poses this question in *Love Wins*. He asks, "If our salvation, our future, our destiny is dependent on others bringing the message to us, teaching us, showing us—what happens if they don't do their part—what if the missionary gets a flat tire? . . . Is your future in somebody else's hands?" (Bell, *Love Wins*, 9).

"Now we see but a poor reflection as in a mirror."[136] We will return to this verse and explore it further in chapter 6 (p. 159–161).

We may, perhaps, readily believe that God sees and knows the hearts of those who would have responded if they had heard, or if the darkness and hurt in their lives had been less profound, and that through his mercy and love, they will be saved.

But there are undoubtedly many whose hearts are too hard, too indifferent, or too selfish to respond to Christ, and some appear to comprehend the message but *choose* to reject it, knowing what they are doing—or not doing.

It would seem that the "unrepentant thief" crucified alongside Jesus might fall into this category[137] (though we might ask, did he in fact know who it was that he was blaspheming?) And it is notable that Jesus, who promised the "repentant thief" that he would be with him in paradise "this day,"[138] did not turn to the one who was blaspheming and tell him that he was heading for condemnation or plead with him to repent and believe also. I have heard more than one sermon in which these two men were—rightly—contrasted, and the preacher went on to confidently contrast their eternal fate also. But the fact is that though Jesus promises paradise for the repentant man, we are given no insight into what would happen to the other.

And surely those who actually crucified Jesus should be condemned?

But we read that Jesus pleaded for their forgiveness: "Father, forgive them, for they do not know what they are doing."[139] Some early manuscripts do not include this sentence, but it is entirely in tune with Jesus' appeal to his disciples to forgive "not seven times, but seventy times seven."[140] And if this sentence is added as a gloss, it would point to a tradition that understood that Jesus would desire the forgiveness of those who crucified him.

To some, the demands of following Jesus seem too high, just as they were, unsurprisingly perhaps, for the rich young man from whom Jesus demanded the sale of *everything* to follow him[141]—but I wonder how

136. 1 Cor 13:12.
137. Luke 23:39.
138. Luke 23:43.
139. Luke 23:34.
140. Matt 18:22.
141. Matt 19:21–22; Mark 10:21–22.

many of those of us who claim to be his disciples have in fact sold or given up *everything?*

And how will our Lord judge the scribes and Pharisees (and their modern-day equivalents) against whom Jesus pronounced with great severity: "Woe to you . . . hypocrites"?[142]

Jesus' radical condemnation of the scrupulously religious Pharisees was at least in part because they felt themselves to be above condemnation. His aim was to arouse in them an awareness that they too were guilty and in need of the grace of forgiveness. In this, Jesus was in line with the prophets who denounced religious rites without accompanying justice and fairness.

So it is that Amos thunders:

> I hate, I despise your religious feasts;
> I cannot stand your assemblies.
> Even though you bring me burnt offerings and grain offerings,
> I will not accept them.
> Though you bring me choice fellowship offerings,
> I will have no regard for them.
> Away with the noise of your songs!
> I will not listen to the music of your harps.
> But let justice roll on like a river,
> righteousness like a never-failing stream![143]

Jesus, like Amos and the other prophets, was aiming to arouse a sense of guilt in those who felt that, because of their religiosity, they were holy and upright, beyond guilt. Only by becoming aware that they too needed to repent would they be in a position to access the grace of forgiveness and inward transformation.

The psychotherapist Paul Tournier, discussing the story of the woman taken in the act of adultery,[144] writes:

> It is as if the presence of Christ brought about the strangest of inversions: He wipes out the guilt in the woman who was crushed by it, and arouses guilt in those who felt none . . . Before Jesus there are not two opposed human categories, the guilty and the righteous; there are only the guilty—the woman to whom

142. See Matt 23:13–29; Luke 11:42–52.
143. Amos 5:21–24.
144. John 8:1–11.

Jesus speaks God's pardon, and the men who will receive it in their turn, since by their silent withdrawal they admit their own guilt. Such is the great reversal . . . which is found throughout the Bible. In psychological terms, we could formulate it thus: God blots out conscious fault, but He brings to consciousness repressed guilt[145] . . . To offer grace only is to cut off half the Gospel. Grace is for the woman trembling at her guilt. But her accusers will be able to find grace only by rediscovering for themselves the shudder of guilt . . . Jesus does not awaken guilt in order to condemn, but to save, for grace is given to him who humbles himself, and becomes aware of his guilt.

Jesus himself formulates this paradoxical inversion of things in these words: "So the last will be first, and the first last" (Matt 20:16).

There is not only the rehabilitation of the scorned, but the humiliation of the scornful. To the latter the Bible, and Jesus Christ Himself, speaks with an implacable severity which . . . can only be understood if we are aware of its ultimate aim. It aims, not to suppress the arrogant sinner, but to arouse his sense of guilt, and so to humble him, thereby opening for him the way to grace.[146]

And how will Jesus judge Judas, who was one of his chosen disciples, and yet betrayed him?

In his monumental *Church Dogmatics*, Karl Barth includes a long and interesting section on "the rejected"; i.e., those who have rejected Jesus so that they themselves warrant being rejected by God. He focuses on Judas as the model of one who was truly elected and yet, because he betrayed Christ, who also epitomized one who was rejected. Barth writes:

It is a serious matter to be threatened by hell, sentenced to hell, worthy of hell, and already on the road to hell. On the other hand we must not minimize the fact that we actually know of only one certain triumph of hell—the handing-over of Jesus—and that this triumph of hell took place in order that it would never again be able to triumph over anyone . . . Jesus Christ is *the* Rejected of God, for God makes Himself rejected in Him, and has Himself alone tasted to the depths all that rejection means . . . Scripture speaks of countless men, as it does of Judas, in such a way that we must assume that they have lived and died without even the possibility, let alone the fulfillment, of any saving repentance . . .

145. Tournier, *Guilt and Grace*, 111–12.
146. Ibid., 142.

whatever God may inflict on them, He certainly does not inflict
what He inflicted on Himself by delivering up Jesus Christ. For
He has done it for them, in order that they should not suffer the
judgment which accompanies the cleansing of the world's sin,
and therefore should not be lost . . . in view of the efficacy of this
event, we must not lose sight of the hope of the future deliverance of the rejected at the very frontier of perdition.[147]

Barth sees Jesus Christ, God's chosen servant, as both *the* Elect of
God (in whom we are elected) and also *the* Rejected of God who carries
on the cross God's rejection of sin—the sin of Judas and of all the rest of
mankind. Jesus was damned in our place.

The closing dialogue of Graham Greene's *Brighton Rock* hauntingly
captures the passionate love of God that is revealed in the crucifixion
of the Christ.

Pinkie, a boy-gang leader and murderer, had married Rose in a
cold-blooded attempt to stop her giving evidence against him and had
persuaded her to join him in a suicide pact. He has just committed suicide. What should Rose do?

In her confusion and distress, she goes to see an old priest:

She says, "I wish I'd killed myself. I ought to 'ave killed myself
. . . I'm not asking for absolution. I don't want absolution. I want
to be like him—damned" . . . She would have found the courage
now to kill herself if she hadn't been afraid that somewhere in
that obscure countryside of death they might miss each other—
mercy operating somehow for one and not for the other . . .
The old priest suddenly began to talk . . . "There was a man, a
Frenchman, you wouldn't know about him, my child, who had
the same idea as you. He was a good man, a holy man, and he
lived in sin all through his life, because he couldn't bear the idea
that any soul could suffer damnation . . . This man decided that if
any soul was going to be damned, he would be damned too. He
never took the sacraments; he never married his wife in church.
I don't know, my child, but some people think he was—well, a
saint . . . You can't conceive, my child, nor can I or anyone, the
appalling . . . strangeness of the mercy of God . . . It was a case
of greater love hath no man than this that he lay down his soul
for his friend."[148]

147. Barth, *Doctrine of God*, 496–97. The whole section on "the determination of
the rejected" is relevant (ibid., 449–506.)

148. Greene, *Brighton Rock*, 267–68.

I too have sometimes felt that if the gospel includes damnation, then I should seek not salvation but damnation in solidarity with the "rejected"—those who have rejected the offered salvation or who do not know about it, and so have become "the Rejected."

For how can I, or anyone, believe that I have been saved, while others have not?

Paul says much the same: "I have great sorrow and unceasing anguish in my heart. For I could wish that I myself were cursed and cut off from Christ for the sake of my brothers, those of my own race."[149]

But this is what Christ has already done. He was damned in our place.

The Bible Speaks of Judgment, Wrath, and Evil Things Happening

It has always been difficult for humans to come to terms with the evil and suffering that mars our beautiful world.

A fundamental tenet of both Christianity and Judaism is the belief that God is *good*. He is a God of *love* and does not inflict pain and misfortune out of bad temper, capriciousness, or vindictiveness just to show how great and important he is (as many pagan "gods," some earthly fathers, and some earthly rulers do). But it can be very hard to believe that God is Love when life is tough, and though many Christians testify that they have experienced God's love as gentle kindness in their lives and sense his tender help in times of trial, grief, or pain, many experience only his absence—and the apparent sternness of life itself. C. S. Lewis relates the devastating anguish of God's apparent indifference to his need for comfort when his wife died:

> Meanwhile, where is God? . . . When you are happy . . . and turn to Him with gratitude and praise, you will be—or so it feels—welcomed with open arms. But go to him when your need is desperate, when all other help is vain, and what do you find? A door slammed in your face, and a sound of bolting and double bolting on the inside. After that, silence . . . Why is He so present a commander in our time of prosperity and so very absent a helper in time of trouble?[150]

149. Rom 9:2–3. Similarly, Moses pleaded to be "blotted out of God's book" instead of the Israelites (Exod 32:30–32).

150. Lewis, *Grief Observed*, 9.

From our position on earth, bound by space and time, it is hard to reconcile the fact of sin and pain with faith in a good and omnipotent God who we can call Father. This tension has caused many sincere Christians (including myself at times) to doubt their faith and caused many others to find faith impossible. The atheist can simply say, "the confusion, imperfection and chaos is what you would expect when everything happens by chance," while the agnostic simply admits that he does not understand. Many Christian thinkers have attempted to deal with this dilemma,[151] and we can only look briefly at this massive subject here.

We have seen that the early chapters of the Bible show that sin was active from the beginning, as was its result—God's wrath, and suffering—but we also see mitigating touches of mercy active from the beginning. Adam and Eve are rejected from the garden of Eden, but "God made them garments of skin . . . and clothed them."[152] Cain was under a curse for killing his brother, but "the Lord put a mark on Cain so that no one who found him would kill him."[153] After the great flood that Noah rode out in his ark (with his family and the animals) God promised that "never again will the waters become a flood to destroy all life,"[154] and Peter tells us that between his death and resurrection, Jesus preached to those "spirits in prison" who had been drowned by the flood.[155]

Some biblical authors assume that evil and suffering happen as a result of God's wrath—which is directed at those who rebel against him, or who worship other gods, or who act unjustly to their fellow men and women, or who fail to show mercy to the downtrodden and weak—and that his wrath is also directed against nations that threaten the chosen people of God.[156]

But the idea that suffering is the *result of sin* is also challenged by the Bible, especially in some psalms and classically in the book of Job, which is a famous ancient exploration of the problem. The prologue portrays Satan challenging God to allow Job, the "blameless and upright" servant of God, to be tested by one calamity after another. Job's friends all believe that God is punishing him for some hidden sin and urge him to repent,

151. For example, see Lewis, *Problem of Pain*; Jones, *Why Do People Suffer?*; and Hick, *Evil and the God of Love*; and there are many more.

152. Gen 3:21–24.

153. Gen 4:15.

154. Gen 9:15.

155. 1 Pet 3:20.

156. The classic statement of this is found in Deut 28.

but Job hotly denies this and declares his uprightness. In the end, God appears to Job, and the only answer to his suffering that is given (in a poem of awesome beauty) is the inscrutable one that God is the God of creation and beyond the understanding of mankind. Almost as an afterthought (and some scholars therefore believe that the "afterword" is added by a later redactor), Job's fortunes are ultimately restored, and "the Lord blessed the latter part of Job's life more than the first."[157]

In the New Testament, suffering is often considered to be a means of testing faith and developing character, showing that God is not unlike an earthly parent. He watches with a father's care, he reproves with a father's tenderness, and he corrects us as a good father will sometimes need to correct his children, but only and always for their ultimate good.[158] Those of us who have been responsible for children as parents, grandparents, teachers, or caregivers know that we have to be both gentle and firm when dealing with children. We call it "tough love" when a parent does not swerve from saying "No" to a whining, wheedling child who wants sweets or something else not in their best interests, or when a parent imposes sanctions for disobedience, but such firmness often seems to be severe and even ruthless to the child.

The Bible tells us that God is Love, and sometimes his love can seem to us mortals to be very tough indeed. Though many experience his love as gentle kindness and have sensed being held tenderly in times of trial, grief, and pain, there are many others who (like C. S. Lewis, quoted above) experience only his absence and the severity of life itself.

Life's problems can indeed be tough.

God does not stop our foolishness from causing us problems. He does not prevent the harmful consequences that result from unwise, careless, or downright sinful actions of mankind. To use Paul's phrase, he "gives people up" to pursue their self-destructive, sinful desires.[159]

If we put our hand in the fire, we get burnt. If we smoke, we increase our risk of cancer. If we drink too much, we may damage our health, our careers, and our relationships. If we spend more than we can afford, we risk serious debt and losing what we have. If we cheat, we risk being found out and losing our jobs or, again, ruining our relationships. If we are

157. Job 42:12.
158. See Rom 5:3–5; Jas 1:3–4; 1 Pet 1:6–7; 5:10.
159. Rom 1:18–32.

promiscuous, we damage relationships again and risk acquiring sexually transmitted diseases, including the modern worldwide plague of AIDS.

It is worth pausing at this point to briefly consider the awful lessons posed to the world by the AIDS epidemic that has devastated large swathes of Africa and is becoming more widespread in the West, especially amongst the homosexual community. The statistics are frightening. In 2013, the World Health Organization estimated that thirty-five million people are living with AIDS, while 1.5 million people died of the disease, 190,000 of whom were children under fifteen.[160]

Is this a horrendous example of the principle stated in the Ten Commandments that "I the Lord your God, am a jealous God, punishing the children for the sin of the fathers to the third and fourth generation of those who hate me"?[161] The epidemic would dry up in a couple of generations if human beings worldwide were faithful to one sexual partner for life (either heterosexual or homosexual, provided that promiscuity and unfaithfulness came to an end). Is God shouting at a deaf and promiscuous world that the way we are living is not how he planned it? We are failing to live as God intended, not only in the area of sexuality, but in many other ways as well (such as economic greed, exploitation, and violence, to name but a few).

But the AIDS epidemic is not only a warning to the world; it is also a call to the world to act with compassion—and, all too slowly, the world is responding. An unsung army of brave and hard-working grandparents have from the beginning taken on responsibility for many of the orphans in Africa. Gradually, society is learning not to shun the sufferers, but to accept, embrace, and help them. (The Terence Higgins Trust and the late Princess Diana led the way in acceptance; sadly the Christian churches were often more condemning than accepting in the early days of the pandemic.) Many sufferers are the innocent victims of the careless actions of others, and even the "guilty" partners or parents are often just unfortunate insofar as many others behave in the same way without contracting disease. And most of us are in no position to throw stones, but can only think, "there but for the grace of God go I" (though it must be admitted that God's grace often seems quite unpredictable in its protective effects). In face of the threat to "developed" nations, medicines have been developed to keep the illness at bay so that the sufferer can enjoy a

160. World Health Organization, "Global Summary of the AIDS Epidemic: 2013," July 21, 2014, http://www.who.int/hiv/data/epi_core_dec2014.png?ua=1.

161. Exod 20:5.

near-normal lifespan. Gradually, these medicines are being made available in impoverished nations and to at least some of those who cannot afford to pay, and many organizations have been set up to combat the disease.

The AIDS epidemic is an example of how a threat can act as both a judgment and a warning, yet also as a call to humanity to act with compassion and grace.

Global warming also calls to the world: both with a threat of judgment for our carelessness and as a call to act with restraint and careful stewardship of the world's resources—not only for our own sake, but for the sake of other nations and for the generations that will follow us.

But none of this really solves the problem when the chips are down and we are faced with personal tragedy of some kind. At such times, there may be some comfort in remembering that God in Christ not only bears the world's sin, but also shares the world's pain in the broken body of the Christ. (see p. 14–17) Suffering is finite. It will end (in death if not before), and we are promised that there will ultimately come a time when "He will wipe every tear from their eyes. There will be no more death or mourning or crying or pain, for the old order of things has passed away."[162]

The Views of Irenaeus

As we have seen (p. 35), many Christians (especially in the West, and especially since Augustine in the fourth century) have linked sin, suffering, and the imperfections of the world to the so-called "fall of mankind." The thought is that God created a good and perfect world, but Adam and Eve's disobedience, recounted in the second and third chapters of Genesis, somehow spoiled everything. This fall has been reversed by Christ as far as sin is concerned and will ultimately be fully reversed at the end of time when God creates a new heaven and a new earth.

But an earlier explanation was proposed by Irenaeus in the second century AD.

Irenaeus thought that the world is not finished yet; God's purpose was not to construct a paradise free of pain and suffering, but a place where soul-development could take place. The human race was created in a state of imperfection, but with an immense capacity for spiritual and moral development that gives us the capacity to be transformed into "children

---

162. Rev 21:4. See also chapter 7.

of God." Human goodness comes from moral decisions made in an imperfect world; resisting temptation teaches us valuable lessons. There is a tension between the selfish need for survival and the spiritual and moral need to rise above our self-centeredness, and in this war of life, choices we make can aid our development into creatures more in the likeness of God: "God did not design the universe as a cushion but as a challenge."[163]

These ideas resonate with experience, with the Bible, with the thinking of modern Judaism, and with a modern scientific understanding of creation. The world that we know is still being made—evolution is still progressing. As Paul writes, "The whole creation is groaning and travailing in pain."[164] We live with the promise of the new heaven and new earth to inspire and motivate us, but though the world is amazing and teeming with life, and though God has declared it to be "very good,"[165] yet it is clearly imperfect. Nature is "red in tooth and claw." There are tornadoes and floods and tsunamis.

We are, as the psalmist exclaims in awe, "fearfully and wonderfully made,"[166] and our bodies are equipped with astonishing and intricate healing properties, without which medicine and surgery would be impossible. Nevertheless, things often go wrong, and there is much disease and suffering, not all of which can be cured, and all living beings will ultimately die.

The views of the scientist and Anglican priest John Polkinghorne[167] seem to be in tune with Irenaeian theodicy: God has made a creation in which creatures can make themselves, which in his opinion is a greater good than a ready-made world. "A God of love is not simply a cosmic puppet master who pulls every string. He must allow creatures to be themselves and make themselves. There is an inevitable shadow side to the evolutionary process." The world we know is "a world with ragged edges where order and disorder interlace with each other, and where the exploration of possibility by chance will lead not only to the evolution of systems of increasing complexity, but also the evolution of systems imperfectly formed and malfunctioning."[168]

163. Barclay, *Apostles' Creed*, 24.

164. Rom 8:22.

165. Gen 1:31.

166. Ps 139:14.

167. The Reverend John Charlton Polkinghorne, KBE, FRS, is an English theoretical physicist, theologian, writer, and Anglican priest. He has written five books on physics, and twenty-six on the relationship between science and religion.

168. Polkinghorne, *Science and Providence*, 67.

Cancer is the result of those "ragged edges." It is important that DNA copying is not perfect because if it were, evolution would not be possible, but the downside of the creative potential of DNA copying's imperfections is the possibility of cancer, congenital malformations, and genetically-driven diseases.

Irenaeus' ideas are complimented by his belief in an afterlife in which the process can be completed. If the idea of hell grew out of the realization that punishment for sin does not happen fully in this life, then the idea of a "cleansing hell," which will be explored in chapter 6, grows from the realization that God clearly does not find, save, or transform everyone in this life. For that reason, a doctrine of a never-ending hell, forever shut off from the love of God and perhaps with untold suffering and anguish thrown in, is inconsistent with the God of justice and relentless love revealed in the Bible.

The Concept of "The Wrath"

In many of his writings, Paul speaks of "the wrath" in an impersonal way, almost as if "wrath" is a proper noun.[169] The magistrate is represented as a divine agent, and "an avenger *for wrath* to the evil-doer."[170] The New King James Version is precise in these situations, but confusingly, many of the modern English versions often insert "of God" when it is absent in the Greek.[171]

Dodd points out that Paul is in line with the psalmists and prophets in this respect:

> It would be fair to say that in speaking of wrath and judgment, the prophets and psalmists have their minds mainly on events, actual or expected, conceived as the *inevitable* results of sin; and when they speak of mercy, they are thinking mainly of the personal relation between God and His people. Wrath is *the effect of* human sin: mercy is not the effect of human goodness, but is inherent in the character of God. When they speak of His righteousness . . . they find it consummated in a merciful deliverance of His people from the power and oppression of sin—in fact, from "the Wrath" . . . [Paul] retains the concept of "the Wrath of God" . . . not to

169. Rom 2:5; 3:5; 5:9; 12:19; 13: 5; 1 Thess 2:16.

170. Rom 13:4.

171. Paul only uses the phrase "the wrath *of God*" in three places: Rom 1:18; Col 3:6; Eph 5:6.

describe the attitude of God to man, but to describe an *inevitable process of cause and effect in a moral universe.*[172]

But even if "the wrath" infers that painful consequences of our actions are often innate to a moral universe rather than the result of an angry God punishing us for our misdemeanors, there are many passages in both testaments that imply a final judgment, a "coming wrath."[173] Believers escape the wrath because they "receive salvation through our Lord Jesus Christ."[174] We previously considered John's declaration that whoever does not believe stands "condemned already." (See p. 37–38.) There are many other passages in the New Testament that say that without faith in Christ, mankind as a whole, as well as individuals in their particularity, are in danger of hell or destruction, often by fire,[175] are cursed, or are thrown out of the kingdom of heaven.[176] They are dead in trespasses and sins[177] or are in some unspecified way in danger of divine wrath.[178]

Is it possible to accept the truth of such passages, which imply divine retribution for those who do not accept the salvation that is offered, *and also* to maintain that those other passages which portray ultimate salvation for all will one day be true?

The church has wrestled with such questions ever since it came into being, and the majority view—at least since Augustine in the fourth century—has usually been that the "universal salvation" passages will not be fulfilled, and there will indeed be many who suffer not only from the results of "wrath" in this life, but also from divine retribution in the life to come. This has often been interpreted as a very literal, fiery hell, where the wicked suffer in some way forever, or perhaps (rather more mercifully) that they will simply be destroyed. Death will be the end, and for them there will be no resurrection and no eternal life.

In a recent television series entitled "How God Made the English"[179] the historian Diarmaid MacCulloch expressed the view that the medieval

---

172. Dodd, *Romans*, 49–50, emphasis mine.

173. Matt 3:7; 1 Thess 1:10.

174. 1 Thess 5:9.

175. See Matt 10:28; 18:6; 25:41.

176. Luke 13: 24–30.

177. Col 2:13.

178. See Rom 2:8–9; Eph 5:6; Col 3:6; 1 Thess 2:16, to mention but a few.

179. A series of three programs shown on BBC Two on the evenings of March 17, 24, and 31, 2012, http://www.bbc.co.uk/programmes/b01hbkvt.

fear of a very literal hell was behind the terrible persecutions and burn-ings of those whom the contemporary authorities considered to be he-retical. After all, the thinking went, if God is going to send heretics to hell for all eternity, human authorities are acting mercifully when they consign heretics to the brief flames of an earthly burning, while also demonstrating to the rest of the population the sinfulness and danger of heresy. (Whether it was Protestants or Catholics who were considered to be heretical depended on the faith of the ruling monarch.)

Our society has finally become more tolerant, and few people now live in fear of hell, but there are still many whose belief systems might lead one to think that we should fear it more.

As I have been thinking through these issues over many years, I have come to the conclusion that the only way it is possible to understand the "wrath passages" of the Bible together with the "ultimate salvation" pas-sages, is if "hell" and "condemnation" are functions of *restorative justice* by our God of love, whose aim is to purge his beloved creation of sin and evil.

God's aim is always the restoration of the reprobate, not retribution. This would mean that condemnation, and even hell itself, are not the last words; condemnation would be temporary, and hell a place of cleans-ing and purging. With these thoughts in mind, I researched and wrote chapter 6 of this book first: "Deliver Us from Evil—Perhaps through a Cleansing Hell." The subtitle explains the content: "Exploring the idea that hell may be a place of cleansing, with final redemption as its aim." I had decided to proceed with this book only if I could be satisfied that such a view is at least compatible with the witness of the Bible and historical understanding

As I have researched the matter, I have become convinced that this is indeed a reasonable position to hold, in view of the whole witness of the Bible, as well as Jewish and Christian beliefs since the last biblical books were written—particularly during the critical early centuries of Christianity.

Having completed a first draft of chapter 6, I felt able to proceed with the book.

The Evangelical Universalist

I had completed the first draft of chapter 6 and more than half completed most chapters of the book when, early in 2012, I came across Gregory

MacDonald's most helpful book *The Evangelical Universalist*.[180] MacDonald traces his dissatisfaction with traditional understanding in a way that resonates with my own feelings. He carefully explores both the Old and New Testaments and points out that again and again God's judgment falls on Israel, or "the nations"—the idolatrous nations that are Israel's enemies and are robustly condemned—but there are repeated promises of blessing and restoration *after* the judgment and the condemnation. He traces the same pattern in the book of Revelation, seeing parallels with the prophecies of Isaiah and Jeremiah. He has come to a position he calls a "hopeful dogmatic universalist"[181]

A diagrammatic representation and summary of this most relevant thesis is reproduced with permission, on p. 142.

A pivotal chapter in *The Evangelical Universalist* is entitled "To Hell and Back," in which MacDonald argues that:

> The hell texts do not actually affirm *everlasting* damnation but warn of a terrible but *temporary* fate. This is the classical Christian universalist position found in Origen, Gregory of Nyssa, and many subsequent Christian universalists in Christian history.[182]

In a later chapter he writes:

> I understand hell to be a postmortem situation in which God brings home to us the terrible consequences of sin, and this makes sense for someone who has lived a sinful life and needs such an education . . . those in hell are experiencing the wrath of God, but such wrath is not the *absence* of divine love but the *severity* of a divine love that allows the obstinate to experience the consequences of unwise life-styles with the aim of ultimately redeeming them . . . Hell is a manifestation of divine justice, holiness, wisdom, love, and mercy . . . This is not difficult to see if universalism is true, but it is very hard to see how one could understand hell in such terms if traditional doctrines of hell are correct. How could tormenting sinners forever and ever be seen as a loving action?[183]

---

180. See MacDonald, *Evangelical Universalist*.

181. Ibid., 4, 176.

182. Ibid., 135.

183. Ibid., 162–64.

Like MacDonald, I conclude that hell is a function of redeeming love, and that redemption from and even *by means of* hell is possible— indeed, it is to be expected in view of the wideness and power of God's mercy and love.

Ultimately, redemption is for all.

Before moving to the next chapter, let us take a brief look at four Biblical pictures of our God that reveal the extent and commitment of his love for us.

1. A Covenant-Keeping God

God is a covenant-making, and covenant-keeping God, who is in despair because his people do not keep their side of the covenant. The idea of *covenant* is rich and complex. It is based on the Hebrew concept of *berith*, which means a contract or bond between individuals or groups that goes beyond blood relationships. As we have already seen (p. 34), God made an unconditional covenant with creation after the flood to never again destroy it—a promise of pure grace: unconditional, universal and eternal.[184]

God realizes that humans will always be sinful, but he will care for them anyway.[185]

The later covenant between God and Israel rests on God's promise that "I will be your God and you shall be my people."[186] But this covenant was conditional: in return, Israel was expected to be obedient to God and to keep his laws. The prophets portray the exile as the punishment for their failure to do God's will, but they also foresee a final return from exile and give glimpses of the ultimate redemption of all people, nations, and creation itself. The punishments of Israel and the other nations could be understood as a period of restorative justice, followed by ultimate re- demption not only for Israel, but also for "the nations."[187]

In Rom 9–11, Paul picks up the theme of God's covenant with Israel. They have rebelled, says Paul, but "because of their transgression, salva- tion has come to the Gentiles,"[188] and "as far as the gospel is concerned,

184. Gen 9:8–17.
185. Gen 8:21.
186. Jer 7:23; 31:33.
187. See Isa 2:1–5; 35; 45:22–25; 55:5; 66:23, and diagram on p. 142.
188. Rom 11:12.

they are enemies on your account, but as far as election is concerned, they are loved on account of the patriarchs, for God's gifts and his call are irrevocable."[189] In the end God's covenant will prevail, and Israel will return and be saved: "For God has bound all men over to disobedience so that he may have mercy on them all."[190]

In the New Testament the covenant is widened to include the church, and like an unfolding flower, we begin to see that it is potentially with all peoples and all individuals. God chooses some to be his witnesses, and so to reveal him to all people. God chose the Jews, not to save just them and ditch the rest, but to show his ways to the rest of the nations.[191] Now the church takes on the role of being his witnesses to the world. We will look at this more closely in the next chapter.

2. God Pictured as a Husband Who Loves His Unfaithful Wife

The tragic personal story of the prophet Hosea mirrors the dilemma of God, who is portrayed as a loving, wronged husband who continues to love *despite* his anger and despair at Israel, who, like an unfaithful wife, is pursuing her idolatrous affairs.

To capture this tension, let us look at some passages from Hos 9–11:

> Because of all their wickedness in Gilgal,
> I hated them there.
> Because of their sinful deeds,
> I will drive them out of my house.
> I will no longer love them;
> all their leaders are rebellious . . .
> Even if they bear children,
> I will slay their cherished offspring.

189. Rom 11:28.

190. Rom 11:32.

191. There has been a tendency for Jews to believe that they are *exclusively* loved by God. Thus the Babylonian Talmud Gerion 1:1 states: "The world was created for the sake of Israel, and only Israel were called children of God, and only Israel are dear before God." This was admittedly written after the Jewish revolts, when Jewish identity became even more of an issue, but such sentiments would have been anathema to Saint Paul. Sadly, the Christian church has often thought similarly that the world was created for the sake of the church and that only members of the church are children of God or dear to God!

My God will reject them
because they have not obeyed him . . .
How can I give you up, Ephraim?
How can I hand you over, Israel? . . .
My heart is changed within me;
all my compassion is aroused.
I will not carry out my fierce anger,
nor will I turn and devastate Ephraim.
For I am God, and not man—
the Holy One among you.
I will not come in wrath.[192]

The image of Israel, or the church, as the bride and God as bridegroom is threaded through Scripture. Song of Songs can be read both as a tender and erotic human love poem, but also as a song about the love of God for his bride, while Isaiah paints a tender image: "as a bridegroom rejoices over his bride, so will you God rejoice over you."[193]

Though the New Testament often speaks of the necessity of humanity being reconciled to God, "it never speaks about God being reconciled to man, for in the heart of God there is this unwavering and unconquerable and outgoing kindness to man."[194] However, Jesus strikes a warning note in his parable of the wedding feast, where Christ is the bridegroom and his church is the bride. Sadly, some who are not ready are shut out of the feast,[195] and in the closing chapters of the New Testament, where John has a vision of the cleansed and sparkling "Holy City, the new Jerusalem, coming down out of heaven from God, prepared as a bride beautifully dressed for he husband."[196] Some are not allowed into the city.[197]

But the gates of the city are never shut.[198] This image is explored further in chapter 7.

192. Hos 9:15–17; 11:8–9.
193. Isa 62:5.
194. Barclay, *Apostles' Creed*, 32.
195. Matt 25:1–13.
196. Rev 21:2, 9–26.
197. Rev 21:8, 27; 22:15.
198. Rev 21:25.

3. God as a Loving Father

God is referred to as "father" some fifteen times in the Old Testament, usually in relationship to the nation of Israel. For example, "You O Lord, are our Father, our Redeemer from of old is your name."[199] Malachi extends God's fatherhood to *all* the people he has created: "Have we not all one Father? Hath not one God created us?"[200]

In the Old Testament, God's fatherhood referred mainly to the *nation* of Israel (and in Malachi, to other nations, because God is their Creator), but between the testaments during the second century BC, Ben Sira glimpses God as his own *personal* Father. He writes, "O Lord, Father and Master of my life . . . Father and God of my life."[201]

Jesus further deepened this intimate understanding of God as a personal father, a real family figure. He consistently called God his father, or *Pater* (over a hundred times in John and sixty-five times in the synoptic gospels), and taught his disciples—and us—to pray to "Our Father who art in heaven." On the eve of his crucifixion, praying in agony in the garden of Gethsemane, Mark records Jesus' heartfelt cry to "*Abba*, Father," pleading, "everything is possible to you. Take this cup from me . . . yet not what I will but what you will."[202]

Abba, like our "Daddy," is a word used by young children to express intimacy and love. Jesus was intimate with his father and taught his disciples—and us—to be intimate with him too.

Paul also occasionally uses "*Abba*, Father."[203] We are not God's slaves, serving him out of fear, but sons and daughters, obeying with cooperation and love.

But there is another aspect to God's fatherly love of his children that, at first sight, is not very comforting: as we have already seen, the Bible portrays God as a father who cares enough to discipline and train us. Quoting from Proverbs, the writer of the letter to the Hebrews says, "Endure hardship as discipline; God is treating you as sons. For what

199. Isa 63:16.

200. Mal 2:10.

201. Sir 23:1, 4.

202. Mark 14:36.

203. "You did not receive a spirit that makes you slaves again to fear, but you received the Spirit of sonship. And by him we cry, 'Abba,' Father" (Rom 8:15). And "Because you are sons, God sent the Spirit of His Son into our hearts, the spirit who calls out, 'Abba, Father.' So you are no longer a slave but a son; and since you are a son, God has made you also an heir" (Gal 4:6).

son is not disciplined by his father? If you are not disciplined (and everyone undergoes discipline), then you are illegitimate children and not true sons . . . God disciplines us for our good, that we may share in his holiness."[204] Sadly, we all know that earthly fathers can be abusive, controlling, cold, violent, or absent. Because earthly fathers (and sometimes mothers) have too often been harsh or cruel in their efforts to control their children, our generation has become uneasy about this whole area; smacking is taboo, and society has perhaps swung too far in the direction of permissiveness. However, the Bible was written in a different age, and the writer of Hebrews clearly sees that *not* to discipline our children is a sign of indifference, not love.

Our God is not a controlling father; he is not a God to be feared in the wrong sense. Though the Bible speaks often about "the fear of the Lord," what is encouraged is the fear of reverence and love, not the fear of terror. Because of God's fatherly love, we can learn from and grow through the hardships, problems, and sorrows that face us. This is not to say that every problem that faces us is from God. We live in a fallen world, and the power of evil is evident. It was evil and sin that caused the cross of Christ, but God has turned it to the greatest good for the world. So too, as we trust God's fatherly care, he can redeem our pain and grief and turn them to good for us.

The biblical picture of a father who disciplines us "for our good" can sometimes feel ruthless and harsh, but there is no harshness in Jesus' story about a father whose two sons both cause him major problems.[205] It is perhaps the most profound and well-loved picture of God in the Bible.

The younger son squandered his inheritance "in wild living," even before he was due to have it. Under Jewish law, the younger son was entitled to one third of his father's property—but only when the father died.[206] It seems that he had reached an age where he could legally receive the money, but such a request would have met with anger and denunciation in the majority of Jewish homes both then and now. It was almost as if the son were saying that he wished his father dead—and first-century Judaism was a society with much greater expectation of filial subservience than our own. Indeed, according to the law, the parents of such a son "shall take hold of him and bring him to the elders at the gate of his town.

---

204. Heb 12:7–10.

205. Luke 15:11–31.

206. Deut 21:16–17.

They shall say to the elders, 'This son of ours is stubborn and rebellious, He will not obey us. He is a profligate and a drunkard.' Then all the men of his town shall stone him to death."[207]

But the father that Jesus portrays does not take his son before the elders to be stoned, nor does he attempt to stop him from leaving. He instead gives him the inheritance he asks for, apparently without hassle, arm-twisting, or demur. God has given us free will and allows us, if we wish, to go and "squander our wealth in wild living" just as the younger son did.[208]

Our God, too, lets us wander away with a sad heart. But like the father in the story, he longs for us to return, sees our first stumbling steps towards him, and runs to meet us, then showers us with complete forgiveness and restoration.

The reaction of the older brother was predictable, human, and sinful. He was jealous and angry, full of pride, bitterness, and self-righteousness. He answered his father, "Look! All these years I've been slaving for you and never disobeyed your orders. Yet you never gave me even a young goat so I could celebrate with my friends. But when this son of yours who has squandered your property with prostitutes comes home, you kill the fattened calf for him!"[209]

Thus, the dutiful older brother is revealed as a sinner too—a different kind of sinner, less obviously sinful, noble and good in the eyes of the world, but in fact every bit as sinful as his profligate brother. And he too is loved and sought out by his father, who "went out and pleaded with him." There is tenderness and love in his words: "My son . . . you are always with me, and everything I have is yours. But we had to celebrate and be glad, because this brother of yours was dead and is alive again; he was lost and is found."[210]

The father seeks to bring reconciliation not only between himself and his older son, but also between his two sons. We are not told of the older son's final reaction, but we are left in no doubt of the unconditional love of this father for *both* his sinful sons.

The younger son could have chosen to stay away from the father's home, while the older son could still decide to storm out in a rage, but the father's love will continue to reach out and seek reconciliation.

207. Deut 21:19–21.

208. Luke 15:13.

209. Luke 15:29–30.

210. Luke 15:25–32. I fear that there may be many in the church who have more affinity with the older brother than the younger "prodigal son"!

This is Christ's portrait of our Father God, to whom he taught us to pray, "Our Father."

4. God Pictured as a Good Shepherd

Another picture threaded through the Bible is that of God as a good shepherd who cares, tends, guides, leads, seeks, and saves those who are lost—like lost sheep.

Psalm 23, "The Lord is my shepherd, I shall not want," is surely one of the most beloved passages of Scripture; David sees his Lord—his God—leading him through both the "green pastures" of life and also through the rough "valley of the shadow of death."

Ezekiel pictures God as a shepherd who steps in himself to seek the scattered sheep when the leaders fail in their task.[211] And Isaiah sees the sovereign Lord, "who comes with power," yet also "tends his flock like a shepherd, gathers the lambs in is arms, and carries them close to his heart."[212]

Jesus takes this portrait of God upon himself, saying, "I am the good shepherd . . . and I lay down my life for the sheep."[213] He likens the heavenly Father to a shepherd who leaves ninety-nine sheep in the open country and goes in search of one lost sheep. The father in the story *waited* with longing for his lost son to return, but the shepherd goes even further: he will *search* for a lost sheep until he finds it. "Suppose one of you has a hundred sheep and loses one of them," says Jesus, "Does he not leave the ninety-nine in the open country and go after the lost sheep until he finds it? And when he finds it, he joyfully puts it on his shoulders and goes home, then he calls his friends and neighbors together and says, 'Rejoice with me; I have found my lost sheep.'"[214] The one lost sheep matters so much that the shepherd goes after the missing one *until he has found it*. How delighted he is then!

The Jews knew that God would invite the sinner back and that he would welcome back the penitent sinner, "but the idea of a God who

---

211. Ezek 34:7–31.

212. Isa 40:11.

213. John 10:14.

214. Luke 15:3–7; see also Matt 18:12–14.

will go and *seek* for the sinner, and who wants men to do the same is something completely new."[215]

And I wonder—why should this waiting, this seeking, stop at death?

If, as the bible teaches us, there *is* a resurrection, if there *is* life after death, if all this is a reality, then will not our loving, longing, Father-God, our Shepherd, caring seeker-God, continue to wait with longing, and continue to go on seeking for his lost ones to return—even for *aionios*, for eternity?

As the Protestant Dr. Nigel Wright writes:

> A controlling belief . . . which is very firmly held, but which I am questioning, is that death seals a person's destiny and that the condition in which a person dies is that in which they will for ever remain after death . . . The key question is, not so much whether human beings can be redeemed beyond death as whether God's search for his fallen creatures is thwarted by death or continues beyond it.[216]

And as William Barclay writes:

> One of the supreme tragedies of human love is frustration . . . we may love a person and we may yet be quite unable to influence that person . . . and we may have to stand by and see him making ruin and shipwreck of life. But the very fact that the love of God is backed by the power of God is the guarantee that ultimately and in the end the love of God cannot be frustrated. It can be hindered; it can be delayed; it can be grieved; it can be disappointed, but in the end it cannot be defeated, for we must remember that the infinite power of God has not only infinite might, but has also infinite time, all eternity, in which to work.
>
> When we say that we believe in God the Father almighty we say that we believe in a God whose infinite might is ever used in his undefeatable love . . . whose love for us some time in time or eternity will triumphantly work out its purposes.[217]

215. Barclay, *Apostles' Creed*, 34.

216. Wright, *Radical Evangelical*, 98–99.

217. Barclay, *Apostles' Creed*, 34–36.

The Bible

I have quoted freely from the Bible, but before moving to the next chapter, I would like to pause briefly to think about the book that we call our Bible.

It is of course a collection of books, a library of many different books, written in many different modes, by many different authors, over a millennium or so. It has two parts, the Tanakh (the Hebrew Scriptures), which Christians have retained as their Old Testament, and the New Testament, which concentrates on the life, death, and resurrection of Jesus Christ and gives us some insights into the life and thinking of the early church. The biblical scholar James Barr comments:

> In biblical times, the books were separate individual scrolls, A "Bible" was not a volume one could hold in the hand, but a cupboard[218] or chest with pigeonholes, or a room or cave with a lot of individual scrolls. The boundary between what was Scripture and what were other holy books was thus more difficult to indicate, and so was the order of the books and the organization (if any) of the canon.[219]

We could compare the Bible we now have to a symphony; different tones are often juxtaposed even within one book, one chapter, or even one verse. Or we could compare the Bible to a movie in which some scenes contrast with, or seem to be in conflict with, the final and abiding message. Likewise, we could compare it to a tapestry woven of many colored threads; it is possible to give a totally wrong impression of the whole picture by picking out threads of just one color. Contrasting themes weave in and out. The threads may travel in parallel for a little way, then disappear, only to reappear in a slightly different hue—a different setting, a different situation, a different author.

There are stories, visions, poetry, history, apocalyptic myths. Sometimes it is difficult for us in the twenty-first century to enter into the mindset of those who wrote thousands of years ago. That is where the many commentaries and guides by biblical scholars can help, and I thank God for them.

The Bible is not a book of theology but rather a series of many-layered accounts of how human beings have encountered and known the divine. It contains many "theologies," or many ways of seeking to

218. Even today, Jewish synagogues keep their sacred scrolls in a sort of cupboard with pigeonholes.

219. Barr, *Holy Scripture*, quoted in Garner, *On Being Saved*, 68.

understand and express that which is, in an absolute sense, beyond our
understanding. But all the Bible's books[220] were written by those who
believed themselves to be on the side of God and against what they saw
(and believed God saw) to be the sinfulness of mankind—including, and
perhaps especially, the sinfulness of God's chosen people, the Jews. There
are also many prophecies directed against the enemies of Israel.[221]

It is not surprising, therefore, that there is a wide diversity of understanding within the many groupings of the Christian church. It is as
though the white light of God's revelation is split into separate colors.
"It is red," cries one. "No! No! It is green," cries another. And there are
also many shades of opinion amongst Christians on how to approach the
Bible, which is the central text of Christianity.

I have often balked at some of the more unpalatable bits of the Bible,
and I suspect that I am not alone in this. We recoil in horror at some
of its stories[222] and wonder whether the God we believe we worship is
really like *that*. And if he is, should we not be rejecting him rather than
worshipping him? There are some things in the bible that confuse and
disturb me and that I wish were not there.

One day in August 2009, I was reading from Deuteronomy the command to the people of Israel:

> if you hear . . . that scoundrels from among you have gone out
> and led the inhabitants of [a] town astray, saying, "Let us go
> and worship other gods" whom you have not known, then . . .
> if the charge is established . . . you shall put the inhabitants of
> that town to the sword, utterly destroying it and everything in

---

220. The Bible Western Protestant Christians are most likely to read contains sixty-
six books (thirty-nine in the Old Testament and twenty-seven in the New Testament).
Roman Catholics include seven more books in their Old Testament, and the Greek
Orthodox Church includes twelve more, while the Ethiopian Church includes fifteen
more in their Old Testament. The Protestant churches consider these extra books to
be of doubtful authority and term them "apocryphal." They are not included in the
Hebrew Tanakh, but the extra books in the Roman Catholic Church were all in the
Septuagint (the Greek translation of the Old Testament).

221. See Amos 1:3–2:3; Zeph 2, and many other passages.

222. For example, the command to absolutely destroy the Canaanite nations
(Deut 2:34; 3:6; 7:2,5; 13:15-18; 1 Sam 15) and the citizens of Jericho (Josh 6:17–27).
Joshua was then commanded to wipe out all the people of Canaan. This ethnic cleansing is portrayed as God's will. It is totally abhorrent to modern sensibilities and would
be judged as a war crime today. See also n.13 on p.117.

it—even putting its livestock to the sword . . . as a whole burnt-offering to the Lord your God.[223]

A few hours later I heard that eight Christians had been killed by Islamist fundamentalists in Gojra, Pakistan, in the name of Allah "the all merciful" because of a rumor (which was denied) that Christians had desecrated a Koran. The Western world was of course as shocked by this event as I was, but my shock was compounded by what I had read a few hours earlier. The Jews in my reading from Deuteronomy had been commanded to be far more drastic than the modern Islamist fundamentalists had been. Should we allow ourselves to be shocked as we read our Old Testament?

Have ethics changed? Has God's will changed?

I find myself wondering whether some of those who so confidently spoke and acted in the name of the Lord (even in the Bible) were mistaken in what they believed the Lord said and in what they believed he had told them to do. We human beings are all too capable of speaking and acting upon our own thoughts and opinions in the *genuine*, but *mistaken belief* that what we say and do is God's will—when in fact it is not. We have evidence enough of this in the present day.

I do not believe that our Lord God Almighty, who revealed himself in Jesus of Nazareth, wants young, believing Muslims to blow up themselves and many others by committing suicidal *jihad* in the name of Allah (*if* Allah is another name for the God Almighty we worship; there are many Christians who would argue that he is not. This question is beyond the scope of this book, and I do not, in any case, feel qualified to address it.)

And was Moses truly representing the mind of our Lord God in his commands to the people of Israel in Deut 13:12–16 quoted above? (See also n.223.)

Jewish friends tell me that they still see themselves, even now in the twenty-first century, as the covenant people of God, who are called to be a light to the world.[224]

Perhaps it was because the Jews were *not* shining brightly enough (Had they radically misunderstood God's will?) that God acted in the most profound way possible by sending Jesus to come in the flesh, to come as the true light,[225] and fulfill the calling of the people of Israel.

223. Deut 13:12–16.

224. It is thought-provoking to realize that Christians say the same both of Christ, and of their own calling!

225. Luke 2:32; John 1:4–9.

The biblical history of the people of Israel was written on the basis that God is "a warrior" who is "mighty in battle"[226] and that he is *on their side* in their military conflicts—as long as they obeyed him and kept his covenant.[227] So we read in Exodus how God rescued the children of Israel from Egypt; we read in Joshua and Judges how the people conquered the land of Canaan, the promised land, and in the rest of the Old Testament, how they defeated their enemies. Their defeat by the Babylonians and subsequent exile was seen as a result of their sinfulness.

King David was the idealized warrior-king, and the Messiah was expected to be similarly mighty in battle, with the warrior-God on his side.

If the Jews' expectation of a *military* Messiah who would overthrow the Romans had been correct, that is what Jesus the Messiah would have done—but, as we have seen, (p. 11–12,) he turned that expectation on its head and completely opposed any idea of military intervention.

If the people of Israel could be as wrong as we Christians think they were about the Messiah, then it is perhaps not unreasonable to think that when an attitude that is attributed to God is contradictory to the attitude of God as revealed in Jesus, then what was said or done "in the name of the Lord" was probably not in fact what our Lord God really wanted or desired.

My faith as a young Christian was nurtured through the Inter-Varsity Fellowship, which is now known as UCCF, or Universities and Colleges Christian Fellowship. One of their basic beliefs is that "the Bible, as originally given, is the inspired and infallible Word of God."[228]

However, for many reasons, not least of which is the ethical dilemma just posed, I find that I cannot now believe that the Bible is *infallible*, though I believe that it is inspired and take it very seriously, and what I write is based on the biblical witness.

It seems to me that we can see an analogy between the inspiration of the Bible and the way that the Holy Spirit is at work in the church.

The history of the Christian church is permeated not only with wonderful insights and understandings, but also with terrible mistakes and misunderstandings.

Both noble and terrible things have been done in the name of Christ and his church, and "Christian" countries have never been free from devastating conflicts and awful injustices. The God of the Bible is passionate

226. Exod 15:3; Ps 24:8.

227. As we have seen, this premise is outlined starkly in Deut 28.

228. Universities and Colleges Christian Fellowship, "About: Doctrinal Basis," http://www.uccf.org.uk/about/doctrinal-basis.htm.

about justice and the way that human beings treat one another, especially the oppressed and marginalized.[229] The two things that kindle God's anger most are failure to acknowledge him as God and failure to treat fellow humans rightly. So it is that the two greatest commandments of the Jewish law, endorsed by Jesus, were "'Love the Lord your God with all you heart and with all your soul and with all your mind.' This is the first and greatest commandment. And the second is like it: 'Love your neighbor as yourself.' All the Law and the Prophets hang on these two commandments."[230]

It is sobering to ponder the fact that until the time of Emperor Constantine in the fourth century, Christians believed that they could not keep the second commandment and still bear arms, so Christians were almost universally pacifist.[231] One wonders what the history of the world would have looked like if Constantine and other leaders of so-called "Christian" states and nations down the centuries had interpreted the command to "Love your neighbor as yourself" as endorsing a pacifist policy.

The church is not infallible; we can see the process of both revelation and distortion as we look at her history. God has not miraculously prevented her from believing, teaching, or practicing error. "Men of God," both in biblical times and down subsequent centuries until the present day, have frequently understood, but sometimes misunderstood, God's will. Writers seeking to explain the divine mind have revealed, but sometimes obscured, the truth. They have made plain, but sometimes distorted the true will of the eternal God.

Yet despite her lack of infallibility, the church remains "the Body of Christ,"[232] and the Holy Spirit of Christ is at work in and through her.

The nonplussed father of a six-year-old girl with an inquiring mind who wrote a letter that asked, "Dear God, who invented you?" sent her inquiry to various religious leaders. He was so touched by the reply of the then-Archbishop of Canterbury, Rowan Williams, that he had it printed in *The Times*:

Dear Lulu,

Your dad has sent on your letter and asked if I have any answers.

229. Justice, especially for the poor, forms the backdrop to the whole Israeli law; the prophets declare the anger of God against injustice. For example, see Isa 58:1–9; Amos 4:1; 5:11–15, 21–24; 8:4–10; Matt 25:31–46.

230. Deut 6:5 and Lev 19:18, quoted in Matt 22:37–40.

231. Macgregor, *New Testament Basis*, 124–27.

232. 1 Cor 12:12–27; Eph 4:4.

It is a difficult one! But I think God might reply a bit like this—

'Dear Lulu—nobody invented me—but lots of people discovered me and were quite surprised. They discovered me when they looked round at the world and thought it was really beautiful or really mysterious and wondered where it come from. They discovered me when they were very, very quiet on their own and felt a sort of peace and love they hadn't expected.

Then they invented ideas about me—some of them sensible and some of them not very sensible. From time to time I sent them some hints—especially in the life of Jesus—to help them get closer to what I'm really like.

But there was nothing and nobody around before me to invent me. Rather like somebody who writes a story in a book, I started making up the story of the world and eventually invented human beings like you who could ask me awkward questions!'

And then he'd send you lots of love and sign off.

I know he doesn't usually write letters, so I have to do the best I can on his behalf.

Lots of love from me too,

—Archbishop Rowan [233]

I have quoted this letter not only because of its lovely simplicity, but also because it reflects a wise view of how we can understand both the Bible and the church in a way that leaves scope for the possibility that there are some parts of both that perhaps distort the nature of God.

We see most clearly what God is like in the face of Jesus Christ, but even with the whole Biblical witness, including the gospels, we can only get "*closer* to what [he] is really like."

All of this is humbling, and a warning to me as I write this book.

I hope that what I write will be tested by others, and perhaps become a voice in the current debate about the scope of God's redeeming grace. I cannot hope that what I write is without error, but I do sincerely hope and pray that I am not distorting the truth too much as I continue to explore not only for myself, but also for others, something of the purposes of God in his dealings with the world and with humanity

233. Alex Renton, "A Letter to God—and a Reply from Lambeth," *The Times*, April 22, 2011, http://www.thetimes.co.uk/tto/faith/article2994878.ece.

Conclusion

In this chapter I have tried to face up to some of the problems presented by the Biblical portrait of our God.

Before we move on, let us stand back and gaze what is revealed through the incarnation, life, and death of Jesus Christ.

We see a God who reveals his humility by being born in human flesh.

He reveals his identification with the poor by being born in an animal trough, by eating and drinking with "sinners," and by allowing himself to be executed between two rebels.

He reveals his servant-heart by washing the feet of the disciples in an age when rulers were despotic and showed their power by killing their rivals.

He refuses to take the expected route of armed rebellion but instead submits himself to an unjust death imposed on him by those in power—both the Jewish religious leaders and the Roman ruler, Pontius Pilate, and his soldiers.

He told his disciples to turn the other cheek, and he ordered Peter to put away his sword.

His resurrection revealed that his crucifixion was a victory and not the defeat it appeared to be. By his death, Jesus had dealt a death-blow to sin and to the adversary, the devil.

And he told his disciples to follow his example.

We shall see more of what this means in the next chapter.

2

Your Kingdom Come, Your Will Be Done, on Earth as It Is in Heaven

This, then, is how the elect and others differ from one another: the former by witnessing in their lives to the truth, the latter by lying against the same truth.

—KARL BARTH[1]

The church is supposed to be God's new society, the living embodiment of the gospel, a sign of the kingdom of God.

—JOHN STOTT[2]

Justification is ultimately about justice, about God putting the world to rights, with his chosen and called people as the advance guard of that new creation, charged with being and bringing signs of hope, of restorative justice, to the world.

—N. T. WRIGHT[3]

1. Barth, *Doctrine of God*, 346.
2. Stott, *Living Church*, 68.
3. Wright, "New Perspectives on Paul."

JESUS BURSTS INTO THE first chapter of Mark's Gospel, proclaiming that "the kingdom of God is near."[4] The first-century Jews who heard this message did not think, as some Christians today might, that the "kingdom of God" (or "the kingdom of heaven," to use Matthew's phrase) would be somewhere that good people (or perhaps those who have been saved) would go when they die. The Jews hoped and expected that God would rule *on earth*, and many of his listeners would have taken Jesus' announcement to mean that he was claiming to be the long-awaited Messiah who would bring about God's earthly rule.

Christians believe that this is exactly what Jesus was claiming, and exactly what his coming was about—but it would not happen in the way that the Jews expected.

The kingdom of God is where God reigns, where his will is done, and the coming of Jesus brought that kingdom *near*—within reach. The life of God and the Holy Spirit is available through Jesus, even now in the twenty-first century as it was in the first century, but as we have seen in chapter 1, we are all sinners by nature. To enter the kingdom of God, we have to turn away from all that is not pleasing to God and turn towards Jesus. In other words, to enter this now-accessible kingdom of God, we have to "Repent and believe the good news!" as Jesus goes on to say.[5]

In his earthly life, Jesus demonstrated what the kingdom of God is like. He healed people, ate with those who were considered to be "publicans and sinners," and taught people, often using parables about the kingdom. His coming was a foretaste and a preview of the age to come; we can enter it now, yet it will not come in its fullness until the end of the age.

So it is that in the Anglican Communion service we often declare:

Christ has died,

Christ is risen,

Christ will come again.[6]

At the present time, we are living between the second and third of these declarations. We are "living between the victory achieved by Jesus and the ultimate renewal of all things . . . we are called not just to understand the problem of evil and the justice of God, but also to be part of the

4. Mark 1:15.

5. Mark 1:15.

6. The people's response to the declaration, "Great is the mystery of faith" (Church of England. *Common Worship*, 176).

solution to it. We are called to live between the cross and resurrection on the one hand and the new world on the other . . . we are called to bring the two together in prayer, holiness, and action within the wider world."[7]

What we believe about the "age to come" shapes our understanding of what the church is about in the here and now as well as what it means to be praying and working for God's kingdom to come.

So, the two questions we need to address are:

1. What is God's kingdom, and who can enter it?

2. How can we live now, in this interim time, in a way that reflects and brings nearer that for which we pray—that God's kingdom come "on earth as it is in heaven"?

1. What Is God's Kingdom, and Who Can Enter It?

Jesus, the master storyteller, often taught about the kingdom by means of memorable parables[8]—sometimes to reveal a difficult or challenging idea under the cover of an apparently simple story, sometimes to give a cryptic message, in a sort of code, so that his disciples would understand but the authorities would not (or if they did, they would not have sufficient evidence against him to condemn him before the time was right).

The parables look at the kingdom of God from a variety of perspectives, as if using a selection of lenses. They might perhaps be called "kingdom analogies." (Similarly, we explored the meaning of Christ's death through a variety of "redemptive analogies." Perhaps we always need to use analogy as we approach the mysteries of God.)

It is beyond the scope of this book to look at all of Jesus' parables in detail, but to begin to answer the questions I have just posed, it will be helpful to look briefly through the lens of seven of Jesus' parables gathered by Matthew in chapter 13 of his gospel.

7. Wright, *Evil and the Justice*, 82–83.

8. The word "parable" comes from the Greek *parabolē*, meaning "comparison, illustration, analogy." Greek rhetoricians used it for any illustration in the form of a brief fictitious narrative, generally referring to something that might naturally occur. Often spiritual and moral matters were conveyed in this way.

a. The Parable of the Sower[9]

This story mirrors what anyone who tries to spread the good news of God's kingdom soon finds out: not everybody responds in the same way. Some will be hard-hearted, and the message will make no impact; some will respond briefly, but their response will not survive "trouble or persecution." For some, "the worries of this life and the deceitfulness of wealth" choke the message.[10]

However, there will be some who understand and respond, "yielding a hundred, sixty or thirty times what was sown,"[11] and they will become ambassadors for the kingdom, and so the Good News will spread.

b. Two Parables That Refer to the Coming Judgment

The kingdom of God is where God's will is carried out.

Those who know, and are living in awareness of the kingdom of God, are those for whom Jesus is Lord,[12] but many people do not honor him as Lord in this life.

If it *is* in fact true, as we believe, that Jesus is Lord of all and will one day be proclaimed as Lord by all,[13] it is certainly not a truth acknowledged by everybody at the present time, and it is very evident that not everybody lives by kingdom ethics.

Many are not, in this present age, fit to be in God's kingdom, and those who *are* fit are only fit because of God's grace, received by faith.[14]

With these thoughts in mind, let us look at the next two parables in this chapter of Matthew, which paint a picture of the judgment "at the end of the age."[15]

Weeds are sown by an "enemy," or the devil, in a field of wheat. The wheat and the weeds are left to grow together until the harvest, when they are separated. Then the weeds are burnt and the wheat is brought into the barn.

9. Matt 13:1–22.

10. Matt 13:19–22.

11. Matt 13:23.

12. See Rom 10:9–11. Perhaps "Jesus is LORD" was an early creed. See also Matt 10:32 and Luke 12:8.

13. See, for example, Phil 2:10–11; Rom 14:9; Rev 5:13.

14. Eph 2:8.

15. Matt 13:24–29.

Jesus explained to his disciples, "As the weeds are pulled up and burned in the fire, so it will be at the end of the age. The Son of Man will send out his angels, and they will weed out of his kingdom everything that causes sin and all who do evil. They will throw them into the fiery furnace, where there will be weeping and gnashing of teeth. Then the righteous will shine like the sun in the kingdom of their Father."[16]

The last parable in the chapter has a similar message and is based on a catch of good and bad fish, an analogy that would resonate with his fishermen colleagues.

These rejection-from-the-kingdom analogies (to coin yet another phrase), as well as other parables picturing a judgment of fire,[17] have traditionally been interpreted as predicting everlasting hell for those who will be judged as unfit for the kingdom of God. A widely accepted alternative interpretation is annihilation or destruction for the rejected ones (because after all, fire *destroys* that which it burns) and "conditional immortality," or eternal life only for those who are classed as "wheat" or "good fish" (or "sheep" as opposed to "goats" in Matt 25:31–46, or branches "abiding in the vine" in John 15:1–8).

However, I am suggesting that perhaps these analogies point neither to a fiery punishment that lasts forever and ever (whatever that means), nor to annihilation. A third interpretation, which was widely held in the first few centuries of the church and by some interpreters since, sees these pictures of fire pointing to a *temporary* period of redemptive punishment by which the rejected (the "weeds," the "bad fish," the "goats," and the "branches" that do not bear grapes) are faced with the terrible consequences of their sin and are thus cleansed, "but only as one escaping through the flames."[18] Fire destroys only that which can be burned up; it *purifies* such substances as gold and other metals. Paul points out that in the future age, we will not only see God clearly, but also see our own lives with the same clarity that God does. He writes, "Now we see but a poor reflection in a mirror, but then face to face. Now I know in part; then I shall know fully, even as I am fully known."[19] (see p. 39, and chapters 5 and 6.)

16. Matt 13:41–42.

17. See Matt 25 and John 15:1–8.

18. 1 Cor 3:15.

19. 1 Cor 13:12.

c. Two Parables about Waiting

Jesus likens the kingdom of God to a mustard seed that grows from a tiny seed to a large tree, and to yeast that makes dough rise.[20] These are things that do not happen instantly; they take time.

I am writing this in early May, that exhilarating time of year when some of the trees are fully clad in fresh new leaves, some still etch bare branches against the sky, and some are just beginning to burst into life. And the branches of each tree come to life erratically: some branches have just a few leaves here and there, while on the same tree there are still many bare branches; yet other branches are almost in full leaf. Here is another little kingdom parable; the kingdom comes in different stages and different rates in different situations.

d. Two Parables Showing How Precious and Costly the Kingdom Is

The kingdom of God is like a treasure hidden in a field, or like a pearl of great value.[21]

We cannot do everything in life; we have to make choices.

It is costly to enter the kingdom of God, and if we chose to make God the king of our lives and live by his standards, some things will have to go. The Christian way of life is counter-cultural, and there will be some things that Christians will *not* do that "the world" will do. But we will not regret it because of the great value of the kingdom of heaven in our hearts.

Having briefly thought about the meaning of the kingdom of God and who may enter it, we need to ask ourselves our second question:

2. How Can We Live Now, in This Interim Time, in a Way That Reflects and Brings Nearer That For Which We Pray—That God's Kingdom Come "on Earth as It Is in Heaven"?

To begin to answer this question, we first need to consider the purpose of the church.

20. Matt 13:31–33.
21. Matt 13:44–46.

a. The Church Is a Royal Priesthood

Peter writes to "God's elect," that is, to Christians scattered throughout Asia Minor, "you are a chosen people, a royal priesthood, a holy nation, a people belonging to God, that you may declare the praises of him who called you out of darkness into his wonderful light,"[22] echoing God's promise given by Moses to the people of Israel at Sinai: "if you obey me fully and keep my covenant, then out of all nations you will be my treasured possession. Although the whole earth is mine, you will be for me a kingdom of priests and a holy nation."[23] Likewise, John declares to the "seven churches in the province of Asia," that they have been made "a kingdom and priests to serve his God and Father."[24]

So it seems that the church participates to some extent in Jesus' own double role. As Messiah, he is both a king and a priest.

The aim of a good king (in times when they had authority) was to rule justly and to promote peace and equity, so if Christians are in some way "rulers" in God's kingdom, we should work for justice, peace, and equity. It does not necessarily mean having a role in worldly power systems, though often that is the best way to change things for the better. As we shall see, many Christians have worked tirelessly through government to work for a society that is more just.

The role of priests is to lift up before God the world, in all its pain and sin, and to pour into that world on behalf of God his grace, his healing, and his forgiveness—that is, his salvation. This is supremely the role of Jesus Christ, "our great high priest,"[25] but it is also the role of the whole church, not just of those who have been ordained to the liturgical and sacramental role of priests. The whole body of Christ is a "kingdom of priests."

b. The Church Is Called to Be Salt and Light in the World

Jesus calls his disciples "the salt of the earth . . . the light of the world."[26]

22. 1 Pet 2:9.
23. Exod 19:5–6.
24. Rev 1:6.
25. Heb 4:14.
26. Matt 5:13–14.

Salt acts as a preservative and makes good food taste even better, while light reveals dirt and extinguishes darkness. These pictures are miniature parables of our calling.

We are called to make the world a better place, more like the kingdom of God.

Thus, most of the New Testament letters are addressed not, as traditional theology might lead us to expect, to "the ones who have been saved," but to those who are "called to be holy"[27] or to "the saints" in a certain place,[28] which means the same thing because the holiness and love of Christ is at work in those in whom Christ lives by his Spirit.

This does not mean that Christians should withdraw from the world to avoid contamination but rather that, like our Lord, we should seek to restore the world by engaging with it. As we saw in chapter 1, our calling includes sharing the darkness. It also includes seeking to alleviate the darkness wherever we can.

c. The Church Is the Body of Christ, Active in the World

Paul describes the church as the body of Christ.[29] As such, she is called to reveal Christ to the world. She is not a community of the "saved ones" over against those outside who are "unsaved" or "condemned," but a community of those in whom the Spirit of Christ dwells and who *know* that they have been saved and also know that their Lord's will is to bring salvation and wholeness to the whole world, not just the church. As the great twentieth-century Swiss-German theologian Karl Barth wrote, "This, then, is how the elect and others differ from one another: the former by witnessing in their lives to the truth, the latter by lying against the same truth."[30]

d. The Church Is the Forerunner of the Reconciliation the Whole of Creation Will One Day Experience

In *The Evangelical Universalist*, MacDonald discusses the theology of the first chapter of Paul's letter to the Colossians and describes the reconciled

27. 1 Cor 1:2; Col 1:2.
28. Rom 1:7; Eph 1:1; Phil 1:1.
29. 1 Cor 10:17; 12:12–31; Rom 12:4–5.
30. Barth, *Doctrine of God*, 346.

church as the forerunner of the reconciliation that will one day be experienced by the whole of creation:

> The reconciliation of creation is . . . already achieved in Christ
> and yet is only experienced as a reality by those in Christ by
> faith . . . They are the first to taste the reconciliation that has
> been won for all. The church, then, is a present sign of the rec-
> onciliation that the whole creation will one day experience . . .
> The Church must live by the values of, and proclaim the coming
> of, the kingdom age in the present evil age as a sign to a hostile
> world . . . Colossians . . . holds before us a confident hope in
> the salvation of the whole creation. It is God's covenant purpose
> that his world will one day be reconciled in Christ. For now,
> only the Church shares in that privilege, but this is not a posi-
> tion God has granted his people so they can gloat over the world.
> On the contrary, the Church must live by gospel standards and
> proclaim its gospel message so that the world will come to share
> in the saving work of Christ.[31]

The chart reproduced with permission on p. 142 conceptualizes this and shows the place of the church in the outworking of God's kingdom plans.

Until that final age dawns, we live, and can only live, in the present imperfect age.

Both the crucifixion and the resurrection are at work. All too often it seems as if evil is triumphant, and we are surrounded by events that point to the reasons that led to Christ's crucifixion. But if our gospel is true, this is a temporary triumph, and we also see glimpses of God's kingdom happening, like oases in a desert, wherever love reigns, wherever justice prevails, wherever God is honored and worshipped. And the job of God's people is to pray and work to increase the extent of God's kingdom here on earth in the *now* in which we live. We do this in as many ways as possible: by proclaiming, preaching, and sharing the message of the king-dom; by loving and caring for our families and neighbors (even when they reject Jesus, the king we serve); and by working wherever we can for justice through social and charitable actions (not forgetting political action and practical involvement in world affairs) as well as the massive task of speaking out against what is wrong is society. This is almost always a task that is unpopular with the rich and powerful who benefit from the oppression of the poor, and it is sometimes outright dangerous. We have

---

31. MacDonald, *Evangelical Universalist*, 51–53.

seen that Martin Luther King Jr. was assassinated for campaigning for racial justice in the United States, and there have been countless others who have been martyrs for the sake of the kingdom of God.

e. Working for the "Earthing of Heaven"

The threat of global warming is slowly making us all realize that the resources of our wonderful earth are finite and need to be used responsibly.

We read that "God created man in his own image . . . and said to them, 'be fruitful and increase in number; fill the earth and subdue it. Rule over the fish of the sea and the birds of the air and over every living creature that moves on the ground.'"[32] Christians have too often taken this as a carte blanche gift of natural resources to be plundered at will to enrich ourselves or make life easier. However, in the last decade or two we have woken up to the fact that we are called to be *stewards* with a God-given responsibility to *care for* the earth rather than to use it as an inexhaustible supply of natural resources. Very often indigenous peoples, such as native North American Indians, live closer to the land than we do in the "developed West" and have much to teach us about treating the earth with respect. Slowly, and sometimes reluctantly, Christians have realized that the "Green Movement," which involves people of many faiths and of none, is something that we should all support. To care for the created earth is to work for the kingdom of God.

We are called to look after the natural world of trees and flowers, of fish and birds, of rain forests and rivers, not least because Scripture promises that God's kingdom will be finally fulfilled *on earth* as it is now in heaven—something Bishop James Jones evocatively calls "the earthing of heaven."[33] This is what we look towards, and this is what we must work for.

> Together with other Christians and with people of good will we work . . . for the holistic transformation of the neighborhood, for its regeneration spiritually and physically . . . to pray and to work for the earthing of heaven.[34]

---

32. Gen 1:27–28.

33. Jones, *Jesus and the Earth*, 92. James Jones was bishop of Liverpool from 1998 until his retirement in August 2013.

34. Ibid.

The Christian Response

Over the centuries, the Christian response has varied from pioneer lead-ership in the transformation of societies to dragging feet and Luddite conservatism.

Christian missions have spearheaded the provision of schools and hospitals in many developing countries, and in Britain, Christians have often been involved in the fight for justice for the poor. But at times, the evangelical task has seemed so pressing that anything smacking of social action has been considered secondary to the task of trying to get people "saved." This, I think perhaps in a crudely caricatured form, was the "gos-pel" as understood by the leaders of the Christian Union[35] in the late 1950s, when I was a fledgling Christian at Bristol University; social action was a considered to be a waste of valuable time that could be better spent evangelizing; and I was discouraged from visiting a needy elderly lady and from taking part in "Soup and Bread lunches" because such actions were deemed to be a distraction from the evangelistic task.

Similar reasoning was behind an evangelical mission that had upset and angered a discouraged missionary doctor I met at about the same time. The mission leaders felt that his medical work for needy people in a poor country in Africa should be *subservient* to the preaching of the gospel, whereas he saw it as *valid in its own right*.

The leaders felt that he should use his medicine more or less as a bait to draw the people in for the real thing—which, they believed, was to "hear the gospel." The doctor thought (as I do) that bringing physi-cal healing to those who need it is a valid part of the mission of Christ in itself, because people's bodies matter to us and to God, and to heal someone physically, especially when done with love and compassion in the name of Christ, also reveals God's nature and his kingdom.

Of course, the mission in question was right to stress the impor-tance of preaching the good news about Jesus as well as the importance of seeking to lead people to respond to Christ, but the point I am trying to make is that, just as in the time of Christ, acts of healing and mercy are *also in themselves* valid signs of the kingdom.

In his earthly life, Jesus healed many people, but the gospels only once record that he spoke forgiveness of sins to the one who had been healed.[36] This does not mean that others who were healed were not also

---

35. Bristol University Christian Union is a member of UCCF.

36. Matt 9:2–8.

forgiven, but it seems that the healings themselves were kingdom actions, which the Gospel of John calls "signs."

I have mentioned the ambivalence Christians have sometimes felt towards the social aspects of the gospel, but there are countless inspiring examples of Christian men and women who—motivated by Christian compassion, and realizing that our God is a God of justice whose will it is that society should be just and fair—have been in the forefront of the fight for social justice. We are promised that God's kingdom will ultimately come *on earth*, and to work for values that are resonant with that kingdom, for the healing of individuals, and of society itself, is to do God's will.

I will cite a few outstanding examples to illustrate this point.

The nineteenth century was a time of great contrasts. The Industrial Revolution was in full swing, and the rapid advance in technology meant rising wealth for some, while the many men, women, and children who worked in the factories or down in the coalmines suffered great poverty and terrible living conditions. We may feel a deep stab of guilt that such inequalities were tolerated in a so-called "Christian" country—and are still being tolerated in our very unfair world—but it is heartening to find that there were some outstanding reformers whose Christian faith spurred them to do what they could to improve matters.

Anthony Ashley Cooper (1801–1885)

Anthony Ashley Cooper, Seventh Earl of Shaftsbury, was a notable example. He was a prominent Evangelical Christian and the leading social and industrial reformer of his day, campaigning frequently in Parliament, where he was a member from 1826 to 1847, and then from the House of Lords until his death.

He worked indefatigably, promoting low-cost housing projects for urban workers and many campaigns for reform: to shorten working hours in factories, to prevent women and girls from being employed in the mines, and to prevent young children doing the dangerous and horrible work of climbing chimneys to sweep them. He also championed the "Lunacy Act" of 1845, which recognized that mentally ill people were patients who needed treatment by a physician, not social outcasts who needed to be shut away.

Cooper was also the president of the Ragged Schools Union, which provided free education and food for many thousands of destitute children, and of the British and Foreign Bible Society. He founded numerous Young Men's Christian Associations and Working Men's Institutes and used his personal wealth to financially support many missionary and philanthropic societies.

William Wilberforce (1759–1833)

William Wilberforce was a notable reformer who worked mainly through the British House of Commons to change the law.

After his conversion in 1785, he was thinking of being ordained, but he was strongly advised by the converted former slave trader John Newton to stay in politics and serve God there.

Wilberforce campaigned for numerous good causes, but his most strenuous and best-remembered campaign was against the iniquitous slave trade that was at that time a source of wealth to many people in Britain, the rest of Europe, and the United States. Such a profitable trade would not be given up without a struggle.

Wilberforce and many others worked tirelessly, both in British Parliament and outside it, to abolish the capture and shipment of African men and women across the Atlantic under unbelievably awful conditions. After many failed attempts to push through legislation, they had a partial success in 1807 with the passing of the Slave Trade Act, which made the *trading* of slaves illegal.

The bicentenary of the Slave Trade Act was widely celebrated in 2007, and in my hometown of Liverpool, which was made rich largely through the slave trade, moving acts of confession and apology were held on the very dockside from which so many slave ships had set sail until 1807.

But abolishing the trading of slaves was only part of the task. The abolition campaigns continued until *slavery itself* had been abolished in Britain and the then the British Empire. Wilberforce died just three days after the Slavery Abolition Act was passed in 1833, having spent fifty-six years of strenuous efforts in Parliament. Numerous other concerned citizens backed those in the frontline with much prayer and active campaigning. This was Christianity in action: people were motivated in their fight for justice because they realized that this was in some measure working for the coming of God's kingdom.

Slavery had once been so commonplace that its abolition had seemed almost impossible. Two centuries later, we are amazed that Christian people took so long to be convinced that slavery was unjust and inimical to a society that claimed to be Christian (as both British and American societies finally did in the nineteenth century). However, we cannot become complacent. Although the forced shipment of African slaves to the Americas is now happily a thing of the past, slavery itself is still rampant throughout the world. Sexual trafficking and exploitation of women and young children is still widespread (though largely illegal). Many workers in third-world countries work virtually as slave labor for scandalously low wages and in unsafe conditions that would not be tolerated in "developed countries"—all so that we can buy cheap goods.

There is still much to be done.

Elizabeth Fry (1780–1845)

Elizabeth Fry did not let the fact that, as a woman, she could not even vote, and certainly could not stand for Parliament, stop her from having a massive influence.

Motivated by her Quaker faith, Fry visited prisons, where she was horrified at the conditions she saw. The women's section was overcrowded with female inmates, some of whom had not even received a trial, and their children were in prison with them. They did their own cooking and washing in the small cells in which they slept on straw. She stayed overnight in some of the prisons to experience the conditions for herself.

Fry campaigned for improvements to be made and for schooling for the children in prison, and in 1818 she was the first woman to present evidence to Parliament. This gained her the respect of Queen Victoria and Prime Minister Robert Peel. Her campaigns were later taken to Parliament by her brother-in law, who was a Member of Parliament.

Fry performed many other charitable works, including the distribution of food and clothing to the homeless as well as starting a shelter for homeless children, but she is always remembered primarily for her pioneering efforts to reform prisons. She saw that prisons were dark and unsavory places where she tried, with some success, to shine the transforming light of the gospel in practical ways.

Josephine Butler (1828–1906)

Josephine Butler was born into a wealthy family. Her father had a passion for social reform and a hatred of injustice that greatly influenced Josephine. Her husband, George Butler, also shared these concerns, and together the couple supported the abolition of slavery and argued for better rights for marginalized women and the socially disadvantaged. They had four children, but tragedy struck when their youngest child, Eva, died after falling from the banisters at the top of their stairs. She was just six years old.

In 1866 George, who by then had been ordained in the Church of England, became the headmaster of Liverpool College, and the couple moved to Liverpool. Josephine was grief-stricken over the death of Eva, so:

> Still suffering from grief and from the depression which would recur throughout her life, Josephine threw herself into working with women in the local workhouse, hoping, as she wrote, to "find some pain keener than my own—to meet with people more unhappy than myself." She had no clear plan, other than to help: "my sole wish," she explained, "was to plunge into the heart of some human misery, and to say (as I now knew I could) to afflicted people, "I understand. I, too, have suffered." As a result of rescuing many young girls from the workhouse, and either finding them homes or taking them into her own household, Josephine worked to set up her own refuge, believing it to be a divine calling.[37]

She wrote books and campaigned for better educational provision for women, becoming President of the North of England Council for the Higher Education of Women and traveling to Cambridge to persuade the University to allow women's admission to study there. As a result, Newnham College for women was set up.

However, Josephine is best remembered for her campaign for the Repeal of the Contagious Diseases Acts of 1864, 1866, and 1869. These acts effectively legalized the sex trade. In an attempt to control the spread of sexually transmitted diseases in the army and navy, all women living near garrison towns and naval ports had to submit to registration and regular internal examinations that were often carried out with brutality and insensitivity.

37. Josephine Butler Memorial Trust, "A Brief Introduction to the Life of Josephine Butler," http://www.josephinebutler.org.uk/a-brief-introduction-to-the-life-of-josephine-butler.

In 1870 Josephine became leader of the Ladies National Association for the Repeal of the Contagious Diseases Act, arguing against the presumption of guilt on the part of the women, and seeking instead both to question the morality of the men involved and to bring them to account for their behaviour. She travelled the country, speaking with incredible force and passion, sometimes putting herself in danger, surprising many with her candour on the taboo subjects of prostitution and sexual morality. Her husband supported her campaigns, despite warnings that it would damage his academic career.[38]

William Booth (1829–1912)

The reformers we have considered so far used their privilege, wealth, and influence to work for social justice for those less fortunate than themselves, but William Booth experienced poverty first-hand, because his father lost his job when he was only thirteen. William had to leave school and work in a pawnbroker's shop in Nottingham. Later he moved to London and joined *The Christian Mission*, working amongst the poor in London, some of whom had been turned away from other churches for being too smelly and dirty.

Booth realized that people wouldn't listen to the gospel message if they were hungry and cold, so he opened food stores and shelters for people to stay in and, with his wife Catherine, founded the Salvation Army, which today still spearheads both evangelism and social action in many different ways.

Pastor Nims Obunge (b. 1965)

A more recent example of Christian action for peace and justice comes from Tottenham in North London, which has for many years suffered a higher than average rate of violent crime. This motivated Nims Obunge, the pastor of the Freedom's Ark Church, into action.

Obunge was born in London, the ninth child of Nigerian parents. His father worked as a diplomat and traveled widely, so Obunge honestly calls himself "a citizen of the world."

In a 2008 BBC interview Obunge said:

38. Ibid.

I was burying young people who had been shot or stabbed and I was speaking at their death, yet I'd never had the opportunity to speak in their lives. So, I felt challenged by God to see whether I could pastor people who I knew would never come to my church . . . We needed to create a response to what was happening, so we started the Peace Alliance, and the London Peace week.[39] We wanted to support the community in dealing with tensions between different cultures so we started "Building Relationships Amongst Cultures Everywhere"—or BRACE.

When we started, there was a huge need because so many young people were being shot or stabbed. It has reduced now and I pray it continues to do so. For me, pastoring is more than sharing on a Sunday morning; it is about social justice . . . The multi-faith community has worked in partnership with the police, council, parents and community and seen a reduction in this type of crime. We created a DVD for schools to share with children how to avoid getting caught up in that spiral of violence but we still must look at the pockets of deprivation in this city . . . I'm Chair of the London Criminal Justice Board IAG (Independent Advisory Group), and in partnership with the police, we're involved in a particular project that looks at young people going into prison and finds out which estates they come from. Then it sees how we can invest resources, financial and otherwise, into these estates and communities.[40]

Despite the apparent improvement in 2008, when Obunge gave this interview, violence escalated in August 2011, and a spate of riots rapidly spread across the country—triggered by the police shooting of a twenty-nine-year-old man in Tottenham. This left the Tottenham area deeply angered and suspicious of the police. Once again Obunge, who is respected by the local population, the police, and civic leaders, was called upon to try to mediate.

His task continues, as does that of the church as the body of Christ, active as salt and light in society.

I have selected only a few outstanding individuals—all British, and all from the last three centuries—so barely a representative sample, but enough perhaps to point to the fact that Christians have often been in

---

39. In September 2001.

40. Nims Obunge, interview by Sarah Kinson, *BBC*, December 5, 2008, http://www.bbc.co.uk/london/content/articles/2008/12/05/londonpeople_nims_obunge.shtml.

the forefront of social action. There have been numerous movements and many charities motivated by the gospel challenge to practical action:

The Anglo-Catholic revival in the late nineteenth century produced many "slum priests" who sought to raise the horizon of the people living in slums of the inner cities.

Many Christians—mainly Methodists—were involved in the early trade union movement's fight for fair conditions for working people.

Dr. Barnardo decided to help the many desperately needy poor and homeless children in nineteenth-century Britain instead of going as a missionary to China. He founded Barnardo's homes, whose work continues today.

The development of street pastors, food banks, and Christians Against Poverty are more recent examples of the church working towards repair of some of the needs of a fractured society. Our mission is both to show and to proclaim the good news about Jesus.

Paul writes in humble amazement, "God, who had set me apart before I was born, and called me through his grace, was pleased to reveal his Son to me, so that I might proclaim him among the Gentiles."[41] But proclaiming means *both* preaching the good news about Jesus with the aim of making new disciples *and also* demonstrating the kingdom in action in some of the ways we have been considering. As I read prayer letters and news items from different groups working around the world, I am continually amazed and humbled by the multitude of creative and imaginative works of grace and restoration in which God's people are involved.

But Christians are certainly not alone in these struggles.

The Jewish idea of *tikkun olam* is very similar in meaning to the ideas outlined above. The phrase goes back at least to the third-century Mishnah, and in modern Judaism it means "world repair" through human action. Human beings are responsible for bettering their own existence and that of others; we should not expect God to do it for us. To some extent, *tikkun olam* has become synonymous with social action and working for social justice. Unless we work for justice, evil and injustice will continue to exist.

Mark L. Winer, the senior rabbi at the West London Synagogue, pinpoints what *tikkun olam* means in the face of the conflicts currently tearing apart the Middle East:

41. Gal 1:15–16.

> Tikkun olam is the expression of justice, compassion and mercy
> in fostering the reconciliation of Shiites, Sunnis and Kurds with-
> in Iraq. Tikkun olam means a Marshall Plan for Iraq to rebuild
> hospitals, schools and public services. Tikkun olam means the
> West's acknowledgement of Arab humiliation and the establish-
> ment of a mutual respect among Christians Jews and our Abra-
> hamic sibling Muslims.[42]

If only such a call for peace-work were followed!

Working Together with Christ

There may be some readers who think I am proposing "a gospel of good
works," but this is not the case. As we have seen in chapter 1, we are saved
because of what Christ has done for us, not because of what we do for
him. But as Christians, we identify with Christ, and to serve him as Lord
means to participate in his redeeming and restorative involvement in the
world. In a much-loved vignette, Jesus called those who were weary and
burdened to come to him "and I will give you rest." Then he continued,
"take my yoke upon you and learn from me, for I am gentle and humble
in heart, and you will find rest for your souls, for my yoke is easy and my
burden is light."[43] I like to visualize being yoked alongside Christ, pulling together as a team of oxen—not striving and straining, not rushing
ahead or lagging behind or trying to achieve impossible tasks in my own
strength and getting worn out (a message to myself that I need to take
on board!). Similarly, Paul speaks of himself as a fellow worker, or "joint
worker" with God.[44]

The understanding that we are fellow-workers with God, yoked
together with Christ, also helps us to understand prayer and, indeed,
motivates us to pray.

I am sometimes tempted to wonder—is there any point in praying?
And do our prayers make any difference? The Bible answers an unequiv-
ocal "Yes" to both these questions, and Jesus made sweeping promises about the efficacy of prayer.[45] But I must confess that because I, like

42. Garner, *On Being Saved*, 94. Garner quotes Mark L. Winer, "*Tikkun Olam*: A
Jewish Theology of 'Repairing the World,'" *Theology* 111 (2008) 439.

43. Matt 11:28–29.

44. 1 Cor 3:9; 2 Cor 6:1.

45. For example, Jesus said, "I tell you the truth, if you have faith and do not
doubt, not only can you do what was done to the fig-tree, but also you can say to this

many others, struggle with the fact that our prayers often go apparently unanswered (or perhaps not answered in the way that we had hoped), I sometimes wish that his promises had not been quite so sweeping! Perhaps my literal twenty-first-century mind is not in tune with Jesus' Eastern use of exaggerated metaphor when he called his followers to move mountains. I hope it is not a cop-out to find John Austin Baker's helpful explanation of prayer more practical and less daunting than Jesus' challenging call to move mountains:

> Once we have grasped clearly what we are doing when we pray for others, we shall see that the most important requirement by far is inner calmness and tranquility. We are not engaged in creating or producing anything, but in becoming aware of what is already the fact, namely that God is immediately and intimately present both to ourselves and to the ones for whom we are praying. Our task is to hold the awareness of this fact in the still centre of our being, to unite our love for them with God's love, in the quiet but total confidence that he will use our love to help bring about the good in them which we both desire . . . we contemplate not God himself, but God in his relationship of love towards those whom we also love; and on the basis or our partnership with him we entrust our love into his hands to be used in harness with his own for their benefit.[46]

I have sometimes tried to help people struggling to overcome addictions to alcohol or drugs, and I have usually found that they are longing for an instant miracle of grace to rescue them from the mess in which they find themselves—a miracle that would involve no effort. I make a point of saying that God's grace is available to them and that God longs to help them and work with them, but they need to get their own will behind the rescue package too. They have to *decide* not to buy another bottle, not to look for another fix, or to take the positive step of applying to a rehabilitation center, depending on where they are in the process of restoration.

Miracles do happen—and I have heard some amazing testimonies of miraculous healing—but they are rare. (If they happened routinely, they would cease to be miracles.) For most people struggling for restoration, it is slow upward struggle. Even for those who are actively seeking to

---

mountain, 'go throw yourself into the sea,' and it will be done. If you believe, you will receive whatever you ask for in prayer" (Matt 21:21–22). See also Matt 17:20.

46. Baker, *Foolishness of* God, 385–86, quoted in Garner, *On Being Saved*, 91.

overcome challenges by working in partnership with God, the mountain is moved little by little, spade-full by spade-full.

When we pray for those who are struggling, it is good to remind ourselves of Austin Baker's exhortation to "entrust our love into his hands to be used in harness with his own for their benefit."

Conclusion

Christians are not just the "saved ones" who are trying their utmost to turn as many "unsaved" people as possible into "saved" people. Christians are those who *know* that they are being saved, (that is, being made whole) by grace, through faith.[47] They look forward to, and work for, the promised time when salvation will be fully realized for all humanity and all creation "on earth as it is in heaven."

Like our Lord and Savior, Jesus Christ, we are called to identify with the pain of the world. Perhaps this is part of what Jesus meant when he said that "whoever does not take up the cross and follow me is not worthy of me."[48] We are his hands and his feet, and we have a special responsibility to care for the vulnerable and the sick, for widows and orphans, for refugees and children, and for all those who find themselves at the bottom of the pile, rejected by the world. We are called to be salt and light, to show that grace, love, justice, and mercy lie at the heart of the gospel.

We are called to look after the earth with the hope and vision of a renewed earth ever before us.

The Bible is full of concern for justice, but it also calls the individual to repentance and faith. Christianity, at its best, has always been both a personal and a social religion.

Isaiah was personally touched and cleansed by a coal from the fire in the temple before being commissioned as a prophet who spoke out passionately about social issues.

The Jesus who denounced the social injustice of the Pharisees who "eat up the property of widows" is the same Jesus who shows us the loving heart of God and calls us to belief in himself.

Christians are, by both our words *and* our deeds, witnesses of God's kingdom and of his saving grace in the world, but we also have the task of warning the world that there will be a judgment that for some will result

47. Eph 2:8.
48. Matt 10:38.

in experiencing the severe side of a divine love that aims to ultimately redeem them.

I have been constantly challenged as I have written this chapter: Am I living as a coworker with Christ? Am I motivated by the values of the kingdom of God?

It therefore seems apt to close with a prayer:

> Lord of all life
> Help us to work together for that day
> When your kingdom comes
> And justice and mercy will be seen in all the earth.[49]

Addendum

If Christians are after all mistaken and this life is all there is, then the call to live for the kingdom of God—for the dream that will never happen—is still a valid call to a way of life that is worthwhile for the good of others and for the whole world. Such a mistaken vision will still have a real benefit for the world and will have given us a sense of purpose.

If I am mistaken, I am still glad that I have dreamed a dream.

49. Church of England, *Common Worship*, 197.

3

Give Us This Day Our Daily Bread

(Just Enough) Bread for the Journey

The secret things belong to the Lord our God, but the things revealed belong to us and to our children forever, that we may follow all the words of this law.

—DEUT 29:29

"My thoughts are not your thoughts, neither are your ways my ways," declares the Lord. "As the heavens are higher that the earth, so are my ways higher than your ways, and my thoughts than your thoughts."

—ISA 55:8–9

Do not try to understand things that are too difficult for you, or try to discover what is beyond your powers. Concentrate on what has been assigned you, you have no need to worry over mysteries.

—ECCL 3:21–22

JANE[1] WAS CRIPPLED WITH anxiety. She would worry about her children every minute they were out of her sight; she constantly felt insecure and frequently suffered from depression. She worried about her health and about what would happen when she became old. Would she have a stroke? Or get cancer? And then what would happen to her children?

All this worry was needless, as she was in fact quite healthy.

With the help of a Christian counselor, Jane looked at various traumatic events of her childhood, asking God to heal past hurts and painful memories. Her somewhat tentative faith grew as she brought her past to God for healing prayer. She learned to start each day first by relaxing her body and then consciously inviting God into her life *to be with her that day*. She gave the problems of *that day* into his hands and asked him to release her from worry *that day* and to replace her anxiety with his peace *that day*.

So she began to live one day at a time,[2] and gradually, her fear lessoned. She became more relaxed. Her understanding of theology is rudimentary, and she would be unable to explain what the atonement is about—(I doubt whether she has ever heard the word;) but she is learning to receive daily bread from the Lord.

Jane's story reminds us that the Christian message is basically very simple: God is *for us*.

He is on our side: "The Son of God, Jesus Christ . . . was not 'Yes and No'; but in him it is always 'Yes.'"[3] If we come to him in simple trust, he will help us live our lives one day at a time, one step at a time.

Jesus taught his disciples to pray for (just enough) *daily bread* for the journey. Not for full larders and bulging freezers, not for cake and caviar— he taught them to pray for what they needed for *that day*, not for everything they might need in future or wish for as luxuries in the here and now.

It is a prayer that is highly relevant to our physical and psychological health (as we have just seen in Jane's story), but in the rest of this chapter, I will focus on the spiritual and theological lessons that we can also draw from this prayer.

Our daily spiritual bread is to *know* Jesus (made known by the Holy Spirit) as a living presence in our hearts. We do not really need to know more than this.

---

1. Name has been changed.

2. As recommended by Jesus in Matt 6:24: "Therefore do not worry about tomorrow, for tomorrow will worry about itself. Each day has enough trouble of its own."

3. 2 Cor 1:19.

So is there a dangerous irrelevance in my quest to understand the scope of salvation? Am I treading where angels fear to tread? Is this like a request for cake and caviar rather than bread?

Should I accept the traditional teaching of the majority of the church down the centuries (even if with a conflicted heart and gritted teeth)? Or should I simply acknowledge that there will be a judgment, and leave the result of that judgment totally in God's hands, as something that we should inquire into no further? God will do what God wills to do—and to try to discern what that might be could be considered at best a useless waste of time, and at worst, bordering on the blasphemous.

But I find that the "excruciating tensions and inner contradictions imposed by traditional theology," to use MacDonald's apt phrase,[4] will not allow me to relinquish my quest.

I do not believe that the gospel, when rightly understood, should cause excruciating tensions and inner contradictions for Christ's followers.

And much harm has sometimes been done by the terrifying teachings about hell. This is less prevalent at the present time than it has been in the past because the concept is now so alien to modern sensibilities that even those who have a strong *theology* of "everlasting condemnation" are perhaps more reluctant to preach it than they were in the past (which could be interpreted as a sign that the Holy Spirit is prompting the church to think again about these matters).

Paul Tournier[5] practiced as a psychotherapist and physician during the middle of the twentieth century, working mainly in the strongly Calvinist city of Geneva. He commented,

> Gospel means "good news" of the grace of God. Yet there has been freely cultivated in Christendom a fear of eternal punishment. I do not think we can measure exactly the part it plays in the fear of death. Nevertheless, it seems that the fear of death is greater in the Christian West than in the Far East. The fear of hell can assume incredible proportions with some patients.[6]

I believe that harm has also been done to the ideas that people hold about the nature of God. Perhaps the heart of my quest is for the honor of God's name of Love.

---

4. MacDonald, *Evangelical Universalist*, 55.

5. Tournier died in 1986 at the age of eighty-eight.

6. Tournier, *Guilt and Grace*, 155.

Thoughts such as this prompt me to continue this exploration, but with the acute awareness that in the end we have no option but to leave the matter in God's hands. God will do what he wills to do, and we can have confidence that what he does will ultimately be perfectly loving and perfectly just.

There Is Mystery at the Heart of the Gospel

We worship an invisible God who can be known only by faith—and finding faith could be compared to following the footsteps of the wind.[7]

God's footsteps can be seen in creation if we open our eyes to its wonderous artistry and do not allow the theory that it all happened by chance to steal our sense of awe at the immensity of God's creativity—of vast galaxies of stars and planets, the unimaginably minute detail in the structure of cells and snowflakes, atoms and electrons, biochemical processes, enzymes and genes—and the patience of a God who is humble enough and patient enough to work through the slow, painful processes of evolution.[8]

In the person of Jesus Christ, God draws near and knocks at the door of our hearts.[9] When we invite him into our hearts in faith, then by grace he will come and make his presence and his salvation known to us.

As we read our bibles and pray, receive the sacraments, and share fellowship with other Christians, that faith will grow. Yet mystery will always remain, for "great is the mystery of faith."[10]

To change the metaphor, we are finding our way through a deep and beautiful forest, crisscrossed by many paths, with vistas of high peaks suddenly glimpsed through the trees. It would be easy to get lost here. But Jesus is, as it were, the path through the forest. He is "the Way, the Truth and the Life,"[11] and as we come to him each day, we can follow the path

---

7. Both in Hebrew (*ruah*) and Greek (*pneuma*) the word for "wind" and "Spirit" is the same.

8. The scientific evidence for evolution seems to be compelling. My understanding is that God created *through evolution*. In my opinion "creationism"—in the usual sense of the term (accepting a more or less literal interpretation of the Genesis account of creation, and an anti-evolution stance)—is not tenable if we accept that truth comes to us in many ways, not least through science.

9. Rev 3:20.

10. This acclamation is used in the Anglican Communion service.

11. John 14:6.

through the wood, and, (returning to our original metaphor,) we receive our daily bread for the journey.

But the high peaks are only glimpsed through the trees, and mystery remains.

Even Moses, who spoke to the Lord "face to face, as a man speaks to his friend,"[12] was denied a fuller vision of God.

Moses wanted even more reassurance that God was with him and asked to see God's glory, but this was not allowed. God said, "when my glory passes by, I will put you in a cleft in the rock and cover you with my hand until I have passed by. Then I will remove my hand and you will see my back; but my face must not be seen."[13]

Like Moses, we only see God's "back," even while we see and feel and believe that there is evidence enough to inform our faith—even our faith with its shadow of doubt.

I am promised that after the resurrection I will see "face to face" and "know fully, even as I am known,"[14] but until then I have to be content with "but a poor reflection, as in a mirror," and like Moses, only see God's back. Even John, who is generally thought to be the "beloved disciple" who lay on Jesus' breast at the last supper, wrote in his letter to early Christians, "No one has ever seen God."[15]

Paul sometimes seems to be almost overpowered by the depths of the message he is trying to convey. In his letter to the Ephesians, he exuberates about "the unsearchable riches of Christ . . . this mystery . . . how wide and long and high and deep is the love of Christ . . . which . . . surpasses knowledge."[16] Modern young people often enthuse "It's awesome!" in a phrase that catches the mystery and sense of wonder that Paul is trying to convey.

The Greco-Roman world in Paul's time had many "mystery religions," whose hidden secrets were known only by the initiated, but Paul was not trying to keep mysterious truths *hidden* from all but the few initiates but rather to *reveal* that which had been previously hidden. He talks

---

12. Exod 33:11.

13. Exod 33:22. Interestingly, in the story of Jacob, who wrestled all night with a man he later thought was God, Jacob exclaimed in amazement: "I saw God face to face, and yet my life was spared" (Gen 32:30).

14. 1 Cor 13:12.

15. John 13:23, 1 John 4:12.

16. Eph 3:8–19.

about the mystery *being made known* and understood. For example, he writes to the Colossians:

> I . . . present to you the word of God in its fullness—the mystery that has been kept hidden for ages and generations, but is now disclosed to the saints. To them God has chosen to make known among the Gentiles the glorious riches of this mystery, which is Christ in you, the hope of glory.[17]

But mystery remains. As Augustine of Hippo (354–430) said in one of his sermons, "We are speaking of God; what marvel, if thou do not comprehend? For if thou comprehend, He is not God."[18]

It is indeed dangerous to deceive ourselves into thinking that we can fully understand the things of God or that we can encapsulate our God in our theology, but there is an opposite danger in hiding behind the idea of mystery rather than rigorously searching the Scriptures to explore what has been revealed to us. We admit that our amazing gospel remains at its heart a mystery and that we have to live with unanswered questions, but we know enough to follow "the Way"[19] of Christ.

John Stott urges us to be dogmatic about those things that have been plainly revealed:

> God has not revealed everything; he has deliberately kept some things secret (Deut 29:29). This is why Christians combine elements of dogmatism and agnosticism. We should be dogmatic about those things which have been plainly revealed, and agnostic about those things which have been kept secret. Our troubles arise when our dogmatism trespasses into the secret things, and our agnosticism into the revealed things. Moreover even what God has revealed is not always plain . . . [Even] the apostle Peter confessed that there were some things in Paul's letters which he found hard to understand (2 Pet 3:15–16).[20]

---

17. Col 1:25–27.

18. Augustine, "Sermons," 117:5. See also ibid., 5:2, 6.

19. Jesus called himself "the Way, the Truth and the Life" (John 14:6), and "the Way" was the oldest name given to the Christian church (Acts 9:2; 19:9, 23; 22:4; 24:14, 22). Similarly, the Old Testament pictures God's people being led along God's way (Ps 23; Isa 40:3, 10–11). In Matt 7:13–14, Jesus challenges his hearers to choose between the two possible paths open to them (and to us).

20. Stott, *Living Church*, 108.

A Summary of the Things I Believe
Have Been Plainly Revealed

Following Stott's advice, I will summarize those things—explored in Chapter 1—that in my opinion we need to know in order to feed on Christ, who is our daily bread:

1. God is our creator and redeemer, and he loves the creation he has made.

2. Jesus Christ lived and died in first-century Palestine to reveal God more completely and to make the kingdom of God more accessible to humanity.

3. Jesus died on the cross as a result of human sin, revealing the extent of God's love. In God's eternal plan, his death was a means of identifying with the pain of the world and of dealing with its sin.

4. The whole Godhead was involved in the cross.

5. Christ's resurrection from death reveals the fact that the cross was a victory, not a defeat, and that one day we shall all be raised from the dead.

6. His death demands a response from us.

7. We will all—believer and unbeliever alike—be judged by Jesus Christ.

Our Hope

The Bible assures us that those who have received Christ will, through God's grace, receive eternal life both in this age and in the age to come.

But there are many who have never heard the gospel, or who have heard but do not understand or do not care, or who see and at least partially understand but nevertheless reject Christ and what he offers. The ultimate fate of these people, who are sometimes termed "the rejected" (or perhaps more accurately, "those who reject"), is less clear, and the Bible seems to say different things in different places. We are given pictures and symbolisms, guideposts and signs, and glimpses of enormous hope.

And our hope is enlarged when we remember that Christ, who will judge us all, is also the one who died for the salvation of the world.

The judge is the savior.

But if this book seems to have exchanged one set of dogmatic certainties with another, then I have failed in my task.

4

Forgive Us Our Sins, For We Also Forgive Everyone Who Sins against Us

If you forgive men when they sin against you, your heavenly Father will also forgive you. But if you do not forgive men their sins, your Father will not forgive your sins.

—MATT 6:14–15

Be kind and compassionate to one another, forgiving each other, just as in Christ God forgave you.

—EPH 4:32

"If the Messiah isn't raised, then your faith is futile and you are still in your sins." In other words, with the resurrection of Jesus a new world has dawned in which forgiveness of sins is not simply a private experience; it is a fact about the cosmos . . . The resurrection is neither an isolated and out-of-character divine "miracle," nor simply the promise of eternal life beyond the grave. It is, rather, the decisive start of the world-wide rule of the Jewish Messiah, in which sins are already forgiven and the promise of the eventual new world of justice and incorruptible life are assured.

—TOM WRIGHT[1]

1. Wright, *Surprised by Hope*, 259, discussing 1 Cor 15: 17.

FORGIVENESS IS AT THE heart of the gospel.

The good news is that despite our sinfulness, God forgives us because Jesus Christ has suffered for us on the cross. He has carried away our guilt and released God's grace: "The redemption is redemption from punishment which man has merited and deserved into a forgiveness and grace which he has not merited and which he has not deserved."[2] We are a forgiven people, and we are called in our turn to be a people who forgive.

The more deeply we realize that we are forgiven, the more we receive God's healing and saving forgiveness, and the more we forgive those who have hurt us—then the more God is able to form us anew into his image: more holy, more loving, more forgiving, and more like Jesus—more like we were intended to be.

But the natural way of the world is not forgiveness but revenge.

For several years I lived with my husband and family in Papua New Guinea, where traditional society (especially in the highlands) had often operated in a system of escalating "payback" that might go something like this: someone from tribe A accidentally (or on purpose) kills a pig from tribe B, so tribe B mounts a "payback" raid, killing several pigs from tribe A or perhaps carrying off one or two of the women. In revenge, the warriors of tribe A make a return raid and kill several warriors from tribe B, so the fighting rapidly escalates into all-out tribal warfare . . . The situation may have changed, but at that time (during the 1970s,) we were repeatedly warned never to stop if we accidentally injured an indigenous person when driving on the road, because we might rapidly be lynched by the family or tribesman of the injured person. Fortunately, we never had to put this warning to the test and never heard of such an event actually happening.

Human nature is the same all over the world.

In southeast Kenya, there have been long-standing disputes between the Pokomo and Orma tribes over access to water and land for grazing cattle. The following report on August 23, 2012 reminded me of the situation in Papua New Guinea in the 1970s:

> There have been problems simmering for a while . . . About 10 days ago three Pokomo were killed by the Orma community . . . In revenge, the Orma raided villages occupied by the Pokomo and burnt down more than 100 houses. Now the Pokomo have once again revenged by killing about 50 people. These are purely revenge attacks.[3]

2. Barclay, *Mind of St. Paul*, 63.

3. Agence France-Presse, "Dozens of Kenyans Hacked, Burnt to

If we think that we in the "civilized" West are above that kind of thing, we have only to read our newspapers to be disillusioned. The cry for revenge, for compensation, for somebody else to pay the price of our injury—and to pay it in full, with interest—is usually at the forefront.

Against a background of primitive payback morality, perhaps not unlike that which I have sketched from Papua New Guinea and in the situation between the Pokomo and Orma in Kenya, the Old Testament injunction to limit revenge to the equivalent injury (and no more) represents a real step towards justice. The law says, "Life for life, eye for eye, tooth for tooth, hand for hand, foot for foot, burn for burn, wound for wound, bruise for bruise."[4]

But Jesus preached and practiced a radically different philosophy:

> You have heard that it was said, "Eye for eye, and tooth for tooth." But I tell you, Do not resist an evil person. If someone strikes you on the right cheek, turn to him the other also. And if someone wants to sue you and take your tunic, let him have your cloak as well . . . Love your enemies and pray for those who persecute you, that you may be sons of your Father in heaven.[5]

Jesus marvelously demonstrated what he preached when he prayed from the cross: "Father, forgive them, for they do not know what they are doing."[6]

When Jesus uttered this prayer, it was for the confused and mistaken people who had him condemned to death, and for the soldiers who—acting under orders—beat him and nailed him to the cross. I do not think it is fanciful to visualize our Lord's prayer sending a stream of forgiveness through the centuries to confused and unbelieving mankind, to those of us in the churches who have got it wrong, and to those outside who haven't a clue what it is all about.

Jesus' teachings and example have inspired his followers to practice forgiveness, sometimes to a remarkable extent. Soon after Jesus' crucifixion, Stephen echoed Jesus' prayer. While the stones that would kill him

---

Death," August 23, 2012, www.thenational.ae/news/world/africa/
dozens-of-kenyans-hacked-burnt-to-death.

4. Exod 21:23–25.

5. Matt 5:38–40, 43.

6. Luke 23:34.

were being hurled he cried, "Lord, do not hold this sin against them."[7] And many others have sought to live lives of forgiveness.

I have mentioned traditional "payback" attitudes in Papua New Guinea; however, in 2009 the Women's World Day of Prayer Service,[8] written that year by the women of Papua New Guinea, included the following powerful story of forgiveness:

> *Maria's Story:* Maria is my name and I come from the highlands of Papua New Guinea where tribal fighting is a worry for many mothers and children. For a long time the fighting had been traditional with bows and arrows but now it is with modern firearms. My husband became a victim when he was killed by another tribe. Our tribal members were ready to retaliate. However this revenge did not take place due to the Christian commitment of family members and also to the prayers of the many women and children who pray continually for peace. Instead, forgiveness and reconciliation were extended towards the enemy.[9]

Another inspiring example of forgiveness came a few years ago from Merseyside, England.

Anthony Walker was a black British A-level student who was murdered with an ice axe in a racist attack in July 2005. He was a practicing Christian and keen on sports. Remarkably, his family publicly forgave the killers, and they have set up a foundation to promote racial harmony. Anthony's mother, Gee Walker, who is much in demand as a speaker, stresses that children are not born racist—sadly, this is something they learn from adults.

In a welcome letter on the foundation's website, Gee writes:

> The Foundation is committed to making a difference, to challenge prejudice, discrimination, inequality, and instead promote peace, harmony and integrity . . .
>
> It has not always been easy, many tears have been shed over the years, but happily when I see the response in people, especially young children, there have also been tears of joy and laughter . . . It's not easy and we must strive hard to show our

7. Acts 7:60.

8. The Women's World Day of Prayer movement was started around 1887 when women from different denominations joined to organize days of prayer for missionary work. The movement has grown, and now a service of prayer is planned each year by women from a different country.

9. Papua New Guinea World Day of Prayer Committee, Women's World Day of Prayer Service Booklet, March 6, 2009, 12.

forgiveness, our compassion, our love. I can speak from personal experience about how difficult this is, however, I hold fast to my dreams. What we consider once impossible can become possible if we believe, if we have faith, and we work together.[10]

The attitude of positive forgiveness and reconciliation this brave and compassionate Christian family has shown has made a massive impact in the troubled area in which they live.

It is heartening to hear recent news from the chaotic situation in the Middle East about churches responding to attack with forgiveness and acts of reconciliation. For example, in 2013 churches and Christian bookshops were burned by extremists in Egypt, but Christians did not retaliate. "Instead they gathered to pray for those who did the damage. God gave the strength to forgive, and their neighbours have noticed."[11] Likewise, churches in Lebanon, Jordan, and Egypt have been helping displaced people. This has not been easy: "Initial resentment gave way to realizing God is in these movements. So they've welcomed refugees, given food, clothes and simple education, and offered them Scriptures and Christian teaching."[12]

Another event from 1986 has stuck in my mind. A gang of burglars broke into the Reverend Michael Saward's vicarage in Ealing England, and beat up Michael and his daughter Jill's boyfriend, fracturing both their skulls. Then they tied them up, robbed the home, and brutally raped Jill.

To general amazement, Michael publically declared that the family forgave those brutal men, but he demanded that they should receive a stiff sentence because even though they had been forgiven, justice still needed to be done.

Jill was severely traumatized and she was shocked when the judge gave a more lenient sentence for the rape than for the burglary. She has since campaigned to change society's attitude to sexual offences and has established a charity to help rape victims.

The following is a recent post about Forgiveness and Justice from Jill's website:

> Forgiveness and justice, although from a similar stable, are *not* the same. This point is often forgotten or misunderstood by

10. Anthony Walker Foundation, "Welcome from Gee Walker," http://www.anthonywalkerfoundation.com/welcome-from-gee.

11. Parker, "God Gave Them Strength," 18.

12. Ibid.

many people. When I forgave the men that raped me I did it,
calling on God's strength to get me through, and his supernatural power to sustain me. I did it so that I wouldn't have to live
with anger and hatred festering away and eating me up inside.
I did it to be free of the burden of bitterness. I had been down
that path in the past; it was painful; it was horrible and I didn't
want to go there again. I was reminded of how close I had come
to not being able to do that just days before the rape. And I did it
because that's what the Bible tells us to do. "Vengeance is mine,"
says the Lord. That frees me from having to decide what level of
retribution is satisfactory.

I will never know what made my attackers do what they
did. They can never justify what they did with an answer that
will be satisfactory, there isn't one.

But I did want justice. I wanted the men to be caught. I
wanted them to be sentenced, I wanted them to be locked up so
that they couldn't hurt others, and I wanted them to know that
what they did was wrong.[13]

Jesus demonstrated almost unbelievable forgiveness and taught us
to forgive, but anyone who has been seriously hurt or wounded either
mentally or physically knows, as Jill Saward found out, how difficult this
is in practice. The desire for revenge is strong and innately hardwired
within us, while forgiveness and love for our enemies runs counter to
unredeemed human nature.

We need God's grace to be able to forgive.

One could ask, "Where is the justice in forgiving?" To forgive means
to refuse to seek personal revenge or harbor bitterness. But it does not
mean that the wounds inflicted don't hurt, or that justice can be passed
over. Jill's rape was massively traumatizing and it was evil in the extreme.
The perpetrators certainly deserve to be brought to justice, which is in
line with biblical principles.

The Sawards' case provoked much media attention at the time, and
we discussed the issues involved in a small group that I was then involved
in. We were discussing the section of the Lord's Prayer that heads this
chapter, as well as Jesus' accompanying comment:

Forgive us our debts, as we also have forgiven our debtors . . .
"If you forgive men when they sin against you, your heavenly

13. Jill Saward, "4 Thought," *Jill Saward* (blog), April 7, 2012, http://saward.
org/2012/04/07/4-thought/.

Father will also forgive you. But if you do not forgive men their
sins, your Father will not forgive your sins."[14]

We looked at the dilemma and reactions of the Saward family as a
case study. We were not asking whether forgiveness annulled the need
for justice, for as Jill Saward states with such clarity, it does not. But we
were asking whether there could be any forgiveness without repentance
or remorse on the part of the wrongdoer, and we were in disagreement.

Some thought that the Sawards were right to extend forgiveness unconditionally, even for such horrendous acts, as a sign that they bore no
bitterness or desire for revenge against those wicked men (though they
were indeed very wicked). But other group members felt that forgiveness
should not, and indeed could not, be offered without some evidence of a
change of heart on the part of the wrongdoers. We all agreed that there
could be no reconciliation, no possibility of establishing a relationship
(even if it were desired), unless the perpetrators repented profoundly
with deep and heartfelt sorrow for the hurt that they had caused.

The discussion we had all those years ago is very pertinent to the
question in hand: Jesus' words seem to imply that God will only forgive
us *if* we forgive our enemies. This is very much on a par with the understanding that we will only be saved *if* we repent and believe (or are born
again, or ask Jesus into our heart, or an equivalent concept).

We are often told that God loves us unconditionally—and yet, we
seem to see conditions imposed on God's love by our Lord's own words:
"*If* you forgive men when they sin against you, your heavenly Father will
also forgive you. But *if* you do not forgive men their sins, your Father will
not forgive your sins."[15]

And Jesus tells Peter that he should forgive his brother, not a mere
seven times, but seventy-seven times.[16] Some manuscripts have "seventy
times seven," but the meaning is clear: Peter was in fact told to go on and
on forgiving. Jesus then goes on to tell a challenging parable about a troubled servant whose massive debt was forgiven by the king. Going out from
the king's presence, he immediately found a fellow servant who owed him
a much smaller sum and "grabbed him and began to choke him, 'Pay back
what you owe me!' he demanded." When his fellow servant beseeched him
for mercy, he refused, and instead had him thrown into prison.

14. Matt 6:12; 14–15.
15. Matt 6:14–15.
16. Matt 18:22.

When the king found out, he called him in. "You wicked servant," he said. "I cancelled all that debt of yours because you begged me to, shouldn't you have had mercy on your fellow-servant just as I had on you?" In anger, his master turned him over to the jailers to be tortured until he should pay back all he owed. Then comes the crunch: "this is how my heavenly Father will treat each of you unless you forgive your brother from your heart."[17]

Sobering teaching indeed! We are all imperfect, and we all need forgiveness from each other and from God. If we are to receive God's forgiveness, it is vital that we ourselves forgive our fellow human beings. Does this mean that unless we forgive others, we will be forever condemned and lose the salvation that Jesus came to effect?

I turn again to the insights of the psychotherapist Paul Tournier, who writes with the experience of one who has heard many accounts of deep hurt and anguish:

> I do not think that in the mouth of Jesus Christ repentance has the force of a condition but rather of a route. Jesus seems to me to be a penetrating and realistic observer of men, who describes things as they take place . . . in the Lord's Prayer Jesus has taught us to ask God to forgive us "as we also have forgiven our debtors" (Matt 6:12). And he clearly adds: "If you forgive men their trespasses, your heavenly Father also will forgive you: but if you do not forgive men their trespasses, neither will your Father forgive your trespasses" (Matt 6:14–15). These words could therefore be taken in the sense of a "condition," a right, a meritorious demand, for a forgiveness which we gain by the forgiveness which we ourselves grant to others.
>
> How tragic that would be for us! What a burden would press upon us! One has to be a psychotherapist to know how rare the forgiveness of others is, and how aggressiveness can be repressed behind false forgiveness. Here we have all the drama of moralism again. For if forgiveness of others is the condition for God's love, then we must appear to forgive, we must do our outmost to forgive, we must camouflage or repress our aggressiveness under friendly words, and the repressed aggressiveness eats within the soul, becomes the source of false guilt and morbid anxiety, and bars the way to salvation . . .
>
> The very thought of it makes me shudder. What a drama is there! For what false love, what false forgivenesses between men—and particularly in the Churches and in religious

17. Matt 18:23–35.

families—and for what anxieties these repressions are responsible . . . And all this happens because that piece of Christ's
teaching has been taken in an infantile way, and God has been
credited with a conditional love, which places the condition of
salvation back upon our own shoulders; because we try hard to
fulfill the condition, and when we are not able we feign it.[18]

So what is the answer to this conundrum? Tournier continues:

These words of Christ can be understood as a factual description of the way things happen, of the route that is followed . . .
when we grasp the fact that God's love is unconditional, we find
the power to forgive others; for God does not love us because we
love Him and obey him, and in that way fulfill some condition,
but, as St. John says, "because he first loved us" (1 John 4:19).[19]

Tournier describes a dynamic process: when we grasp the fact that
God loves us unconditionally and forgives us unconditionally, not because we deserve to be forgiven (by its very nature, forgiveness is not deserved—condemnation and "payback" is what is deserved) but because
the condemnation and "payback" has been carried within the Godhead
on the cross of Christ. Then, knowing that we are forgiven *by undeserved
grace*, we are more able to forgive in our turn—even acts that do not
deserve to be forgiven. Our forgiveness does not earn God's forgiveness
as a merit but springs instead from a heart that has been set free from
"payback" morality and so is enabled to forgive others. This dynamic is
expressed in the exhortation to the Ephesians: "Be kind and compassionate to one another, forgiving each other, just as in Christ God forgave
you,"[20] and is powerfully illustrated in the life of Bishop Festo Kivengere.

Kivengere was a Ugandan who was transformed by the East African
Revival movement. He became a bishop in 1973 and was soon forced
to flee from Idi Amin, who was threatening to kill him for speaking out
against his tyrannical regime. Kivengere died in 1988.

Sometime in the 1970s I read his compelling book *Revolutionary
Love*, and the following delightful account has stayed with me. In a sim-
ple narrative style, Kivengere recounts how he became able to forgive Idi
Amin once he knew that his own sin of unforgiveness had been forgiven:

18. Tournier, *Guilt and Grace*, 190–91.
19. Ibid., 191.
20. Eph 4:32.

That first Good Friday after our escape from Uganda, we were in England and the newspapers were reporting daily the increased persecution back home. The six young actors who were to have represented the early martyrs of Uganda in a play for the church's Centennial Celebration were found dead together in a field. And on and on . . .

I felt something was strangling me spiritually . . . I grew increasingly bitter toward Amin . . . I slipped into the back of All Souls Church in London to listen to the meditation on the seven last words of Christ on the cross.

The first word was read distinctly: "Father, forgive them; for they do not know what they are doing."[21] So said my Lord when the cruel nails were being driven into His hands . . .

To me He was saying, "You can't forgive Amin?"

"No, Lord."

"Suppose he had been one of those soldiers driving the nails into my hands. He could have been, you know."

"Yes Lord, he could."

"Do you think I would have prayed, 'Father, forgive them, all except that Idi Amin?'"

I shook my head. "No, Master. Even he would have come within the embrace of Your boundless love." I bowed, asking forgiveness, and although I frequently had to repent and pray again for forgiveness, I rose that day with a liberated heart and have been able to share Calvary love in freedom.

Yes, because of His immeasurable grace to me, I do love Idi Amin, have forgiven him, and am still praying for him to escape the terrible spiritual prison he is in.[22]

Forgiveness can indeed be deeply healing, as Jason[23] found out. He suffered for months from general anxiety and terrible nightmares from which he awoke in terror. His job began to suffer, his marriage was deteriorating, and he sank into a deep depression.

The nightmares had started after a car crash, and his wife kept reminding him that he had been lucky to escape from the crash with only a minor whiplash injury to his neck. But Jason's wife was also angry with him because the car that he had crashed belonged to her; she was ambitious, capable, had a better job than him, and earned more money. And she was constantly putting him down.

21. Luke 23:34.

22. Kivengere, *Revolutionary Love*, 80.

23. Name has been changed.

Finally, Jason admitted that he was consumed with suppressed bitterness and anger. Eventually he came to realize that the only way that he could escape from the cycle of bitterness was through forgiveness. Over several weeks he forgave his wife, and little by little, his anger melted, his sleep pattern improved, and his anxiety and depression lifted. His marriage also improved, and his wife started to treat him with more respect.

By forgiving deep hurts, Jason had found healing for his own bitterness and depression.

The unforgiving heart is like a clenched fist, ready to strike back in revenge and anger, which is easy to understand when the hurt inflicted by another has been grievous. As long as the fist is clenched, it is unable to give or receive the grace of forgiveness, for only an open hand can receive.

To let go of grievous hurt is never easy, but it is a route of healing for the one who has been hurt. This is also why Jesus told us to pray for our enemies.[24] It may be possible to pray for those who have hurt us even before we are able to forgive them. Prayer may be a step on the road to forgiveness and towards healing of our own hurting, wounded hearts.

C. S. Lewis, with his usual clarity of perception, found on one occasion that

> forgiving (that man's cruelty) and being forgiven (my resentment) were the very same thing. "Forgive and you shall be forgiven" sounds like a bargain. But perhaps it is something much more. By heavenly standards, that is, for pure intelligence, it is perhaps a tautology—forgiving and being forgiven are two names for the same thing. The important thing is that a discord has been resolved, and it is certainly the great Resolver who has done it.[25]

It is interesting to see the close connection between healing and salvation, both in experience and in the meaning of the Greek word in the New Testament. *Sozo* is a word that is usually translated as "save," but it is also quite frequently used to mean "to heal, or make whole."[26] To be fully healed in mind, body, and spirit is to be made whole. To be made whole in the deepest sense includes what is usually thought of in theological terms as "being saved." It includes both forgiving and being forgiven.

Forgiveness can be a costly option, as we have seen in the personal stories we have looked at, and above all, in the crucifixion of Christ.

24. Matt 5:44.

25. Lewis, *Letters to Malcolm*, 137–38.

26. For example, Matt 9:21–22; Mark 5:23, 28, 34; 6:56; Luke 8:36; Acts 14:9.

Forgiveness is not a cheap denial of what has happened. It involves admit-
ting that everything is *not* alright but that the vicious cycle of escalating
anger and hurt can only be broken by one side refusing to take revenge or
harbor bitterness, and so the wrongdoer and the one who has been wronged
are released from the venom of hate, anger, and the fear of reprisal.

As the anger and hate slip away, we begin to become aware of some
of our own attitudes that need to be forgiven, and we are able to receive
more forgiveness and to become more able to forgive. And so the healing
process continues.

Forgiveness continues to hold out a hand offering reconciliation to
those who have committed the hurt, but reconciliation can only happen
when *both* partners want it to happen and when the one who has committed the offence admits the fault and asks for pardon. Then the future
is set free from being forever blighted by the pain of the past.

As Desmond and Mpho Tutu write in their very helpful book, *The
Book of Forgiving*, "Without forgiveness, we create patterns of violence
and hurt that get repeated in neighborhoods and cities and between
countries for decades and even centuries."[27]

If any reader is struggling to forgive deep wounds and hurts, I would
commend the Tutus' book, written by a father and daughter who have
both experienced deep traumas in their lives that they have been able
to forgive. The book is at once simple and profound, and describes the
fourfold path to be taken to reach the healing of forgiveness. It draws on
the experience of the Truth and Reconciliation Commission set up in the
aftermath of apartheid in South Africa—which is often credited with the
fact that South Africa did *not* descend into a bloodbath once majority
rule was achieved and apartheid was overcome.

Let us look again at Jesus' Parable of the Prodigal Son.[28] See also
chapter 1 (p. 57–59). The father forgave his son long before he returned
(Perhaps even as he walked away?) and was longing for his return with a
sorrowful heart. He did not forgive his son because of his halting words of
remorse, instead he "ran to his son, threw his arms around him and kissed
him" before the words were spoken—because he had already forgiven.

I believe that this is also true for each one of us. Our salvation is based
on the forgiveness of our sins. Though the Bible constantly speaks of God's
wrath and anger, this is against the sin, not the sinner, and is dealt with on

27. Tutu and Tutu, *Book of Forgiving*, 224.
28. Luke 15:11–32.

the cross. Christ died instead of the "notorious prisoner" Barabbas, "who had committed murder in the uprising."[29] "God demonstrates his own love for us in this: While we were still sinners, Christ died for us."[30] God holds out forgiveness and salvation that is not conditional on our repentance or our faith. But in Jesus' parable, although the father had forgiven his errant son and waited with sorrowful love for his return, there could be no *reconciliation* between them until the son returned from the "distant country" and *accepted* the offered forgiveness, the robe, the ring, and the celebration.

The father had not cut him off or rejected him; it was the son who had walked away and rejected his father's house and his love.

This also is how it is between us and God. To be *reconciled* with God, to experience and enter into the salvation that is offered, we need to believe and accept what Christ has done. We need to receive his forgiveness with faith. As Paul explains to the Ephesians, "it is by grace you have been saved, through faith—and this not from yourselves, it is the gift of God—not by works, so that no one can boast."[31]

We have seen through the eyes of the Saward family that the need for justice is not erased because of forgiveness. In the final accounting of God, if it is justice we ask for, we will all stand condemned—a condemnation that is carried on the cross so that justice is done but mercy can yet prevail, because God longs to be reconciled with every person in the world.

As Paul writes to the Corinthians, "God was reconciling the world to himself in Christ, not counting men's sins against them . . . We implore you on Christ's behalf: Be reconciled to God. God made him who had no sin to be sin for us, so that in him we might become the righteousness of God."[32]

Not long ago I came across the following anonymous prayer, which was found in the clothing of a dead child at the Ravensbrück concentration camp. It shows the fruit that can be yeilded at a human level when injury is met with forgiveness rather than revenge, and I found it deeply moving:

> O Lord, remember not only the men and women of good will, but also those of ill will.
> But do not remember all of the suffering they have inflicted upon us:

---

29. Matt 27:16; Mark 15:7. See also Luke 23:18; John 18:40.
30. Rom 5:8.
31. Eph 2:8–9.
32. 2 Cor 5:19–21.

instead, remember the fruits we have borne because of this
suffering—

Our fellowship, our loyalty to one another, our humility, our
courage, our generosity, the greatness of heart that has grown
from this trouble.

When our persecutors come to be judged by you,

Let all of these fruits that we have borne be their forgiveness.[33]

Finally, a Disturbing Question

Before closing this chapter I want to look at a very disturbing question:
Can there, *in the end*, be forgiveness for those who show no repentance
or remorse?

We have seen how sometimes human beings find the grace to forgive horrendous crimes inflicted against them and those they love. The
Saward family, the family of Anthony Walker, a group of Christian women
in Papua New Guinea, Festo Kivengere, and many others have forgiven
those who have wronged them in appalling ways, and we have just read
the moving prayer of forgiveness found in the clothing of a dead child.

But we have no evidence that the perpetrators of these horrendous
crimes repented for their actions. Dare we ask whether God will forgive
them in the final judgment? Or has he already forgiven them because of
the cosmic effects of Christ's cross? Or is that forgiveness "put on hold"
until they are finally aware of their need—until they repent and turn to
the God who is still waiting and seeking their response?

For example: can there be eternal forgiveness for Anders Behring
Breivik, the thirty-three-year-old right-wing extremist who, on July 22,
2011, killed eight people when he blew up a car parked in the government
block in Oslo, then systematically gunned down sixty-nine young people
at a Labor party camp in Norway. Like Hitler attempting to annihilate
the Jewish race, like many fanatical Islamist suicide bombers, and like
many others in history who have slaughtered those they consider to be
their enemies, Breivik claimed to be acting "righteously." He showed no
remorse at his trial and claimed that the massacre was "a preventive attack
against state traitors" guilty of "ethnic cleansing" due to their support for
a multicultural society. He had spent years planning the attack, which he

33. "Prayer no. 668" in Castle, *Treasury of Prayer*.

called "cruel but necessary." His lawyer has said that Breivik "laments not going further."[34]

Most of us find such thinking and such actions to be horrifying and terrifying. Did Breivik, in the deepest sense of the word, know what he was doing? And are the atrocities of war, sanctioned by society and usually blessed by the church, any less horrifying? The atomic bombs dropped on Hiroshima and Nagasaki probably ended World War II. Far more people were killed in a much more painful way than the victims of the lone Breivik, with his clean bullet-shots to the head. Was such a slaughter really necessary? Was it a "righteous act" in a "just war"? How will God judge those who ordered the bombs to be dropped? Or those who actually dropped them? My point is that Anders felt justified in what he did (wrongly in the view of the vast majority). Awful acts are committed in war too, and those who commit them believe that they are justified. In the end only God can judge.

We are getting into deep and troubled waters here.

For such grossly evil acts, hell or annihilation would seem, from a human perspective, to be just—at least until the perpetrators have seen what they have done and repented of it.

But what of those whose nagging pettiness drip bitterness into their families for years? Or those filled with lust, envy, hate, anger? The list goes on until it becomes as long and as wide as the human race. And it includes me, and each of my readers.

Thank God, we can only leave such questions with him in the knowledge that he will judge with righteousness and mercy.

But perhaps for some, the awareness of the need to be forgiven may only come in that clarity of vision that we believe will be brought about by the full revelation of God and his piercing view of our lives in the resurrection life that is to come.

We will look again at this in chapter 6, where we explore the possibility that in hell we will meet God and, as Paul says, "then I shall know fully, even as I am known."[35] Perhaps we will see then with horrifying clarity the effects of our actions—and perhaps seeing will lead to repentance in a sort of Godly restorative justice, a painful cleansing process that will finally lead to restoration and salvation.

34. "Anders Behring Breivik: The Boy Next Door Turned Serial Killer," *The Telegraph*, April 16, 2012, http://www.telegraph.co.uk/news/worldnews/europe/norway/9206108/Anders-Behring-Breivik-the-boy-next-door-turned-serial-killer.html?mobile=basic.

35. 1 Cor 13:12.

We are not explicitly told that this will be so, but we do know that "God our Savior . . . wants all men to be saved and to come to knowledge of the truth. For there is one God and one mediator between God and men, the man Christ Jesus, who gave himself as a ransom for all men."[36]

Conclusion

Following the psychotherapist Paul Tournier, I have argued that when Jesus says, "If you forgive men when they sin against you, your heavenly Father will also forgive you, but if you do not forgive men their sins, your Father will not forgive your sins,"[37] he is describing *the way things happen*: God's forgiveness of us is not conditional on our forgiveness of others, but *the route* that we take. When we realize that we are forgiven, we are released by grace and can finally forgive others.

And when we forgive, we are able to receive forgiveness. By forgiving others, we open our hearts to healing and forgiveness so that the increasing spiral of payback and vengeance is replaced by a widening circle of healing and forgiveness.

Forgiveness releases a great power for healing in the world, not least of all for the one who forgives, and is thus released from the bitterness and anger of a "payback" morality.

In chapter 1, we looked at how the cross of Christ carries the sins and deepest hurts of the world, releasing a cosmic stream of healing and forgiveness into the world. We looked at the account of God making an unconditional covenant with creation *before* he covenanted conditionally with the nation of Israel. We looked at biblical pictures of God that compare him to a husband who longs for his unfaithful wife to return, to a father who waits for his errant son to return, forgiving him and running to meet him long before he hears his stumbling statements of contrition, and to a shepherd who goes in search of one lost sheep even when he has ninety-nine safe in his fold.

This is our God.

We can never fully know "how wide and long and high and deep is the love of Christ," and we can never fully know "this love that surpasses knowledge."[38]

36. 1 Tim 2:4–6.
37. Matt 6: 14–15.
38. Eph 3:18–19.

5

Deliver Us from Evil—through Judgment

Look, the lamb of God who takes away the sin of the world!
—JOHN THE BAPTIST[1]

We do know that no man can be saved except through Christ; we do not know that only those who know him can be saved through Him.
—C. S. LEWIS[2]

In the Hebrew mind, "judge" doesn't mean "condemn." It means to put things right at last, where things have been out of joint. What a judge does is restore order and balance to the world. So God is coming to sort the whole thing out, and the Christian message is—God has actually done that in Jesus.
—TOM WRIGHT[3]

---

1. John 1:29.
2. Lewis, *Mere Christianity*, 62.
3. "N. T. Wright On Mission," interview by Roy Crowne Wright, *Christianity*, November 3, 2011, http://www.hopetogether.org.uk/Groups/188296/HOPE/Media/Press_cuttings/Press_cuttings.aspx.

WHEN TERRIBLE THINGS HAPPEN in the world, when our desires, which seemed to be good and godly, have been thwarted and our hopes for God's kingdom to come in a certain situation are still unfulfilled, we may feel like children who cry, "It's not fair!" when mother refuses to buy that packet of sweets placed so temptingly near the supermarket checkout.

Sorting out children's problems is hard enough, but sorting out the problems within a society or between nations is in a different league altogether—and all too often, human beings fail miserably. We fail because most of us, like the child crying for sweets at the checkout, tend to feel that life should be skewed in our own favor, which of course is not fair after all, because fairness means more for those who have too little to begin with. Therefore, in a world of finite resources, fairness means less for those who, like myself, currently have more than our share of the world's goods. And most of us, like myself, find it difficult to give up more of what we have come to think of as our share of the world's resources.

It may feel unfair to pay more in taxes or give away more to good causes, but in fact it is *justice*, not even charity, that demands that we should do so. Too often our reaction is to hold on tightly, to keep what we already have, and if possible, to try to get more: more power, more of the world's resources; more, more, more . . . It is this drive for more that is behind most of the world's conflicts.

Darwin and his followers have shown that evolution is driven by the "law" of survival of the fittest—which means, in effect, that the strongest thrive and succeed in getting more, while the weak or the marginalized become downtrodden and suffer, or survive only by ingenious strategies of self-defense or protection. This happens not only in nature, but in human society as well. Wealth creates more wealth and power tends to accrue more power, so the poor tend to get poorer and the weak, weaker—unless some action of love and justice intervenes.

The gross inequalities we see in society may be partly explained by the Darwinian theory of survival of the fittest, but that does not mean that they should be accepted as part of God's will or "because that is how he created things." All of us, adults and children alike, have an innate sense that life should be fair, but we also realize that this is not the case. The infamous lines: "The rich man in his castle, the poor man at the gate; God made them high and lowly, and ordered their estate" are now almost universally omitted from the otherwise much-loved hymn "All Things Bright and Beautiful." However, the fact that this false theology was once popular reminds us that Christians, and especially rich Christians, have all too often argued that the inequalities of society are ordained by God, or that they are due to God's blessing on those who do his will. They argue that the rich and powerful should be honored because their riches and their power are evidence that either they or their ancestors kept God's laws and did God's will, whereas the poverty of the poor is somehow their own fault.

The Bible does indeed teach that God blesses those who do his will. This is enshrined in the Ten Commandments.[4] It is spelled out strongly in Deut 28, and it underlies much of the Old Testament.[5] However, the call to "act justly and love mercy"[6] and to support the weak and the oppressed is an even more fundamental call, and one that challenges our complacency. Jesus indeed said, "you always have the poor with you,"[7] but he did not endorse the status quo. He told the rich young ruler, "If you wish to be perfect, go, sell your possessions, and give the money to the poor, and you will have treasure in heaven."[8]

We cannot hide behind the knowledge that God often (but not always) pours economic blessings on those who do his will in an effort to support a too-affluent lifestyle in the face of massive world poverty.

Inequality is stark enough in our own country, but infinitely starker when we look at the whole of "the global community"—a euphemistic phrase that reminds us that the mandate to be "our brother's keeper" extends beyond our own family, friends, and neighbors, and ultimately includes the whole world. As Sheila Cassidy reminds us, "we are all children of the same God, with the same rights to food, shelter, work and freedom. This means that we must care about injustice and poverty and the threat of nuclear war. How we express that caring will depend upon our gifts and resources at any given moment."[9] And there are many who, like Cassidy herself, do care deeply and passionately, work tirelessly, and give generously, trying to do what they can towards righting the unfairness with which we are surrounded.

In chapter 2 we looked at some outstanding examples of individuals who have cared, campaigned, and acted towards making the world a

4. Exod 20:5; 34:7.

5. The book of Job is a notable voice pointing out that this simple dogma does not always work. In reality, "good people" like Job often suffer. Many passages in the psalms express the same thought.

6. Mic 6:8.

7. Matt 26:11.

8. Matt 19:21.

9. Cassidy, *Sharing the Darkness*, 133.

fairer and better place—which is, as we have seen, working towards the coming of God's kingdom *on earth* as in heaven. In chapter 4 we looked not only at some horrendous acts perpetrated by human beings, but also at moving acts of forgiveness offered by others.

The human race is capable not only of appalling violence and naked evil, but also of goodness, compassion, and nobility, and evil loses much of its power over those who are "in Christ."

Yet we must all continue to live in this imperfect world, and even the best of us (whether Christians or not) are prone to niggling selfishness, thoughtlessness, and pettiness. We need to be delivered from a great deal of evil before God's kingdom can come in its fullness.

Throughout the Bible we find tantalizing promises and glimpses of an age to come when, at last, God will eradicate all evil from the world and we will finally be delivered from its clutches.[10] But until That Day we live in a state of partial deliverance.

The Israelites Expected God to Deliver Them from Evil

The primal story of the Israelites is their deliverance from the evil of slavery in Egypt. But this deliverance came at great cost to the Egyptians. Because Pharaoh would not let the Israelites go, the Egyptians suffered many horrible plagues, culminating in the most terrible plague of all: the destruction of their firstborn children and domestic animals. Later, Pharaoh's pursuing army was destroyed in the waters of the Red Sea (or Reed Sea),[11] at which the Israelites sang triumphantly and with great joy:

> I will sing to the Lord,
>   for he is highly exalted.
> The horse and its rider
>   he has hurled into the sea.[12]

---

10. See chapter 7.

11. Exod 12:29, 13:18. Most English translations follow the Greek Septuagint, *erutha thalassa*, or "Red Sea," but the Hebrew Bible uses *yam suph*, which means "Sea of Reeds." Scholars debate the location of the sea; a sea of reeds would have to be freshwater, but the Red Sea could be salt or fresh. Colin J. Humphries devotes chapters 11 and 12 of his book *The Miracles of Exodus* to discussing these issues. He concludes that the northern part of the Gulf of Aqaba is the most likely site of the crossing.

12. Exod 15:1.

Destruction for one nation, liberation for another—a pattern that is repeated throughout history. But this primal story is only the beginning of the story of the Jewish people.

After wandering in the desert for forty years, they were finally established as a nation in the land of Canaan, but this was achieved only at the expense of the almost complete destruction of the resident Canaanite tribes, which has been fairly accurately described as ethnic cleansing.[13] The Israelites were only able to possess their promised land through the overthrow of the "evil" Canaanites and others who were already living there.

However, the Israelites' deliverance, rescue, and establishment as a nation was still incomplete. According to the biblical historians, obedience and righteousness brought them blessing, whereas disobedience and wickedness brought them curses.[14] Under the "golden age" of King David, they eventually came to occupy the whole land promised to Abraham a thousand years before, but they lost it again over the next five hundred years. In 587 BC Jerusalem was overthrown, and many Israelites were taken into exile in Babylon, which the prophets interpreted as a punishment for disobedience. The leaders were acting unjustly towards the deprived members of society and had followed many of the evil practices of the surrounding nations, including idolatry and fertility cults, with their associated ritual prostitution (both male and female) and child sacrifice.

13. I confess that my mind balks at the apparent unfairness of the fact that the "promised land" was "given" to the people of Israel when it was already populated by Canaanites. In Gen 15:16, God promised Abraham that "In the fourth generation your descendants will come back here, for the sin of the Amorites has not yet reached its full measure," and the biblical explanation is: "It is not because of your righteousness or your integrity that you are going in to take possession of their land; but on account of the wickedness of these nations, the Lord your God will drive them out before you, to accomplish what he swore to your fathers, to Abraham, Isaac, and Jacob" (Deut 9:5; see also Deut 18:12 and Lev 18: 25). By the time the Israelites took possession of the land, it appears that the Amorites and other Canaanites were wicked enough to warrant destruction. They practiced fertility cults with male and female prostitutes, and (perhaps unsurprisingly) archaeology has revealed that sexually transmitted disease was common (Pawson, *Unlocking the Bible*, 186). The people also sacrificed children to the god Molech. The Israelites copied many of these practices, which seriously offended God (Jer 32:35). For a detailed discussion of this and other ethical problems associated with the Old Testament, see Copan, *Is God a Moral Monster?*, which sheds some light on this massive ethical problem, though I do not think it can be fully resolved. See also p.62–66.

14. This understanding is spelled out most explicitly in Deut 28, and underlies the theologically-orientated historical books.

And of course, their story is ongoing. As a people, the Jews have suffered rejection, persecution, and genocide—perhaps more than any other nation on earth.

There is an underlying assumption in the Old Testament that God blesses those who do his will, but there is also a strong belief that God is on the side of the poor, the despised, the underprivileged, and the weak—often classified as the "fatherless and the widow."

Holding these two apparently contradictory understandings in the face of the unfair realities he sees around him leads the psalmist to cry:

> Why, O Lord, so you stand far off?
> Why do you hide yourself in times of trouble? . . .
> Arise, Lord! Lift up your hand, O God.
> Do not forget the helpless.
> Why does the wicked man revile God?
> Why does he say to himself,
> "He won't call me to account"?
> But you, O God, do see trouble and grief;
> you consider it to take it in hand
> The victim commits himself to you;
> you are the helper of the fatherless.
> Break the arm of the wicked and evil man;
> call him to account for his wickedness
> that would not be found out.[15]

The cry, "It's not fair!" goes up not only from the psalmist, but in many other places in Scripture—and from our own hearts and lives, and from the poor in the world *now*, in the twenty-first century. All too often the rich and arrogant seem to prosper at the expense of the afflicted.

It's not fair! "Do something about it, God!" we pray.

"Arise, Lord! Lift up your hand, O God. Do not forget the helpless."[16]

Life itself demands judgment. It demands that evil should be punished and routed. It demands that God listen to the cry of the poor and afflicted, and that they be cared for. "Will not the Judge of all the earth do right?" asks Abraham.[17]

---

15. Ps 10:1–3.

16. Ps 10:12.

17. Gen 18:25.

Mary, a good Jew, expected that her son, who was to be called Jesus "because he will save his people from their sins,"[18] would bring justice to an unjust world. Her poem of praise when she meets her cousin Elizabeth expects the righting of many wrongs:

> My soul glorifies the Lord
> and my spirit rejoices in God my savior . . .
> He has scattered those who are proud
> in their inmost thoughts.
> He has brought down rulers from their thrones
> but has lifted up the humble.
> He has filled the hungry with good things
> but has sent the rich away empty.[19]

During his life, Jesus was unimpressed by the arrogance of the pious, self-satisfied, rich Jews of his day, and he made friends with the underdogs of society: lepers, publicans, and "sinners."

As we saw in chapter 2, part of the commission of the church is to follow Jesus' example and to work for justice in this unjust world until "That Day" when Christ returns and ushers in the kingdom in all its fullness:

> The Church . . . is a present sign of the reconciliation that the whole creation will one day experience . . . [and] must live by the values of, and proclaim the coming of, the kingdom age in the present evil age as a sign to a hostile world.[20]

God does not stop our foolishness and sin from causing problems.[21] Often, the judgments of God work out in life itself, but we are still left with the unfair world in which we live. Deep down, most of us hope that, just as our mothers do their best to put things right for their children, our Lord God will ultimately sort out our mess.

To do this, God will, and in fact *must*, act in judgment. Much of what is happening is contrary to his will, and the psalmist envisages God dealing ruthlessly with his enemies when he appears:

---

18. Matt 1:21.

19. Luke 1:46–47, 51–53, a poem that is widely known as the Magnificat.

20. MacDonald, *Evangelical Universalist*, 51.

21. See chapter 1 (p.45–47).

Your hand will lay hold on all your enemies;
your right hand will seize your foes.
At the time of your appearing
you will make them like a fiery furnace.
In his wrath the Lord will swallow them up
and his fire will consume them.[22]

"The Day of the Lord": A Day of Judgment and Salvation

Like a lodestar, the ideal of the kingdom of God leads the people of God forward in hope and expectation, but the hope and expectation are not yet fully realized, and the ringing phrase, "The Day of the Lord," or "That Day," or in the New Testament, "the Day of Christ" carries the eschatological hope, prayer, and expectation that *one day* God will act in judgment and salvation.[23] And when "That Day" finally arrives, the Bible teaches us to hope for a time when the flawed present, with its rampant evil, suffering, and injustice, will finally be transformed and justice, peace, harmony, and universal worship of the living God will prevail.

The "Day of the Lord" is a vision that motivates and inspires us, but paradoxically, it is also to be feared. The Israelites hoped that God's judgments would be in their favor and against the nations that were oppressing them—that *they* would be saved, rescued, and helped to prosper, and that their enemies would be overthrown and destroyed. But like the child who thinks that "fairness" means getting sweets at the checkout (when the parent knows this is not in the child's best interests), so too God, through the prophet Amos, disillusioned the people of Israel:

Woe to you who long for the day of the Lord!
Why do you long for the day of the Lord?
That day will be darkness, not light.[24]

---

22. Ps 21:8–9.

23. "Eschatology" literally means "the study of the last things." Tom Wright argues persuasively that "this does not just refer to death, judgment, heaven and hell, as used to be thought . . . It refers to the strongly held belief of most first-century Jews, and virtually all early Christians, that history was going somewhere under the guidance of God . . . towards God's new world of justice, healing and hope. The transition from the present world to the new one would be a matter not of the destruction of the present space-time universe, but of its radical healing" (Wright, *Surprised by Hope*, 134).

24. Amos 5:18.

Amos had already given his reasons in no uncertain terms: despite being very religious, the rich leaders of Israel had been oppressing the poor and acting unjustly. Moreover, they had been practicing the fertility cults of the surrounding nations:

> They sell the righteous for silver,
> and the needy for a pair of sandals.
> They trample on the heads of the poor
> as upon the dust of the ground
> and deny justice to the oppressed.
> Father and son use the same girl
> and so profane my holy name.
> They lie down beside every alter
> on garments taken in pledge.
> In the house of their god
> they drink wine taken as fines.[25]

For all this, and for more, they would be judged—a judgment that happened when Samaria fell to the Assyrians and the Israelites were taken into captivity (which was one phase of the exile.) But a few chapters later, Amos is prophesying the ultimate restoration of Israel:

> In that day I will restore David's fallen tent.
> I will repair its broken places,
> restore its ruins
> and build it as it used to be.[26]

This pattern—judgment followed by salvation or restoration—is repeated throughout Scripture. Again and again the Bible speaks in one breath of the destruction of wickedness and evil, which is often portrayed as the destruction of wicked and evil individuals or nations, but sometimes, as in the above prophecies of Amos, is seen as a severe judgment to be followed (because of God's great love) by ultimate restoration and salvation. (See diagram on p. 142.)

Isaiah and Jeremiah, writing in the succeeding couple of centuries, warned about the fall of Jerusalem and the deportation of the people of

---

25. Amos 2:6–8.
26. Amos 9:11.

Judah to Babylon. Isaiah pictures "the great double work of redemption and vengeance"[27] of God (or his agent):

> robed in splendor, striding forward in the greatness of his strength . . . for the day of vengeance was in my heart, and the year of my redemption has come . . . so my own arm worked salvation for me, and my own wrath sustained me. I trampled the nations in my anger; in my wrath I made them drunk and poured their blood on the ground.[28]

Like the Old Testament prophets, Jesus spoke devastating words of judgment against sin, and he sometimes prophesied about cataclysmic events to come—prophecies that have often been wrongly interpreted to refer to the final judgment at the end of time. But many of his prophecies of coming judgment referred not to the end times, but to an *imminent* event: the fall of Jerusalem to the Romans, which Jesus realized would happen if the Jews persisted in opposition and rebellion against Rome, and in AD 70 these prophecies were fulfilled. Wright comments:

> The warnings . . . are manifestly and obviously, within their historical context, warnings about a coming national disaster, involving the destruction by Rome of the nation, the city and the Temple. The story of judgment and vindication which Jesus told is very much like the story told by the prophet Jeremiah, invoking the categories of cosmic disaster in order to invest the coming socio-political disaster with its full theological significance.[29] The "normal" way of reading these passages within the Christian tradition has been to see them as references to a *post mortem* judgment in hell; but this betrays a fairly thorough lack of historical understanding.[30]

But to say that "The Day of the Lord," or the day when God acts, can come at any time in history and that "The Wrath" (see p. 49–50) and judgment are constantly at work (and are not confined to the end times) does not exclude a final day of judgment when evil will finally be exposed, judged, and dealt with. Paul clearly looked forward to such a final day, *as well as* seeing God at work in the here and now, and Revelation,

27. Motyer, *Isaiah*, 18.

28. Isa 63:1–6.

29. Jer 4:23–28.

30. Wright, *Jesus and the Victory*, 323. Wright deals with the issue in depth in ibid., chs. 8–10.

the last book of the Bible, is the account of John's apocalyptic visions. These visions include devastating judgment because "the time has come for judging the dead . . . and for destroying those who destroy the earth."[31] To quote Wright again:

> This is the ultimate meaning of God's judgment . . . the judgment of the creator on all that spoils his creation. His purposes, deep-rooted in the vision of chapters 4 and 5 [of Revelation], are for his wonderful creation to be rescued from the forces of antimatter, of anti-creation, of anti-life. It is time for death to die.[32]

We have been looking at some of the ways in which the Bible speaks about God acting both through history and at its consummation in the end-times; let us now think about one of the metaphors used for God himself.

The Lord Your God Is a Consuming Fire . . . Speaking out of Fire

God's call to Moses came out of a burning bush that did not burn up, and his presence with the Israelites in the desert was revealed as a "pillar of fire" leading the way.[33] When the law was given at Mount Sinai, "the Lord descended on it in fire" and "to the Israelites the glory of the Lord looked like a consuming fire on top of the mountain."[34]

We may understand that the fire was a volcanic eruption, but the timing and symbolism of the experience to the unscientific Israelites was intense and molded their ideas about God. So Moses declared, "The Lord your God is a consuming fire . . . speaking out of fire."[35] And the most awe-inspiring visions of God recorded in the Bible— Isa 6, Ezek 1, Dan 7, and Rev 1—all include a central element of fire or blazing metal.[36] It seems that the symbolism of fire was later used to refer to God's very essence, so when the letter to the Hebrews was written more than a millennium later,

---

31. Rev 11:18.

32. Wright, *Revelation for Everyone*, 105.

33. Exod 3, 13:21–22.

34. Exod 19:18, 24:17.

35. Deut 4:24, 33.

36. Ezek 1: 27; Dan 7:9–10; Rev1:14–15.

the writer quotes Moses' declaration: "let us . . . worship God acceptably with reverence and awe, for our 'God is a consuming fire.'"[37]

The Godly Fire Destroys Evil

Malachi proclaims, "Who can stand when he appears? For he will be like a refiner's fire or a launderer's soap. He will sit as a refiner and purifier of silver."[38] And Ezekiel pictures God saying,

> The house of Israel has become dross to me; all of them are the copper, tin, iron and lead left inside a furnace. They are but the dross of silver . . . so I will gather you in my anger and my wrath and put you inside the city and melt you.[39]

Perhaps John the Baptist had such prophesies as these in mind when he said of Jesus:

> He will baptize you with the Holy Spirit and with fire. His winnowing fork is in his hand, and he will clear his threshing-floor, gathering his wheat into the barn and burning up the chaff with unquenchable fire.[40]

It is usually assumed that the wheat and the chaff are different groups of people, but chaff clings to each grain. The picture here is of a grain-by-grain cleansing of the clinging chaff by winnowing. It is the useless chaff that is burnt with unquenchable fire; the precious wheat is saved, lovingly gathered, and stored. The picture is analogous to that used by Saint Paul in his first letter to the Corinthians, which beautifully shows the cleansing action of the fire of God as the rubbish in our lives is revealed and destroyed in the final judgment, "The Day":

> For no one can lay any foundation other than the one already laid, which is Jesus Christ. If any man builds on this foundation using gold, silver, costly stones, wood, hay or straw, his work will be shown for what it is, because the Day will bring it to light.

37. Heb 12:28–29. This idea was not unique to Judaism. The ancient Zoroastrian religion used fire as a central symbol of worship: "Fire, the great purifier, was the sacred symbol of Ahura Mazda, the Zoroastrian supreme god." The rulers built fire temples in their palaces, and the Magi priests were tasked with keeping the sacred fire permanently alight. (O'Grady, *And Man Created God*, 177).

38. Mal 3:2.

39. Ezek 22:18–22.

40. Matt 3:11–12; Luke 3:17.

It will be revealed with fire, and the fire will test the quality of
each man's work. If what he has built survives, he will receive his
reward. If it is burned up, he will suffer loss; he himself will be
saved, but only as one escaping through the flames.[41]

Some of my evangelical friends will tell me that those who will be
saved are only those who are building (albeit of "wood, hay or straw")
on the foundation of Christ. They will say that this passage refers to the
judgment of *Christian* believers, not to all mankind.

But surely the foundation of Christ is laid, whether or not we know
it. In Christ is light, "and that life was the light of men . . . The true light
that gives light to every man was coming into the world."[42] The foundation has been laid for all, whether or not we accept the fact. So it seems to
me that it is valid to refer this to all mankind.

The "Day of the LORD" will reveal what our lives have been.

Anything that is of lasting worth in God's eyes will remain like the
"gold, silver and costly stones" of the metaphor. Faith and trust in Jesus
will ensure that much of our lives *is* of lasting worth. Nevertheless, even
for believers, anything that is useless in God's eyes will be burnt up in
the purifying fire. Yet "he himself will be saved, but only as one escaping
though the flames."

The fire cleanses, burns up the rubbish, and cleans that which is
of eternal worth, so when the Holy Spirit descended at Pentecost, the
disciples saw "what seemed to be tongues of fire that separated and came
to rest on each of them."[43] God not only filled the disciples with his very
being and power, but also purified and purged them of evil.

Many hymns down the ages express a yearning desire to be made
clean, purified by the Holy Spirit fire of God. The ancient hymn of Bianco
da Siena pleads:

> O, comforter draw near, within my heart appear,
> And kindle it, your holy flame bestowing.
> O let if freely burn
> till earthly passions turn
> to dust and ashes in its heat consuming.[44]

41. 1 Cor 3:11–15.

42. John 1:4, 9.

43. Acts 2:3.

44. ©Baughen and Jubilate Hymns, *Hymns for Today's Church*, Hymn 231. This
hymn was translated by R. F. Littledale (1833–1890) after Bianco da Siena (died 1434).

There are many similar hymns. In a modern example, Michael Saward cries out for the "Fire of God, titanic Spirit" to "burn within our hearts," to "cleanse our sin," and "purge the squalidness that shames us, soils the body, taints the soul" so that we may "exhibit holiness in every way," and pleads, "purify us, make us whole."[45]

Such hymns are not referring to final judgment, or "the Day of the Lord," they are yearning for cleansing by the Holy Spirit—the fire of God—to bring transformation and purity in our lives *here and now*—a transformation we cannot achieve even by our best efforts. (Our efforts to live holy lives unaided by God's Holy Spirit are in grave danger of leading to a rigid Pharisaism.) True holiness is the product of the Holy Spirit of the living God, and can only be achieved by his searing cleansing of the soul. So when Isaiah saw the Lord in all his glory, his immediate reaction was to cry out, "Woe to me! . . . I am ruined! For I am a man of unclean lips, and I live among a people of unclean lips, and my eyes have seen the King, the Lord Almighty."[46]

What happened next is a classic example of God cleansing by fire:

> Then one of the seraphs flew to me with a live coal in his hand, which he had taken with tongs from the altar. With it he touched my mouth and said, "See, this has touched you lips; your guilt is taken away and you sin atoned for."[47]

It was only after this experience that Isaiah felt able to respond to the call of God, saying: "Here am I. Send me!"[48] The fire of God destroys evil and cleanses people.

Many years ago I heard a memorable sermon about God's judgment that encapsulated several of these themes. The preacher, Berg Toputain said,

> Karl Marx got it wrong again! He said, "Christianity led to a sub-missive resignation . . . with its promise of pie in the sky later" . . . He obviously did not read about the raging furnace in the sky! . . . Because there is a last day of judgment, then we strive by God's Spirit to change ourselves and to change the lives of others by offering them God's love . . .

45. Ibid., Hymn 234.

46. Isa 6:5.

47. Isa 6:6–7.

48. Isa 6:8.

The last day will mean different things to different people, but not because we are subject to different treatment. It's not sunshine for the goodies and hot ovens for the baddies. Sin and evil must be eradicated from our lives. God does not have a different standard of holiness for his family and those who are outside . . . Even though we are in a forgiven and loving relationship with him, our words and our works will be equally subjected to the refining divine furnace of God's holiness, so that all dross and evil may be eradicated from our beings and that which is of him will endure. The fire that destroys is also the fire that refines . . . If there is nothing of God in our lives, we will be reduced to nothing.[49]

Basing his talk on chapter 4 of Malachi, Berg pointed out that the Last Day will not only be a painful purging and the destruction of all evil from our personalities, but the healing rays of warmth of the Son of God will also bring us to wholeness, releasing us to be what we were meant to be like calves released from their stalls.

Berg then held up two pieces of paper: one was a beautiful piece of Christmas wrapping paper, while the other had dirty scribbles on it but was backed by silvery metal foil. He set light to both. The beautiful wrapping paper was completely burnt up, but the dirty, scribbled-on paper was burnt away to reveal the foil backing—a memorable illustration of the fact that God looks at the heart, and "the Day of the Lord" will reveal what is truly within, not what is seen by men!

Before we rush to conclude that this is simply another way of saying that only those who have received Christ will be saved (because we assume that only they will have a "silver backing" to their lives), let us remember that we are *all* made in the image of God. All men and women have the divine stamp on their natures; Christ died for all, so all have been potentially redeemed. All human beings are, to return to Berg's metaphor, created with a silver backing to their life because they are created in the image of God. This is surely the foundation for Christians' belief in the sanctity of human life, and it forms their main argument against abortion and euthanasia. When we put our trust in Christ, we say "Yes" to the silver backing that is already within us as a part of our very creation, and so the Spirit of Christ will strengthen and increase our inner spiritual beings.

49. Berg Toputain preached this sermon in Christ Church, Clifton in Bristol, UK, on July 17, 1986. Fortunately, his sermon was taped, and I was able to access a locally-produced copy.

If there are some people in whom the silver backing has so disintegrated that even when they see the divine love in all its glory and fullness (which is another way of saying, "when they are exposed to the divine fire"), there is *no* part of their personality left that is capable of responding, then they will be completely annihilated by the fire of God. This is emphatically *not* the same as being everlastingly tormented by the fires of hell. The fire is eternal because the destruction must be eternal and complete.

The witness of the church down the ages is that even in this life, the most apparently sinful men and women are capable of responding to the love of Christ when they are able to fully see it. This leads me to hope that there will be very, very few (if any at all) who do not respond to Christ in the life to come. We will explore this further in the next chapter.

The Bible does frequently speak of the complete destruction by fire of polluted items or evil people. Idols are to be burnt to show their total rejection, while contaminated articles are burnt as an act of cleansing.[50] We may realize the good hygiene behind this practice, but at the time of Moses, this was a ritual, symbolic cleansing rather than a sterilizing process.

The enemies of Israel are frequently destroyed by fire.[51] The famously wicked cities of Sodom and Gomorrah were destroyed by "burning sulphur . . . from the Lord out of the heavens," which probably happened some two thousand years BC.[52] This was perhaps another volcanic eruption or earthquake, but this time it was seen to enact God's wrath.

But despite the apparently complete destruction of the cities and despite being held up as an infamous example of wickedness, the prophet Ezekiel, writing in the sixth century BC, offers a promise of restoration for Sodom. Indeed, not only Sodom, but also Samaria and unfaithful Jerusalem:

> I will restore the fortunes of Sodom and her daughters and of Samaria and her daughters, and your fortunes along with them . . . your sisters, Sodom with her daughters, and Samaria with her daughters, will return to what they were before; and you and your daughters will return to what you were before . . . I will deal with you as you deserve, because you have despised my oath by breaking the covenant. Yet I will remember the covenant I

50. For example, Deut 7:5, Lev 13:52, 57.

51. e.g. Deut 9:3; Josh 6:24; 8:8, 19; 11:11.

52. Gen 19:24–25. Cecil, "Destruction of Sodom and Gomorrah," http://www.bbc.co.uk/history/ancient/cultures/sodom_gomorrah_01.shtml.

made with you in the days of you youth, and I will establish an everlasting covenant with you.[53]

Once again we see that punishment, and even destruction, is not the last word.

Throughout the Old Testament we read oracles of punishment and destruction against the nations followed by oracles that picture those same nations streaming to Jerusalem, or the Lord God, to worship. This is particularly evident in the prophesies of Isaiah, and the pattern can also be discerned in Revelation.[54] (See diagram on p. 142)

Deliverance from Evil in the New Testament

As we saw in chapter 1, the Jews were expecting a warrior-king messiah like David who would deliver them from occupying powers (which in the time of Jesus meant Rome), but Jesus rejected temptations and pressures to fulfill the role of a worldly ruler or warrior.[55] Instead, we see him healing and delivering people from the evil of illness or demonic powers, and in one case, the demons were manifestly destroyed. They invaded a herd of pigs that rushed over a steep bank and drowned in the lake.[56]

The deliverance revealed by Jesus took a very different shape from what was expected, and when we pray: "Deliver us from evil," it is good to remember how Jesus delivered people from the evil of demonic powers, sin, and sickness when he was on earth.

To use language more accessible to us in the twenty-first century, people were set free from those damaging habits, forces, or illnesses that were oppressing or corrupting them.[57] An encounter with Jesus so changed the wealthy and corrupt tax collector Zaccheus that he exclaimed, "Look, Lord! Here and now I give half of my possessions to the

53. Ezek 16:53, 55, 59–60.

54. See chapter 7. For a full discussion of this, see MacDonald, *Evangelical Universalist*, chs. 3, 5.

55. The temptation to receive from the devil "all the kingdoms of the world and their splendor" (Matt 4:8; Luke 4:6) and the rejection of violent conflict in Gethsemane (Matt 26:51–54), may reveal that Jesus was at times tempted to adopt the role of a savior-warrior, but that he rejected this role.

56. Mark 5:1–11; Luke 8:26–33.

57. Even now, in the twenty-first century, there seem to be some cases of definite demonic oppression, where the only cure is deliverance from a demonic spirit or spirits.

poor, and if I have cheated anybody out of anything, I will pay back four times the amount." Jesus then said to him, "Today salvation has come to this house."[58] Zaccheus had been set free from the evil hold that greed and corruption had held over his life. There may be many in our capitalist societies who need a similar deliverance today!

Personal Salvation: A New Way of Life

The writers of the New Testament describe the process of salvation in many different ways. The Greek word *metanoia*, literally meaning to turn around to face a different direction, is used to describe a change of thought and feeling or repentance and a lifestyle transformation.[59] Suddenly or gradually, we are delivered from the evil in our lives, and we are changed and transformed. The related Greek word *metamorphoo* is also used to denote this transformation.[60] This metamorphosis is a process that we believe will be completed in the life to come. Because of the change faith in Jesus inspires, it is also likened to a new birth and a completely new way of life.[61] Paul often describes those who have received salvation as being "in Christ."[62] They have "put on Christ,"[63] they have been made right with God or been "justified,"[64] and they have been "adopted as sons" by God.[65]

Salvation is an ongoing process of repentance and belief that opens our hearts and spirits to the loving, cleansing, renewing action of God and invites his Holy Spirit to bring more and more healing, deliverance, and salvation into our lives so that we can say, "I have been saved from the penalty of sin, because Jesus died for me on the cross; I am being saved from the power of sin in my life, because the Holy Spirit is at work in my life; and I will finally be saved from the presence of sin in the life to come."

58. Luke 19:8–9.

59. See Matt 3:2, 8; Luke 17:3–4; 15:7; Acts 20:21; 2 Tim 2:25; Heb 12:17.

60. It is the root of our English word "metamorphosis," which is used in biology to describe the radical changes that turn a caterpillar into a butterfly or moth. See Matt 17:2; Mark 9:2; Rom 12:2; 2 Cor 3:18.

61. John 3:3–8; 2 Cor 5:17; Jas 1:18; Titus 3:5; 1Pet 1:23; 1 John 3:9.

62. See 2 Cor 5:17; 12:2; Gal 1:22.

63. See Rom 13:14; Gal 3:27; Col 3:5–16.

64. Rom 3, 5, 8; Gal 2, 3, 5; Titus 3:7. See also Jas 2.

65. Rom 8:15, 23.

However, none of this means that Christian believers will not face judgment.

The Bible teaches that all humankind—believers and unbelievers alike—will face the final judgment. Paul wrote to the *believers*, who were members of the church of God in Corinth, "We must all appear before the judgment seat of Christ," and it was to *the church* in Rome that he wrote, "We will all stand before God's judgment seat."[66]

What's in a Name?

The "Judgment Seat" and "Mercy Seat"

In the New Testament, Paul talks about God's "judgment seat," but in the Old Testament, the people of Israel thought that God resided in a special way in the "mercy seat." One might have expected it to be the other way around.

Thinking about this prompted an interesting little journey of discovery through various words and phrases and different versions of Bibles that reminded me once again of the complexity of ideas lying hidden in our Bibles, and how again and again we use analogies (perhaps only half understood) to convey the mysteries of our faith. We explore but the hem of the garment of our God.

The "Judgment Seat"

Sometimes translated as "tribunal," the "judgment seat" was the stone platform, or in Greek, *bema*, from which awards would be given to winning athletes and legal charges against individuals would be judged. Christ stood before Pilate at the *bema* in Jerusalem, and Paul was brought before Gallio, the proconsul of Achaia, at the *bema* in Corinth, where he was accused of "persuading people to worship God in ways contrary to the law."[67]

Paul would doubtless have had this experience in mind when he wrote to the Corinthian Christians, "We must all appear before the judgment seat of Christ, that each one may receive what is due to him for

---

66. 2 Cor 5:10; Rom 14:10.
67. Matt 27:19; John 19:13; Acts 18:12–13.

the things done while in the body, whether good or bad."[68] Some will have done good things and be praised (the equivalent of receiving a laurel wreath) but others will be found wanting at the *bema* of Christ.

In his letter to the Romans, Paul argues that we should not judge one another but should instead leave it to Christ, whose judgment will be just. He then goes on to quote one of the most universalist passages in Isaiah to back up his arguments. In the end, *all* will bow before God in worship, even though they may feel shame in the clear knowledge of what they have done:[69]

> Why do you judge your brother? Or why do you look down on your brother? For we will all stand before God's judgment seat. It is written:
>
> "'As surely as I live,' says the Lord,
> 'Every knee will bow before me;
> every tongue will confess to God.'"
>
> So then each of us will give an account of himself to God.[70]

The "Mercy Seat"

The evocative English phrase "mercy Seat" has a different connotation. It was first use by Tyndale[71] in his sixteenth-century translation to refer to the gold cover of the Ark of the Covenant.[72] Tyndale was fleeing the wrath of the Catholic Church and the government in Britain, and he was forced to go to Germany to publish his translation. He may well have had discussions with Luther over biblical meanings, for Luther was translating the Bible into vernacular German at the time, and "mercy seat" is a near-literal translation of the German term *gnadenstuhl*, which literally means "seat of grace." It is easy to see how the phrase appealed

68. 2 Cor 5:10.

69. MacDonald argues strongly that though the nations are ashamed, they do in the end offer true worship to the Lord (MacDonald, *Evangelical Universalist*, 67–73).

70. Rom 14:10–12, quoting Isa 45:23.

71. Tyndale was an influential pioneer of the Reformation. He wanted ordinary people to be able to read and understand the Bible, which he translated into English at a time when doing so was forbidden. He was eventually strangled, then burned as a heretic in 1536 by the Catholic Church.

72. Exod 25:17–22; Lev 16:2; Heb 9:5, and elsewhere.

to Tyndale, who aimed at a simple, clear style that would be widely understood. "Mercy seat" has been used in many versions of the bible since Tyndale's time, and it helps us to picture a God who, despite his holiness, is nevertheless gracious and merciful in atoning for sin and covering it over. But many other phrases have been used; the Jerusalem Bible uses the powerful "throne of mercy," and the New International Version gives "atonement cover." The New English Bible uses the literal translation, "cover," and the Good News Bible simply gives "lid." The Douay-Rheims version, based on Latin, uses "propitiatory."

This wide range of words and phrases—"propitiatory," "lid," "cover," "atonement cover," "throne of mercy," and "mercy seat"—all give us some insight into how the Jews understood their God. The translations all attempt to render the rich meaning of the Hebrew *kaporeth*, which can simply mean "to cover" in a physical sense but also includes the idea of wiping clean or cleansing, atonement, expiation, or to obliterate. That is, covering over or wiping out wrongdoings. The cognate Arabic term *kaffaret* is used in modern legal contexts to refer to rectifying any illegality ranging from the failure to fast during Ramadan to murder. It can also refer to the freeing of slaves.

The Jews, who could not make any graven images or idols of God, believed that God spoke to Moses in a cloud above the ark, in the inner sanctuary behind the veil of the temple (in "the holy of holies"). This was such a holy place that even Aaron could not go into it on pain of death, except once a year on Yom Kippur, the Day of Atonement, and then only after having undertaken the sacrificial atonement rituals we looked at in chapter 1 (p. 17–21) and censing the mercy seat, then sprinkling it with blood.[73]

Though terrifying in his holiness, God was prepared to make a way of mercy, a way to cover over sins. We can find here the roots of Paul's theology of justification. Yet the mercy seat is only mentioned once in the New Testament, in a retrospective discussion of the first covenant, which the writer describes as "an illustration for the present time, indicating that the gifts and sacrifices being offered were not able to clear the conscience of the worshipper."[74]

Jesus' death was the *real thing* to which the mercy seat pointed. It fulfilled the atonement rituals so that they would no longer be needed. Jesus himself is the Lamb of God, and when he died, "the curtain of the

73. Lev 16:2, 13, 15.
74. Heb 9:5, 9.

temple was torn in two from top to bottom,"[75] revealing that the atonement had been accomplished and a way had been made into the presence of the holiness of God.

What's in a Name? A Look at the Title
of This Book, *The Judge Is the Savior*

I have tried to explore how the portraits of judgment and salvation are entwined.

Salvation involves the overcoming of evil, and so it necessitates judgment, but God's ultimate aim is not judgment but salvation: "God did not send his Son into the world to condemn the world, but to save the world through him."[76] Salvation must involve judgment because evil must be exposed before it can be eradicated. So, John continues, "whoever does not believe stands condemned already . . . this is the verdict: Light has come into the world, but men loved darkness instead of light because their deeds were evil."[77]

I was discussing the chosen title of this book with my husband, who commented that I should reverse the order of the title so that it would read: "The Savior Is the Judge" to guard against the danger of cheap grace; the offer of salvation is there for all, but because we can accept or reject God's offer and will be judged according to our response, the final word is one of judgment.

However, because I passionately believe (and have tried to show) that the God who reveals himself in Jesus is a God of love and mercy whose *ultimate aim* is salvation (through a process of judgment and elimination of evil), I have chosen to keep the title as it stands: *The Judge Is the Savior.*

God's final word is salvation. God's greatest name is Love, and I believe that his mercy will ultimately triumph over all the rebellion of mankind. I have come to believe that, even after the judgment that each of us must face, God in Christ will ever continue to seek and save that which was lost. He will continue to seek those who have "loved darkness," "hated the light," and refused to come to the light during their lifetime

---

75. Matt 27:51.

76. John 3:17.

77. John 3:18–19. (See p.37.)

"for fear that [their] deeds will be exposed,"[78] and have therefore chosen hell and separation from God. I have come to believe that there will be a route of salvation through the cleansing, purging, and redeeming fires of hell itself.

This is not cheap grace, because it may be very painful indeed to see with clarity, in the full light of Christ, the enormity of our sins and the enormity of the price that has been paid for our redemption.

We are perhaps now in a position to pose the question:—

Who in the End Will Be Saved—Delivered from Evil?

Faced with the dilemmas I have tried to explore, Christians down the ages have come to different conclusions about how they believe God will judge and who they believe will be saved. These conclusions might be broadly summarized in the following way, always bearing in mind that opinions cannot be as neatly pigeonholed as this summary implies.

1. Only *some* will be saved.

2. God's will is that all should be saved, and in the end all *will* be saved.

3. We can never know, and must simply leave the entire matter to God and speculate no further.

If there are only *some* who will be saved, there are various views about who will be included and who will be excluded from that salvation. These have been variously thought to be:

a. Only the *baptized* will be saved (or only those who *belong to the church*).

b. Only *those who truly believe in Christ* will be saved. This true faith may come about because of the individual's free choice or God's choice/election—(outlined in [c] and [d] below)

c. Only those who *choose* to have faith will be saved. (The "Armenian" position.)

d. Only those who are *chosen by God*—the elect—will be saved. (The "Calvinist" position.)

e. Only those who *deserve salvation* will be saved; i.e., salvation is earned.

78. John 3:20.

Let us look briefly at each of these views:

a. Only the Baptized Will Be Saved, or Only Those Who Belong to the Church Will Be Saved

Historically, this view was held by mainstream Catholics for many centuries. *Salus extra ecclesiam non est*, or "outside the Church there is no salvation" was an affirmation "often repeated by the Church Fathers,"[79] but no longer held in an absolute sense (if it ever was). This teaching led to the practice of emergency baptism of babies thought to be at risk of dying soon after birth. Paradoxically, it also led to the practice of late baptisms, because believers delayed baptism until they were near to death to leave less time for mortal sins to be committed after baptism that might nullify the saving efficacy of baptism. There are probably few Christians who absolutely hold this view now.

b. Only Those Who Truly Believe in Christ Will Be Saved

This view can be combined with (c) or (d) below, depending on whether or not it is believed that human free will can override God's will. Or to put it another way, depending on whether those who come to "saving faith" do so because they freely choose to believe (whereas others freely choose to reject the offered salvation), or whether God's sovereign will prevails in the case of those who are elect (chosen by God) and only these chosen ones are drawn by the irresistible grace of God, and so come to have faith in Christ. Those who do not believe are, in this view of things, the "non-elect," who have *not* been chosen by God for faith and salvation.

This leads us to look at the contrasting philosophical positions of (c) and (d):

79. Robert M. Haddad, "Justification and Salvation: Catechism of the Catholic Church (1992) No. 846," Catholic Apologetics, October 27, 1996, http://www.theworkofgod.org/Library/Apologtc/R_Haddad/Course/Book1-A.htm.

c. Only Those Who *Choose* to Have Faith Will Be Saved (The "Armenian" Position)

We have freedom to accept or reject the grace and salvation offered by God, and our decision affects our ultimate fate. The "rejected" are those who have freely chosen to reject the offered salvation.

This is probably the majority view of evangelical Christians today, as it seems to be fairer than the "Calvinist" position described below, which seems to most thinking people to be monstrously unfair and incompatible with a God who loves his creation enough to die for it.

However, there is a major problem with the "freedom to choose" argument.

We are all, to a greater or lesser degree, blinded by sin. Our vision of God and understanding of his ways are at best extremely partial. The gospel is hidden from us: "Now we see through a glass darkly, but then face to face. Now I know in part, then will I know even as I am known."[80] We touch but the hem of the garment of our God. MacDonald cites Thomas Talbott's objection to the idea that anyone can make a *fully informed* free decision to reject the gospel:

> Nobody is in a position to understand the gospel adequately, due to the epistemically blinding power of sin. However, God's spirit can overcome the effects of sin and enable a person, any person, to understand. Thus, apart from God's gracious work by his Spirit, nobody is ever adequately informed. But God, being omnibenevolent, will eventually bring all into this position and then a rejection is unimaginable.[81]

d. Only Those Who Are *Chosen by God*—the Elect— Will Be Saved (The "Calvinist" Position)

For years I struggled with the doctrine of election because it seemed totally unworthy of the God that I thought I believed in, but it is difficult to refute the apparent biblical basis of the doctrine.[82]

---

80. 1 Cor 13:21.

81. MacDonald, *Evangelical Universalist*, 29–30.

82. See Matt 24:22, 31; Rom 8:27–39; 9:11–18; 1 Cor 1:9; Eph 1:3–11; 18; 1 Thess 1:4–6; 1 Pet. 1:1–2.

As commonly understood, the doctrine argues that only *some* people are "elect"; that is, chosen by God for salvation. And it is argued that Christ died *for the elect*, and he died *only for these*, not for all. As a young Christian student, the argument seemed to be between the "Calvinist" understanding (thus baldly sketched) and the "Arminian" understanding (outlined in (c) above). However, neither of these theologies seem to do justice to the many passages in the New Testament that proclaim that God's saving love extends to all, so when I came across Karl Barth's understanding of election, it was like a light being switched on in a dark place. Barth sees Jesus as the elected one,[83] and *all people* are elected in him because he died for all. Jesus is also the rejected one—rejected on behalf of those who deserve to be rejected; that is, *on behalf of us all*. He carries that rejection on the cross.

Barth helpfully writes:

> The election of grace is the eternal beginning of all the ways and works of God in Jesus Christ. In Jesus Christ God in His free grace determines Himself for sinful man and sinful man for Himself. He therefore takes upon Himself the rejection of man with all its consequences, and elects man to participation in His own glory.[84]

Barth discusses Judas as a model of one who was a chosen disciple, and so truly elected, but, because he betrayed Christ, he also became one who was rejected. (See chapter 1, p.41–42). Taking Judas as an example, Barth argues that *behind* the rejection of those who reject God (and so become "the rejected") stands the eternal election of God. This understanding, that *the whole of humankind* is elect for salvation in and through Jesus Christ, seems to me to be more in keeping with the witness of Scripture and with the God of love I believe I know than does the limiting doctrine of Calvin: that *only some* are elected, called by an irresistible grace to which they respond and in which they persevere and so are saved, while the rest of mankind, in the sovereignty of God, are condemned for eternity.

Election in terms of being chosen and called by God is not about being the saved ones whereas the rest of humanity is not, but is rather about

---

83. This idea of Jesus as "the elected one" fits in with the similar understanding that Jesus fulfilled the role of the servant of God in the Isaiah "servant songs," including the "suffering servant" portrayed in Isa 53.

84. Barth, *Doctrine of God*, 94.

realizing that we are called and chosen to fulfill the purposes of God. Individuals (e.g., Abram, Isaiah, Jeremiah, Mary, the mother of Jesus, or Saint Paul) and nations are called for *a purpose*: to fulfill a special task.

Abram was called so that "all peoples on earth will be blessed through you."[85] His offspring were of course the Jewish nation, and the enigma of the chosen people becomes less problematic when we realize that this one race was chosen in order that they should reveal the justice and mercy of God through keeping the Mosaic law. So it was that God declared, "Although the whole earth is mine, you will be for me a kingdom of priests and a holy nation."[86] The election of the Jews was not election for salvation while the rest of the world was condemned, but election to reveal God to the nations[87]—a task which, as we have seen, they failed to fulfill but which Jesus, as the chosen servant of God, fulfilled in their stead. Jesus is the servant of God, the Elect One, and we are elect in him.

The task of revealing God to the nations has now been passed to the church, which is the body of Christ active in the world. Peter realized that after the resurrection, Jesus "was not seen by all the people, but by witnesses whom God had already chosen—by us who ate and drank with him after he rose from the dead," and he describes the church as "a chosen people, a royal priesthood, a holy nation, a people belonging to God, that you may declare the praises of him who called you out of darkness into his wonderful light."[88]

As we saw in chapter 2, fulfilling this calling means working for God's kingdom to come.

e. Only Those Who Deserve Salvation Will Be Saved; i.e., Salvation Is Earned

Much biblical teaching appears to support this view. For example, in the parable recorded in Matt 25:31–46, the separation of the sheep (who are accepted) and the goats (who are rejected) is based on actions—or lack of actions. As we have seen, the final judgment will be based on what we

---

85. Gen 12:3.

86. Exod 19:6.

87. I have already highlighted the problem posed by the fact that the chosen people were given a land that was already populated (highlighted in Deut 6:10ff., which triumphantly lists the bounty that they would inherit from other peoples; see too p. 62–64.)

88. Acts 10:41; 1 Peter 2:9.

have done in our lives such "that each one may receive what is due to him for the things done while in the body, whether good or bad,"[89] and Rev 21:8 lists the sins that bar entry to heaven.

This view of things is probably believed, if rather vaguely, by many people—especially those outside the church. However, the danger is that it tends towards a "gospel of good works," which is the antithesis of the gospel of grace.

The trouble is that good and evil run right through each of us. As A. A. Milne charmingly wrote about bears (with humans in mind):

> There were Two little Bears who lived in a Wood
> And one of them was Bad and the other was Good . . .
> And then quite suddenly (just like Us)
> One got Better and the other got Wuss.[90]

And even those who "get better" are never good enough to earn salvation. As Paul puts it, "There is no difference, for all have sinned and fall short of the glory of God,"[91] and even those who "get wuss" are not beyond the reach of our loving heavenly Father, who is ever watching and waiting for the prodigal to return, and of Jesus Christ, who, on the cross, carries the sins of each one of us on his shoulders.

Good and evil run right through each one of us, and sadly, often seem to be unrelated to whether or not we have faith. The "good" are partly bad, and the "bad" are partly good. Christian believers (like the Jewish people of old) are often selfish, bitter, angry, unforgiving, and unjust, and non-believers are often forgiving, compassionate, and just. Ultimately, God's kingdom will be fully established only when *all evil* has been eradicated—a process that will doubtless be uncomfortable for most of us, believers and unbelievers alike. We *all* fail the yardstick of Rev 21:8: "cowardly . . . unbelieving . . . vile . . . murderers . . . sexually immoral . . . those who practice magic arts . . . idolaters . . . all liars—their place will be in the fiery lake of burning sulphur."

Which of us has never told a lie? Never hated anyone, which Jesus says is as bad as murder?[92] Never had a sexually immoral thought, which

---

89. 2 Cor 5:10.

90. Milne, *Now We Are Six*, 81–82.

91. Rom 3:23.

92. Matt 6:21– 22.

Jesus says is as bad as committing the act of adultery or fornication?[93] We are *all* are in need of saving grace.

Let us consider the second way of answering the question:–

God's Will Is That All Should Be Saved, and in the End All *Will* Be Saved

The Bible reveals a God of love who does not want any to perish.[94] Jesus Christ died for the sins *of the world.*[95] Surely we can hope with Paul that there will come a time when *all* will have been saved and will worship him.[96]

But universalism is rejected by many theologians (both Arminian and Calvinist) because they assume that the chance to repent and believe ceases at death, and that God's love no longer reaches out to the sinner after death.

However, this is most unlikely to be true, *if* life after death is a reality.

Paul writes, "now we see through a glass darkly, but then face to face."[97] This implies that after death, our blindness will be removed and our eyes opened. Surely when they fully see his majesty and his love, many, many people, and possibly all those who rejected the gospel during life will fall at the feet of their Savior Christ in repentance and faith,[98] for it is when we "see" with "the eyes of our understanding" that we can believe. It was when Saul met the risen Christ on the road to Damascus

---

93. Matt 6:27–30.

94. 1 John 4:8; 1 Tim 2:4–6.

95. See John 1:29; 4:42; 12:32, 47; Rom 5; 1 Cor 15:22; Col 1:20; Phil 2:11; Eph 1:10; 1 Tim 4:10; 1 John 4:14.

96. Eph 1:10–11; Col 1:20; Phil 2:9–11.

97. 1 Cor 13:12.

98. MacDonald quotes Thomas Talbott, who believes that "nobody is in a position to understand the gospel adequately, due to the epistemically blinding power of sin. However, God's spirit can overcome the effects of sin and enable a person, any person, to understand. Thus, apart from God's gracious work by his Spirit, nobody is ever adequately informed. But God, being omnibenevolent, will eventually bring all into this position and then a rejection is unimaginable . . . If one grants Talbott's arguments about freedom, then a sinner in hell experiencing the real consequences of rejecting God will become better informed of the true significance of his or her life-choices, making continuing to resist God increasingly difficult and, at some point psychologically impossible" (MacDonald, *Evangelical Universalist*, 29–30).

that he was transformed and turned from a persecutor of Christians to one of the most valiant champions that the Christian faith has ever had.

Many stories are told by those who have experienced a "near-death" experience and seen a figure of light, or even Jesus himself, and come back to life transformed. (See Appendix)

My own journey towards a universalist understanding has included a growing belief that *if* God is both just and loving, and powerful enough to raise human beings from death and ultimately to deliver the world from all evil, then we can *expect* that he will continue to seek and save and redeem after death through a cleansing process. We call this cleansing process "hell," for it is like a fire that burns sin and rubbish while cleansing what is imperishable. (See above p.123–28, and the next chapter).

With a similar understanding, MacDonald writes in a chapter appropriately entitled "To Hell and Back Again":

> The traditional view that there are no chances to repent after death is . . . very hard to defend. What possible reason would God have for drawing a line at death and saying, "Beyond this point I will show no mercy?" [99]

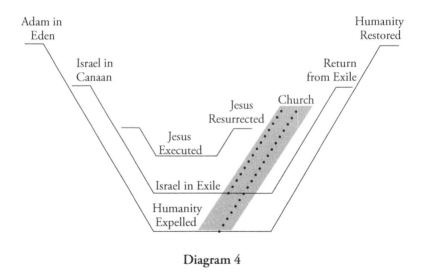

Diagram 4

Diagram from *The Evangelical Universalist* (p.105) summarizing Gregory MacDonald's ideas, reproduced with permission.

99. Ibid., 32.

The death and resurrection of the Christ accomplished a complete victory over the effects of sin for the whole world, making possible its redemption and transformation. It is the ultimate demonstration of the holy justice and fathomless mercy of our God.

Christ is Lord of both the living and the dead; he preached to the spirits in prison and holds the keys to death and hell. He will destroy all enemies of God, the last enemy being death.

For salvation to be fully effective, all sin must be finally unraveled from each life and each heart. This process can begin during our earthly life, but it will only be completed after the final judgment fully reveals what is good and what is evil, eradicates the evil, and restores all things.

Then God will be all in all. Then the words of Paul to the Philippians (based on a prophecy in Isaiah) will come true: "At the name of Jesus every knee should bow, in heaven and on earth and under the earth and every tongue confess that Jesus Christ is Lord, to the glory of God the Father."[100]

But if in the end only *some* will be saved, a second question arises: What does "damnation" look like? Or to put it another way: What happens to the rejected, or those who reject the offered salvation?

There are broadly three answers that are given to this second question:

a. The "rejected" go to everlasting hell.

b. The "rejected" are destroyed or annihilated.

c. The "rejected" go to a purging hell, beyond and through which they are ultimately saved.

Let us now briefly look at these three ideas:

a. The "Rejected" Will Go to Everlasting Hell

Hell has classically been thought of as a place of endless punishment, but much of what one might call the folk images of hell derive from lurid medieval paintings and from literature such as Dante's brilliant but horrifying epic poem, "Inferno." The biblical data is more nuanced and ambivalent. As we will see in chapter 6, a dominant image is Gehenna, the place where rubbish is burned.

---

100. Phil 2:10–11.

It is sometimes described as outer darkness; a place without God and beyond any possibility of repentance. Those who are there have made their choice. They have rejected God and the salvation offered through Jesus, and there is no possibility of choice after death.

b. The "Rejected" Will Be Annihilated: "Conditional Immortality"

Like the other views we have considered, "conditional immortality" limits salvation to believers or to the "good" because, the argument goes, immortality is not innate to every human being but is instead something that is imparted by salvation. It is given only to those who have responded to Jesus Christ, while others will cease to exist after death. To put it another way: they will be annihilated.

Paul speaks of "Christ Jesus, who has destroyed death and has brought life and immortality to light through the gospel."[101] The second-century writings of Tatian, Justin Martyr, Theophilus of Antioch, and Irenaeus tended to teach conditional immortality, while Arnobius was more explicit in his writings.[102] Conditional immortality is the official doctrine of the Christadelphians, and in the last few decades this view has become widely held by many otherwise orthodox evangelical Christians.[103]

The concept is certainly less harsh than the traditional idea of an endless, punishing hell. The "un-saved" simply cease to exist, which is what would be expected in the natural way of things. We know from simple observation that death is the end of life, and it could be argued that nature itself points in this direction by its profligacy. Millions of seeds are scattered, but only a few produce plants. Our garden is surrounded by sycamore trees, and every year millions of seeds fall on the lawn, which we, the gardeners, sweep up to be turned into compost. Then we ruthlessly continue to eradicate the hundreds of seedlings that escape the sweeping process and survive to sprout in the spring.

It is estimated that there are two hundred to six hundred million sperm in one ejaculate of semen, but only one of these will (on the serendipitous

---

101. 2 Tim 1:10.

102. Barclay, *Apostles' Creed*, 190–91.

103. Wenham, "Case for Conditional Immortality," 151–61; ibid., *Enigma of Evil*; Fudge, *Fire That Consumes*; Froom, *Conditionalist Faith*; Atkinson, *Life and Immortality*; Guillebaud, *Righteous Judge*; Edwards and Stott, *Essentials*, 312–19. P. E. Hughes, E. M. B. Green, and many others have publicly endorsed this view.

occasions when this happens) fertilize one female egg cell and conceive a child. So why should not our Lord God offer salvation and eternal life to all, knowing that only a few will respond to that offer, and then simply allow natural death and decay to take its course with the rest? This is some approximation to the understanding of "conditional immortality."

The gospel message includes the expectation that *evil and wickedness* will eventually be destroyed, and many Scriptures imply that wicked *people* will be destroyed.[104] But the death and destruction that are referred to in these passages could also be taken to refer to spiritual death, or the destruction of evil itself, rather than referring to the ultimate fate of the person. As I have argued above, the fire of God destroys evil and cleans up people.

Gulley and Mulholland take a jaundiced but thought-provoking view of this doctrine:

> Ironically, Hitler's desire to purge humanity of those he thought impure and deficient is the extreme manifestations of what many religions affirm—that some people ultimately deserve annihilation. He damned millions to concentration camps and furnaces, convinced he was purifying the world. He did on earth what many expect God to do in the afterlife.[105]

c. The "Rejected" Will Go to a Purging Hell, Beyond and Through Which They Are Ultimately Saved

We keep referring to this viewpoint.

It acknowledges that the final judgment will lead to punishment for many people, but it postulates that the punishment will be restorative and cleansing so that in the end God's will of saving all will be accomplished. The idea will be explored in more depth in the next chapter, which I researched and wrote first, because it seemed to me that it is only possible to accept that both the "hell and condemnation" and the "all will be saved passages" passages of the Bible are true expressions of God's will if the hell and the condemnation are temporary.

---

104. Ezek 18:20; Matt 7:15–19; 13:40; Luke 13:4–5; Rom 6:20–23; 8:6, 13; Phil 3:19; Jas 1:15; 5:20, and many others passages.

105. Gulley and Mulholland, *If Grace Is True*, 164.

There Were Different Views in
Biblical Times, as There Are Today

Perhaps we should not be surprised that Christians have different views on how God is likely to judge, since there have been different views throughout biblical times. As Alan Bernstein comments:

> The Hebrew Bible is composed of many strands, expressions of religious sentiments that vary from person to person and age to age . . . Whatever else this diversity shows, it should warn us of one thing. There is no one statement that can describe the "position" of the Hebrew Bible on a given subject, certainly not on the question of divine punishment and justice . . . Themes within a textual tradition are not static like pillars of a building but more like the nuclei of cells capable of movement, division, reproduction, and lending strength to successive organisms . . . Perhaps they are more like the angles of an optical illusion: the more one focuses on one point, the less clear the others seem; yet, when one focuses on another, even the previous point loses some of its sharpness.[106]

And MacDonald is compelled to confess: "When I claim that universalism is biblical I do *not* mean that all biblical authors were universalists but that the universalist tendencies of some authors provide the big picture within which we can happily accommodate the teachings on hell of all the biblical writers."[107]

Even Paul himself seems to say *both* that all will be saved *and also* that those who do not believe will be condemned or destroyed. Sanders elegantly comments on this, and I will quote at some length because he makes the point so well:

> How could Paul, on the one hand, think that it mattered desperately that people came to faith in Christ, say that it determined whether or not they shared Christ's life, and predict destruction for those who rejected his message (for example, Phil 3:18–19), and, on the other hand, say that God would save everyone and everything? Which did he really think? Both, almost certainly . . . (he was not a philosophical theologian . . .) he was instead an apostle, an ad hoc theologian, a proclaimer, a charismatic who saw visions and spoke in tongues—and a religious genius.

---

106. Bernstein, *Formation of Hell*, 176.

107. MacDonald, *Evangelical Universalist*, 40.

Let us not put him entirely into the straightjacket of logical arrangement.

Paul thought in images and figures . . . One is the image of the throne conceived as a judgment seat. The second is the image of a race or some other kind of athletic contest. When Paul thought in one of these images, he naturally thought in terms of innocence or guilt, and winners or losers . . .

The third image is that of God as creator and omnipotent king. This is a God who gets his way. He created the world, and he will save all that he created. We see this image very clearly in 1 Corinthians 15 and also in Romans 11:36 ("from him are all things"). It is this image which takes control in the closing verses of Romans 11 . . . Of course (he would say) it matters whether or not one becomes part of the body of Christ. Only in that way does one die to sin and live to God. Of course it requires individual commitment. Of course God has chosen some and not others: the elect obtain salvation, the rest are hardened (Rom 11:7). Of course God created all people and all things, and he will not lose anything that is his. All of us and all the creation belong to him . . . God is good and merciful and holds history in his hands: he called Israel and gave the law; he sent Christ to save the world . . .

He forces us, in fact, to pose an extremely serious question: must a religion, in addressing diverse problems, offer answers that are completely consistent with one another? Is it not good to have passionate hopes and commitments which cannot all be reduced to a scheme in which they are arranged in a hierarchical relationship?[108]

William Barclay writes poignantly:

Ultimately God is love. It is his love which directs his power . . . Now if God is love, God cannot be at peace until the last child in his family has come home, and for God the obliteration and annihilation of the rebellious would be not triumph but tragedy, not victory but final and ultimate defeat . . . Eternal punishment, conditional immortality, universal restoration—there will be those who will believe in each of these. But it seems to us that if God is the God who is the God and Father of our Lord Jesus Christ, and if the total impression of the Gospel is true, we may dare to hope that when time ends God's family will be complete, for surely we must think in terms not of a king who is satisfied with a victory which destroys his enemies, but of a Father who

108. Sanders, *Paul*, 126–28.

can never be content when even a single child of his is outside the circle of his love.[109]

The ambiguity of the biblical witness serves to remind us that although we have good grounds for hoping that everyone will be saved, we cannot proclaim this as a dogmatic certainty. But we can say that the biblical pictures of a new heaven and a new earth (explored in chapter 7) portray a time when there will be no more evil and no more suffering, and it seems clear that there will be no room for a never-ending hell.

109. Barclay, *Apostles' Creed*, 200.

6

Deliver Us from Evil—Perhaps through a Cleansing Hell

Exploring the Idea that Hell May Be a Place of Cleansing, with Final Redemption as Its Aim

A wise fire, the means by which sinners are purified and finally saved.

—CLEMENT OF ALEXANDRIA, SECOND CENTURY

Our souls *demand* Purgatory, don't they?

—C. S. LEWIS, TWENTIETH CENTURY[1]

But is there a real choice after death? My Roman Catholic friends would be surprised, for to them souls in Purgatory are already saved. And my Protestant friends would like it no better, for they'd say that the tree lies as it falls.

—C. S. LEWIS, TWENTIETH CENTURY[2]

---

1. Lewis, *Letters to Malcolm*, 140, emphasis Lewis'.
2. Lewis, *Great Divorce*, 63.

JESUS TALKED ABOUT SOMETHING, or somewhere, that our English Bibles
translate "hell." And he talked about it more than anyone else in the New
Testament, or in the Old Testament, for that matter.

Did he mean, as many Christians down the centuries have understood him to mean, a terrible concentration camp or prison, forever lurking in some remote corner of eternity, out of sight of the heavenly land of
the free? But even worse, because it goes on forever and has sometimes
been thought to be a place of literal fire and torture "justly deserved" by
those who are there. If that sort of scenario is not what Jesus meant—then
what *did* he mean, or imply?

The English word "hell" is based on the Anglo-Saxon *helan* or *behe-
lian*, "to hide," and carries the idea of a dark and hidden place, so it is very
similar in meaning to the Hebrew *sheol* and the Greek *Hades*, which both
mean "the unseen world of the dead," and are both usually translated as
"hell" in our Bibles (translating *sheol* in the Old Testament, and *Hades* in
the New Testament.)

"Hell" is also used to translate the figurative use of "Gehenna," or the
valley of Hinnom, which was on the southwest slopes of Jerusalem and
had long been used as a garbage dump where all sorts of rubbish, including the bodies of criminals, were thrown. It smoldered all the time, which
would have reduced putrefaction and the infestation of flies and vermin,
so in some ways the fire cleansed the rubbish dump and limited its nox-
iousness, and because rubbish was thrown there, the rest of the city could
be kept clean. (And even in such a dump, some things such as any gold,
silver, or costly stones would survive, burnished by the smoldering fire.)

The book of Isaiah ends with a prophecy of the restoration of the
earth, when "all mankind will come and bow down before me," rounded
up with a gruesome picture of those who rebelled against God, presum-
ably having been thrown into this loathsome valley—though this is not
stated—where "their worm will not die, nor will their fire be quenched."[3]
This would have been their literal fate as criminals, but it may also carry
overtones of postmortem punishment.

Against this gloomy picture, we can set the optimistic promise by
Jeremiah that "the whole valley where dead bodies and ashes are thrown,
and all the terraces out to the Kidron valley on the east as far as the corner
of the Horse Gate, will be holy to the Lord."[4] If Gehenna came to sym-

3. Isa 66:24.
4. Jer 31: 40.

bolize hell, then we may perhaps be justified in thinking that Jeremiah's picture symbolizes its reclamation.

By the time of Jesus, Gehenna, the garbage dump, had become a metaphor for everything unwanted, unpleasant, and evil that needed to be destroyed, and it was also used as an image of postmortem punishment. This is often the way that Jesus uses it, but sometimes he may have been simply saying something more like "your life is rubbish"—figurative language, rather than theological statement. James writes about "the tongue being set on fire by Gehenna,"[5] which does not make literal sense and is clearly figurative.

Jesus uses "Gehenna" nine times in Matthew's gospel,[6] with parallels in Mark, and once in Luke.[7] He also uses "Hades" twice each in Matthew and Luke. "Hades" is also used twice in Acts and four times in Revelation. John's gospel does not talk about Gehenna or Hades; but there is a lot about choice and judgment in this gospel.

Paul talks about God's wrath, and his punishment—specified in his letter to the Romans as a "giving over to" the evil.[8] God has given us free will and allows us to choose evil; he does not step in to stop the evil results of our choices. However, Paul never uses "Gehenna," but in a somewhat similar metaphor (which we looked at in the previous chapter,) he compares God's judgment to being tested by fire, envisaging a fire that does not destroy the individual. Rather, what the person has done with his or her life is either destroyed by the fire of judgment or revealed as something that will endure the flames:

> For no one can lay any foundation other than the one already laid, which is Jesus Christ. If any man builds on this foundation using gold, silver, costly stones, wood, hay or straw, his work will be shown for what it is, because the Day will bring it to light. It will be revealed with fire, and the fire will test the quality of each man's work. If what he has built survives, he will receive his reward. If it is burned up, he will suffer loss; he himself will be saved, but only as one escaping through the flames.[9]

5. Jas 3:6.

6. Matt 5:22, 29, 30; 10:28; 18:9; 23:15, 33; Mark 9:43, 45, 47; Luke 12:5.

7. Luke 12:5.

8. Rom 1:24, 26, 28.

9. 1 Cor 3:11–15.

The phrase "he himself will be saved, but only as one escaping through the flames" points to a postmortem cleansing process. Paul is using an image that was well known both in Judaism and in Greek philosophy.

As we saw in the previous chapter, God is described as "a consuming fire," (p. 124–29) and the concept of the wrath of God being like fire is widespread in the Old Testament, yet the Jews do not have any conception of a fiery hell. A Jewish friend said to me, "It is Christians who have invented hell." Again and again in both the Old and the New Testaments, pictures of wonderful restoration are immediately followed or preceded by pictures of devastating judgment, destruction, pruning, burning, or eradicating of all that is evil.

The judge is the savior. To save a people or an individual, evil must be eradicated; that is part of the saving process. An alcoholic needs to throw out his remaining alcohol and renounce it if he is to be restored. The surgeon has to completely excise a cancerous growth to cure his patients, and if excision is incomplete, the outlook is less favorable.

There are other passages in the New Testament where the image of fire (not specified as Gehenna) is used as a metaphor for judgment: John the Baptist declares that every tree that does not bear good fruit will be thrown into the fire and that Jesus, who is coming, will baptize with the Holy Spirit and with fire—cleansing and renewing his people like wheat being separated from the chaff, which will be burned.[10] Chaff, of course, clings to *each* grain, so here the picture looks like the cleansing of individuals.

The gospel of John does not refer to Gehenna, but Jesus uses a similar fire motif when he speaks of unfruitful branches being pruned out of the vine and burned,[11] and in the synoptic gospels, he tells a parable of weeds that are allowed to grow together with the good crop but are finally separated out and burned—a clear picture of judgment.[12] In another parable of the final judgment, those without compassion are thrown into the fire prepared for the devil and his angels.[13]

---

10. Matt 3:10–12 and parallels.

11. John 15:6.

12. Matt 13:24–30, 40–42, and parallels.

13. Matt 25:41, but see also the comments below (p. 172–74) on the meaning of *kolasis* and *aeonios*, which throws a more optimistic light on the conclusion of this parable.

So have we come back to the traditional horror-inspiring ideas about the fate of the damned that have formed the backdrop to much orthodox Christian thought, as well as the basis of much terrifying teaching and preaching down the centuries? Fire is clearly being used metaphorically, but what does the metaphor symbolize?

In Paul's analogy above, the fire destroys and burns to ash perishable things (such as wood, hay, or straw, which seem to symbolize a life lived for self and not for God), but it reveals and purifies imperishable things (such as gold, silver, or costly stones, which seem to symbolize a life lived in and for Christ or others). If there is a mixture of the perishable and the imperishable, as is the case in most situations and for most people, then what is equivalent to wood, hay, and straw will be incinerated, and what is equivalent to gold, silver, and precious stones will remain.

What will *not* happen is that the "wood, hay, stubble" element will continue burning painfully forever. Even the recent massive bush-fires in Southern Australia burnt themselves out, leaving stark, stripped tree trunks and ashy rubble where houses once stood. But they did not continue to burn forever.

Many Christian thinkers from the early church right up to the present day have believed that the fires of hell are cleansing and restorative, and in the end destructive only of what cannot and will not be restored, rather than endlessly punitive—though, as we have seen, opinions about the afterlife have always been varied. Indeed, they had varied throughout the Old Testament period, and varied in the time of Jesus.

There were those like Tertullian in the second century—when to be a practicing Christian often meant martyrdom—who relished the thought of those who persecuted Christians being destroyed in flames:

> But there are yet other spectacles to come—that day of the Last Judgment with its everlasting issues, unlooked for by the heathen, the object of their derision, when the hoary age of the world and all its generations will be consumed in one file.
>
> What a panorama of spectacle on that day! Which sight shall excite my wonder? Which, my laughter? Where shall I rejoice, where exult—as I see so many and so mighty kings, whose ascent to heaven used to be made known by public announcement, now along with Jupiter himself, along with the very witnesses of their ascent, groaning in the depths of darkness? Governors of provinces, too, who persecuted the name of the Lord, melting in

flames fiercer than those they themselves kindled in their rage against the Christians braving them with contempt? [14]

But many other church fathers[15] taught the possibility of spiritual cleansing after death and believed that in the end all things would be restored to harmony and fruitfulness as in the beginning of creation.[16] They envisaged Christ's love stretching beyond the grave for those who did not see or did not respond to Christ's offer of salvation during life, and they also saw free will extending beyond the grave, because freedom is not lost and God's love cannot fail to go on reaching out.

Clement of Alexandria in the second century called the fires of hell "a 'wise' fire, the means by which sinners are purified and finally saved."[17]

Two centuries later, Gregory of Nyssa (AD 335–395) argued strongly for universal restoration. In addition to the usual refining fire analogy, he compares the purging process to pulling bodies out of the ruins of an earthquake:

> Crushed by the mounds of rubbish . . . mangled and torn . . . the divine force, for God's very love of man, drags that which belongs to Him from the ruins of the irrational and material, not in hatred or revenge for a wicked life . . . He is only claiming and drawing to Himself whatever, to please him, came into existence . . . Just as those who refine gold from the dross which it contains not only get this base alloy to melt in the fire, but are obliged to melt the pure gold along with the alloy, and then while this last is being consumed the gold remains, so, while evil is being consumed in the purgatorial fire the soul that is welded to this evil must inevitably be in the fire too, until the spurious material alloy is consumed and annihilated by this fire.[18]

In a third metaphor, Gregory pictures a rope that is deeply plastered by clay, needing to be pulled forcibly through a narrow hole:

14. Tertullian, ch. 30, http://www.pseudepigrapha.com/LostBooks/tertullian_spectacles.htm.

15. Notable examples are Clement of Alexandria Origen, Gregory of Nyssa, Gregory Nyzantias, and the Cappadocean Fathers.

16. This is the *apokatastasis*, or restoration of all things, which will be explored in the next chapter.

17. Andreas Andreopoulos, "Eschatology and Final Restoration (*apokatastasis*) in Origen, Gregory of Nyssa and Maximos the Confessor," http://www.romancatholicism.org/maximos-apokatastasis.html.

18. Gregory of Nyssa, *Purgatory and Resurrection*, quoted in *Christian Testament Since the Bible*, 55.

> We may imagine the agonised strugglings of that soul which has wrapped itself up in material passions, when God is drawing it, his own one, to Himself, and the foreign matter which has somehow grown into its substance has to be scraped from it by brute force . . . therefore it seems that it is not punishment chiefly and principally that the deity, as judge, afflicts sinners with, but He operates only to get the good separated from the evil and to attract it into the communion of blessedness.[19]

Gregory believed in universal restoration for three reasons, which are as valid now as they were then:

1. The character of God: Because God is good, he has pity for fallen man, and because God is wise, he knows the means of man's recovery.[20]

2. The nature of Evil: Evil is negative; it does not exist in the same essential sense that good exists. "In any and every case, evil must be removed out of existence, so that the absolutely non-existent would cease to be at all."[21]

3. The nature of God's punishment: Gregory believed that God's punishment is always disciplinary and remedial, and thus part of the process of redemption.

In his popular fantasy *The Great Divorce*, C. S. Lewis imagines himself in hell with a lot of argumentative and very ethereal ghosts, queuing for a bus to visit heaven, where they will have a chance to stay, if they wish—and if they are prepared to undergo the (temporarily) painful process of purging and cleansing. Most of the ghosts choose to return to hell on the bus, while a few dwindle away to nothingness and disappear. There are penetrating vignettes of "respectable" sinfulness in many guises, revealing how entrenched human sinfulness can be and how resistant to the abrasive cleansing power of truth, joy, and love. One who does remain in heaven has to allow his lust to be painfully killed before both he and his sinfulness are wonderfully transformed. Lewis comments:

> I do not think that all who choose wrong paths perish; but their rescue consists in being put back on the right road . . . Evil can be undone. The spell must be unwound, bit by bit . . . if we accept

19. Ibid.

20. *The Great Catechism*, ch. 21, quoted in Barclay, *Apostles' Creed*, 196.

21. Gregory of Nyssa, *Concerning the Soul*, quoted in Barclay, *Apostles' Creed*, 196.

Heaven we shall not be able to retain even the smallest and most intimate souvenirs of Hell.[22]

In a meditation entitled "Wickedness and Judgment," Rod Garner wrestles with the question of how God might judge the late chairman Mao Zedong of China. Garner compares Mao to the biblical King Jehoiakim, who died unlamented, his body cast out of the gates of the city.

Jehoiakim's punishment was to be buried like the carcass of a donkey, whereas Mao is still revered in China, despite the fact that he was responsible for over seventy million deaths in peacetime, more than any other twentieth-century leader, and twelve times the number of Jews killed in the Holocaust.[23]

Garner asks, "How do we begin to speak of judgment or the possibility of moral restitution when such wickedness has gone unpunished?" His tentative answer is that ultimately each of us will be faced:

> with the searing knowledge of who and what we really are and how we passed our days on earth as givers or takers. "Purgatory" is the name for this chastening experience and it is hard to imagine how even a taker such as Mao could remain impervious to the consequences of his deeds once exposed to their chill . . . We must assume that until the opposite proved to be the case for Mao, he would forever remain beyond that sovereign Love which longs to draw even the greatest of sinners to itself.[24]

Garner envisages Mao Zedong "exposed to the chill" of his deeds— the seventy million souls he had killed to impose his will on the nation. Can a human being perpetrate such awful deeds while fully understanding their impact? And for Mao Zedong, read also Hitler, Pol Pot, the Moors Murderer, Harold Shipman . . . the list could go on and on, for it includes many less famous and obvious "sinners." It includes the mean, the mercenary, the merciless, those whose hearts are bitter and unforgiving, and it even includes me.

In real life, it is often an *encounter with the reality of Christ,* or some touch by the Holy Spirit that leads to faith and transformation. Spiritual blindness is overcome by the light of Christ and the restoration of

22. Lewis, *Great Divorce,* 7–8.

23. *Jung Chang and Jon Halliday, Mao: The Unknown Story, quoted in* Garner, *Like a Bottle,* 10–12.

24. Garner, *Like a Bottle,* 11.

spiritual sight. This can happen to the most unlikely person—hence the old saying, "from the guttermost to the uttermost."

Such an encounter happened dramatically for the apostle Paul. Blind to the truth that Jesus of Nazareth was the long-awaited Messiah, Paul had been aggressively trying to destroy his followers until he was totally transformed by a profound experience of the risen Christ.[25] He came to believe that the Jews would in the end be saved in exactly the same way as he had been—by encountering Christ. If this could happen to Paul, the destroyer of the church, then surely, when the Lord Jesus Christ appears in glory to all Israel, they will no more be capable of rejecting him than Paul had been.[26]

The majority of Jews do not believe that Jesus of Nazareth is the Christ, or that he is a savior.

But if the Christian gospel is true—if Jesus is indeed the incarnate Son of God, both Messiah and redeemer—they are, in a spiritual sense, deaf and blind to the truth. However, that does not mean that they have been finally rejected by God.[27] Paul was convinced that God could not deny himself; he could not make null his covenant or abandon those whom he had chosen, and so finally "all Israel will be saved." He quotes Isaiah, "The savior will come from Zion and remove all wickedness from the descendants of Jacob. I will make this covenant with them when I take away their sins," and surely this will be true not only for the Jews, but for the whole of mankind. So Paul concludes the densely argued theological section of the first eleven chapters of his letter to the Romans with the amazing conclusion that "God has bound all men over to disobedience so that he may have mercy on them all."[28]

This wonderful conclusion leads him into a paean of praise:

> Oh, the depth of the riches of the wisdom and knowledge of God!
>
> How unsearchable his judgments and his paths beyond tracing out!
>
> Who has known the mind of the Lord?

---

25. Acts 9:3–16; 22:6–16; 26:12–18.

26. I owe this insight into Rom 9–11, especially Rom 11:26–27, to Murphy-O'Connor, *Paul*, 340.

27. Rom 11:1–29.

28. Rom 11:32.

Or who has been his counsellor? [29]

What was true for Paul before his conversion, and is true for the Jews to this day, is also true for the majority of humankind. During life, one of the main stumbling blocks to faith is spiritual blindness and the hiddenness of God.[30]

Looking back to the time when he was a persecutor, Paul comments, "Even though I was once a blasphemer and a persecutor and a violent man, I was shown mercy because I acted in ignorance and unbelief."[31] This echoes Jesus' cry from the cross: "Father, forgive them, for they do not know what they are doing."[32]

Some early manuscripts do not include this sentence, but it is central to our understanding of the cross and is entirely in keeping with Jesus' exhortation to his followers to forgive,[33] and it was probably the model for Stephen's forgiving cry as he was stoned.[34]

I do not think it is fanciful to see those who actually crucified Jesus as representing in some sense all who reject him—most people who reject Christ in this life do not know what they are doing. They do not "see," for their spiritual eyes are blinded. They cannot "see" the truth of the gospel. They cannot "see" Jesus. (None of us can in a physical sense, of course, but I am talking here about spiritual sight.) They cannot "see" that there is a God at all. The world we live in is so messed up as a result of sin, disease, and destruction that belief in a good God can be extraordinarily difficult for any thinking person. I will be surprised if any of my readers has not at times been assailed by doubts. I certainly have been.

The Jewish nation that should have revealed God to the world failed to do so and failed to recognize their Messiah, and so had him crucified. The church, which should reveal Christ to the world, is scandalously divided and has often been critical, judgmental, violent, and unloving. Her history is hardly one that commends her Lord to a world that may be surprisingly discerning. Church history includes power struggles, worldliness, misrepresentation of the gospel, lack of spirituality, lack of

29. Isa 40:13, quoted in Rom 11:33–34.

30. See Deut 29:4; Isa 6:9–10; 29:10, 11; John 12:37–40; Rom 11:8, 25; 2 Cor 3:14; 4:3–4; Eph 4:18–19; 1 John 2:11.

31. 1 Tim 1:13.

32. Luke 23:34.

33. Matt 6:12–15; 18:21–35; Luke 17:3–4.

34. Acts 7:60.

compassion, and apparently widespread sexual abuse. Down the ages, horrendous conflicts, wars, and awful murders (not least against the Jews) have been perpetrated in the name of the Prince of Peace. The church too is partially blind: "Now we see through a glass darkly."[35]

Christ cries out to the Father to forgive those who do not see, do not know, or do not understand, and surely our understanding of the unity of the Godhead must lead us to suppose that this prayer will be answered. But *then*, after death, spiritual blindness will be removed, and we will see clearly, "face to face." How many people, face to face with the risen, glorious Lord in all his love, will still resist him? Especially when they see with clarity the effects of their own lives on others, for that will be clear too. For "then shall I know fully, even as I am fully known."[36]

For good or ill, our deeds will be revealed by the light. The revelation will be both a judgment and a means of transformation, as we see the impact of what we have (or have not) done. This can happen during earthly life, of course, but will perhaps be continued in a greatly enhanced way after death in a cleansing by intense exposure to the light that is God. If this understanding is true, then doubt and unbelief will be possible no more, as the truth of Christ is finally and inescapably seen. The need for faith will be replaced by the reality of the full vision of love. Perhaps it will still be possible to reject, but with that main stumbling block of spiritual blindness removed, in full understanding at last of the extent and horror of their sin, and in full sight of the magnitude of the savior's love and the greatness of the salvation on offer, surely most, if not all men and women will fall at Christ's feet in worship and repentance. Maybe this will happen in an instant at the moment of death, or maybe at some time in the ages to come.

Then, finally, the words of Paul will be fulfilled:

> At the name of Jesus every knee should bow,
> in heaven and on earth, and under the earth,
> and every tongue confess that Jesus Christ is Lord,
> to the glory of God the Father.[37]

---

35. 1 Cor 13:12.
36. 1 Cor 13:12.
37. Phil 2:10.

The Scriptures teach that we will all be judged on the grounds of what we have done (or not done).[38] As I search my own soul, what leads me to repentance is realizing the effects of my words and deeds on others. Spiritual blindness allows us to sin with apparent impunity, but the searchlight of God, and the opening of our eyes to the effects of our sin, leads to repentance and faith, and thus to salvation.

Like Garner, Lewis, and many other Christian theologians stretching back to the early church fathers, as I contemplate our loving Savior, I find myself compelled to believe that his love will reach out with saving power beyond the grave. Is it not reasonable to expect a "second chance"—indeed a third, fourth, and more chances—from the Christ who exhorted his disciples to forgive "seventy times seven"?[39] Consider too his own example of forgiving the sinners that he came into contact with,[40] his cry of forgiveness for those who nailed him onto the cross, and the whole purpose of his coming: "For the Son of Man came to seek and to save what was lost."[41]

Classic evangelical teaching is that if a person dies as an unrepentant sinner, with the offer of salvation rejected, then it will be too late. There will be no second chance. We are told that our fate is sealed at the time of death. Salvation remains on offer during life: "now is the day of salvation." [42] There is always the chance of a deathbed conversion for those who capitulate at the last moment (this may happen even during the sinner's dying gasps—we cannot tell—and distraught friends and relatives can hang on to this wisp of hope for the renegade they love but believe that God will reject because the dying one has always appeared to reject God during life). But for evangelical Christians, it is both useless and unnecessary to pray for the dead; indeed, to do so is a grave mistake, for it may give a false hope about unbelievers who have died or could be seen as diminishing the certainty of salvation for those who died as believers.

However, there are some from the evangelical wing of the church who do question this classic evangelical understanding, as I am doing in

---

38. See Matt 16:27; 25:31–46; John 5:28–29; Rom 2:6–11; Rev 20:12–13; 21:7–8.

39. Matt 18:22.

40. Matt 9:2–6 and parallels; John 8:10–11.

41. Luke 19:10.

42. 2 Cor 6:2. Compare Luke 4:19, where Jesus announces that he has come "to proclaim the year of the Lord's favor," and also Mark 1:15: "The kingdom of God is near."

this book. The Baptist minister Dr. Nigel Wright, previously a lecturer in Christian Doctrine at Spurgeon's College, London, wrote:

> A controlling belief . . . which is very firmly held, but which I am questioning, is that death seals a person's destiny and that the condition in which a person dies is that in which they will for ever remain after death . . . The key question is, not so much whether human beings can be redeemed beyond death as whether God's search for his fallen creatures is thwarted by death or continues beyond it. The judge of all the earth will certainly do right, but from the perspective we currently occupy it is reasonable to suppose that this includes a universal search to win human beings to relationship with himself which does not cease at the point of human death. [43]

What I have been discussing, and what many of the church fathers, and more recently C. S. Lewis, Nigel Wright, Rod Garner, Gregory MacDonald, and many others talk about, is a purgatorial, cleansing, disciplinary hell for those who, during their earthly life, have not entered into the salvation that is freely offered for all.

Cleansing Hell Is Not the Same as the Classic Roman Catholic Doctrine of Purgatory

This is *not* the same concept as the Catholic doctrine of purgatory for *believers* (who are expected to be saved, but still need to be purified and made clean and pure enough for heaven through purgatory). Traditionally, Catholics also believe that there will be some or many who will be eternally lost in hell.[44]

---

43. Wright, *Radical Evangelical*, 98–99. Wright does not assume that people will find it easier to believe once confronted beyond death with the living God. He writes: "For all we know, it may be harder." In view of the removal of spiritual blindness, at death (see my discussion above) I personally believe that it will be easier rather than harder.

44. This is a sweeping generalization. Doctrinal distinctions are more blurred than this implies, and many Catholic theologians are now moving toward a more universalist position, but the orthodox teaching held by many, is that "once the last soul leaves purgatory at the General Resurrection and Judgment, it will be extinguished and only heaven and hell will remain" ("Purgatory and Praying for the Dead," *Catholic Apologetics*, http://www.theworkofgod.org/Library/Apologtc/R_Haddad/Course/Book2-A. htm).

The Catholic doctrine of purgatory developed gradually, becoming an official article of faith at the Council of Florence in 1439. Masses were said for the dead, and indulgences meant to shorten the time spent in purgatory were granted to those who were penitent (or gave money). They could also benefit deceased loved ones, and so "Indulgences were as ubiquitous as the modern lottery ticket."[45]

In Northern Germany, a now infamous Dominican monk named Tetzel persuaded the townsfolk to purchase indulgences with the jingle:

> As soon as the coin in the coffer rings,
> The soul from purgatory springs.
> Will you not then for a quarter of a florin receive these letters
> of indulgence through which you are able to lead a divine and
> immortal soul into the fatherland of paradise?[46]

The church was grossly distorting the gospel. It was acting as though human beings could manipulate what happens after death and the way God would judge, apparently forgetting that "it is mine to avenge; I will repay," says the Lord.[47]

This elaborate fabrication was hugely financially beneficial to the church, which was at that time in financial straits due to its Crusades against Muslims, but it was radically rejected by Martin Luther, who realized that salvation is simply a gift of God's grace, to be received by faith and neither earned nor bought from any human being, even if authorized by the Pope! This was the final trigger of the Reformation, and embedded in most Protestant spirits is a deep distrust of any teaching that might hint at postmortem cleansing or purging; that is, a cleansing purgatory as opposed to an eternal hell. The Roman Catholic teaching is that purgatory is the "final purification of the elect, which is entirely different from the punishment of the damned."[48] (This carries with it the subsidiary debate: Should we pray for the dead? And if so, how should we pray? But this question is beyond the scope of this book.[49]) These issues still divide the church.

45. MacCulloch, *History of Christianity*, 556.

46. Bainton, *Here I Stand*, 60.

47. Deut 32:35, quoted in Rom 12:19.

48. Mike Conway, "Catholic Bible Study Notes for All Souls Day 2007," *Bible Alive*, February 11, 2007.

49. Early Christian theologians prayed for the dead as a matter of course, as a corollary of the belief that there is a chance for salvation after death (e.g., Tertullian, Origen, Cyprian, Lactantius, Eusebius, Cyril, Gregory of Nyssa, Epiphanius, Jerome, Ambrose, John Chrysostom, Augustine, Gregory the Great, the Venerable Bede, and

We have looked at the implications of the biblical image of judgment and cleansing by fire, as well as some of the ways that this has been understood both by the early church fathers and by more modern thinkers. But is there any further biblical or historical support for a process of redemption beyond death?

Let us now turn to look at the views expressed in the Old Testament, between the Testaments, and in the time of Jesus, later Jewish thinking, and finally, in the New Testament.

1. In the Old Testament

The Hebrew Bible, our Old Testament, often seems to imply that death is simply the end, with no possibility of communion with God or of resurrection, and no hint of postmortem judgment, be it punishment or reward.[50]

But there are also glimpses of God being active in *sheol*, which, as we have seen (p. 150), means simply "the unseen world of the dead" and is similar in meaning to the Greek *Hades*. The psalmist, wondering at God's omnipresence, sees him active even in *sheol*:

> If I make my bed in the depths [Hebrew, *sheol*] you are there . . .
> if I say, "Surely the darkness will hide me and the light become
> night around me," even the darkness will not be dark to you;
> the night will shine like the day,
> for darkness is as light to you.[51]

Similarly, Prov 15:11 proclaims: "death and destruction lie open before the Lord," and Job cries, "Death is naked before God; destruction lies uncovered."[52]

The book of Jonah is often understood as a fictional narrative intended to show God's compassion for the wicked city of Nineveh, and by implication, the rest of the non-Jewish world. The story implies that Jonah recalls having been drowned and had actually died before he was

---

second-millennium theologians such as Anselm, Bernard, Aquinas, and Bonaventure). Prayers for the dead are found in early Christian catacombs and in early church liturgies.

50. For example, "As it is with the good man, so it is with the sinner . . . The same destiny overtakes all . . . the dead know nothing; they have no further reward" (Eccl 9:2–6). See also Ps 88:10–12, 115:17; Isa 26:14.

51. Ps 139:8, 11.

52. Job 26:6.

swallowed by the great fish: "seaweed was wrapped around my head. To the roots of the mountains I sank down; the earth beneath me barred me in for ever." He cried out to God from "deep in the world of the dead [Hebrew, *sheol*],"[53] and the Lord heard, and he "ordered the fish to spew Jonah up on the beach," which happened. This implies that the author of the book believed that the dead can pray to God and communicate with him, and that God is willing to respond to that cry.

A rare hope of resurrection seems to be implied in Isaiah, without reference to judgment:

> Your dead shall live, their corpses shall rise.
> O dwellers in the dust, awake and sing for joy!
> For your dew is a radiant dew, and the earth will give birth to
> those long dead.[54]

The most explicit text in the Old Testament about resurrection to judgment is found in Daniel, which was probably written about the same time as the Maccabean revolt in the second century BC, so the theology has developed to be is nearer to that represented by Maccabees:

> There will be a time of distress such as has not happened from the beginning of nations until then. But at that time your people—everyone whose name is found written in the book—will be delivered. Multitudes who sleep in the dust of the earth will awake: some to everlasting life, others to shame and everlasting contempt.[55]

In the Greek version of Daniel, the phrases translated as "everlasting" life or "everlasting contempt" in our bibles, are from αιωνιον, (*aionion*,) which does not mean lasting forever and ever but "of the age to come" or "of God's age." The significance of this will be dealt with in more detail when we look at the New Testament. (p. 169 f.)

---

53. Jonah 2 (GNB). I owe the understanding that Jonah was actually dead to an Easter Saturday talk given by David Pawson, Moor Lane Methodist Church, Merseyside, UK, March 22, 2008.

54. Isa 26:19.

55. Dan 12:1–2.

2. Between the Two Testaments

The book of 2 Maccabees was written in the second century BC to awaken the Jews of Alexandria to the problems of the Palestinian Jews, who were being persecuted in the time of Antiochus Epiphanes. It is clear that at least some Jews of that period believed in the resurrection of the dead, and because of this belief, they prayed for the dead. We read:

> When they found on each of the dead men under their tunics, amulets of the idols taken from Jamnia, which the Law prohibits to Jews . . . all . . . gave themselves to prayer, begging that the sin committed might be fully blotted out . . . and . . . sent to Jerusalem to have a sacrifice for sin offered, an altogether fine and noble action, in which he [Judas Maccabees] took full account of the resurrection. For if he had not expected the fallen to rise again it would have been superfluous and foolish to pray for the dead . . . this was why he had this atonement sacrifice offered for the dead, so that they might be released from their sin.[56]

The writer comments that it would be superfluous and foolish to pray for the dead if Judas Maccabees had not expected them to rise again, but it would also be superfluous and foolish if there were no possibility of God releasing them from their sin (whether in response to Judas' prayers and sacrifices, or in response to the dead men's postmortem repentance, or simply as an act extravagant divine grace).

My Protestant friends will complain that this account is taken from the Apocrypha, which, though accepted by Catholics and Greek Orthodox Christians, is not accepted by Protestants as authoritative. The Jews who fixed the Hebrew Masoretic texts in the seventh to tenth centuries AD rejected the books of Maccabees, largely because the Maccabees fell out of favor when they later embraced Greek culture, which was considered un-Jewish. Protestants accepted the books that had been included in the Masoretic text at the time of the Reformation as the authoritative books of their Old Testament, while other books of the Greek Septuagint were excluded or kept in the appendix we know as the Apocrypha.

However, the Greek Septuagint translation of the Hebrew Tanakh, or our Old Testament, was in use in the first century and included the first and second books of Maccabees. Consequently, Jesus and his disciples would have known these books, as would Paul and the other writers of the New Testament. It seems likely that the thoughts expressed in this

---

56. 2 Macc 12:40–45.

account would have been widely held by those who believed that there would be a resurrection of the dead. Paul uses a similar argument to that found in Maccabees: "Now if there is no resurrection, what will those do who are baptized for the dead? If the dead are not raised at all, why are people baptized for them?"[57]

3. At the Time of Jesus

First-century Jews longed for salvation, but their expectations of what "salvation" meant varied. Many hoped for national survival rather than life after death: "the inauguration of the age to come, liberation from Rome, the restoration of the Temple, and the free enjoyment of their own land."[58] Many expected that a messiah would appear to accomplish this.

Many longed for the "Day of the Lord" (p. 120 f.) when God would renew his covenant with his people and restore all creation, and when his kingdom would come on earth. The nations, especially those that oppressed Israel, would be judged or converted, and God's people would be vindicated.

Expectations of life after death varied:

> In the confusion of non-standardised second-temple Judaism, all sorts of groups and individuals held all sorts of views about life after death . . . some . . . adopted what may be seen as a Hellenized future expectation, that is a hope for a non-physical [or "spiritual"] world to which the righteous and blessed would be summoned after death, and a non-physical place of damnation where the wicked would be tormented. There are some texts which use language of this sort.[59]

There were many first-century Jews who believed that there would be a bodily resurrection for the vindicated covenant people who had died before the great restoration happened (notably the Pharisees). The Sadducees, uniquely, did not believe in either immortality or bodily resurrection.

---

57. 1 Cor 15:29.

58. Wright, *People of God*, 300. The people's hope was based on such biblical passages as Isa 33, 52, 54–55; or Zeph 3:14–20, and was supported by extra-biblical literature.

59. Wright, *People of God*, 321.

Most of those who believed in resurrection thought that some would be left out. For example, in the Psalms of Solomon, sinners are said to be destroyed:

> The destruction of the sinner is for ever,
> and God will not remember him when he visits the righteous.
> This is the portion of sinners for ever;
> but they that fear the Lord shall rise to life eternal, and their
> life shall be in the light of the Lord, and shall come to an end
> no more.[60]

The many different Jewish factions each stressed different ways of making sure that they would be included in the expected salvation on earth or in the resurrection to come. So it is that Wright comments:

> What are the badges of membership that mark one out in the
> group that is to be saved, vindicated, raised to life (in the case
> of members already dead), or exalted to power (in the case of
> those still alive)? For the Pharisees, there was a programme of
> intensification of Torah. For the Essenes, there was a (varying)
> set of communal rules, and an appeal to loyalty to a Teacher. For
> many rebel groups there were subtly differing agendas.[61]

4. Jewish Beliefs about the Afterlife Have Continued to Vary

a. In the first century AD, there were two main schools of thought, following the strict Rabbi Shammah and the more moderate Rabbi Hillel. Rabbi Shammah thought that in the last judgment day there will be three classes of souls: "the righteous shall at once be written down for the life everlasting; the wicked, for Gehenna; but those whose virtues and sins counterbalance one another shall go down to Gehenna and float up and down until they rise purified."[62] The followers of the moderate Rabbi Hillel also speak of an intermediate state, but they stressed that because of God's merciful nature, the balance is inclined toward mercy, and "the intermediates do not

---

60. *Pss. Sol.* 3:11ff. (14ff.), translated by S. P. Brock in Sparks, quoted in Wright, *People of God*, 328.

61. Wright, *People of God*, 335.

62. The Shammaite rabbis quoted Zech 13:9 and 1 Sam 2:6, to justify this opinion.

descend into Gehenna."[63] There were different opinions as to how long purgatory would last. According to some traditions,[64] the souls of the wicked would be consumed and transformed into ashes under the feet of the righteous after twelve months,[65] and the worst sinners would undergo eternal tortures in Gehenna without cessation.[66] The righteous and, some thought, sinners among the people of Israel (for whom Abraham intercedes because they bear the Abrahamic sign of the covenant) will not be harmed by the fire of Gehenna even when they are required to pass through the intermediate state of purgatory.[67]

b. In the twelfth century, the influential Jewish theologian Maimonides complained that observant Jews hold widely differing and totally confused ideas on the subject. He insisted that the teaching should be taken figuratively and that the ultimate reward is the spiritual reunion of the immortal soul with God, while the ultimate punishment for evil doing is the annihilation of the soul.

Current Orthodox Jewish practice centers around the belief that the dead have an awareness of the living.[68] Like Christians, Jews have held a variety of opinions about the fate of the dead, but belief in some type of purging process has been widespread. Current Orthodox practice is for the son of the deceased to recite the Kaddish—which is a prayer of praise—regularly for eleven months after the death:

> Why is Kaddish recited for only eleven months, when the mourning period is twelve months? According to Jewish tradition, the soul must spend some time purifying itself before it can enter heaven. The maximum time required for purification is twelve months, for the most evil person. To recite Kaddish for twelve months would imply that the parent was the type who needed twelve months of

63. T. Sanh. xiii. 3; R. H. 16b; Bacher, "Ag. Tan." i. 18.
64. Tosef., Sanh. xiii. 4–5; R. H. 16b.
65. Based on Mal 4:3 (3:21 in Jewish Bibles).
66. Based on Isa 66:24.
67. 'Er. 19b; Ḥag. 27a.
68. From the Talmud Berachot 18b.

purification! To avoid this implication, the Sages decreed that a son should recite Kaddish for only eleven months.[69]

c. Reformed Jews, like the Sadducees of the first century, usually do not believe in a resurrection. In 1885, the Pittsburgh Platform, which is an important statement of Reformed Jewish belief, includes the statement: "We reject . . . both the beliefs in bodily resurrection and in Gehenna and Eden (Hell and Paradise)."[70] Lionel Blue, the convener of the Beth Din (Rabbinic Court) of the Reform Synagogue of Great Britain writes:

> The Pharisees and their pupils . . . debated the existence of hell. They decided that it probably did not exist, but if it did this was it, this world was . . . a corridor, a waiting room to another world . . . the corridor of course, leads to the door which is death. What is beyond it, is not dogmatically described . . . Yet at the entrance to Jewish cemeteries are the Hebrew letters which stand for "the house of life." Although there is no formal doctrine of purgatory, death . . . did not break the laws of . . . reward and punishment . . . the judgment is a judgment of truth. Yet everything is prepared for the feast! . . . The awe of God is strong among Jews, but fear is rare . . . Death, original sin and hell are not obsessive fears for Jews. Therefore, the Christian message which brings release from all three is not immediately relevant to a Jewish situation. [71]

5. In the New Testament

The hopes and beliefs of the early Christians shifted from the various beliefs of other first-century Jews outlined above, because the resurrection of Jesus changed everything.

The still-future hope of resurrection was vindicated because it had happened already for Jesus. This confirmed the belief that there would

69. American-Israeli Cooperative Enterprise, "Death and Bereavement in Judaism: Death and Mourning," *Jewish Virtual Library*, http://www.jewishvirtuallibrary.org/jsource/Judaism/death.html.

70. Central Conference of American Rabbis, "Declaration of Principles: The Pittsburgh Platform, 1885," October 27, 2004, http://ccarnet.org/rabbis-speak/platforms/declaration-principles/.

71. Blue, *To Heaven*, 100–101.

be a future resurrection for all, but it did not remove the expectation of judgment. The New Testament is permeated with the idea that God, as revealed in Jesus, is both judge and savior. It emphasizes salvation and eternal life through the Christ, starting with life in Christ during earthly life, and continuing in resurrected life in the world to come.

Some of the judgments, such as the fall of Jerusalem in AD 70, take place in history, but there will also be a future judgment in "The Day of the Lord" or the "Day of the Lord Jesus Christ,"[72] when Christ will be fully revealed in his glory and will finally save those who are his.

We will turn now to a few topics in the New Testament that are particularly relevant to this exploration:

a. The meaning of the Greek word *aionios*

b. Condemnation and judgment in the New Testament

c. Is there biblical evidence of the possibility of forgiveness or cleansing in the age to come?

d. Christ's descent into hell and the final defeat of death and hell

The Meaning of the Greek Word
aion, aionios (αιων, αιωνιοζ)

Aion, aionios is usually translated as "eternal" in modern translations, but the Authorized Version was less consistent and uses "everlasting" in several places, which can be misleading. As a young Christian, I was nurtured on the Authorized Version, with its confusing and varied translations of *aionios*, and for many years I thought that "eternal life" or "everlasting life" simply meant living forever and ever with God in heaven, and "eternal fire" or "punishment" or "destruction" meant being punished in some way forever and ever. I suspect that many Christians still think like that

The New International Version (NIV) is more consistent than the Authorized Version and gives "eternal glory,"[73] "eternal life,"[74] and

---

72. See Luke 17:30; Rom 8:19; 1 Cor 1:7–8; 2 Thess 1:6–10; 1 Pet 1:13, 4:13; 2 Pet 3:12–13. See chapter 5.

73. 1 Pet 5:10.

74. See Matt 19:29; Luke 18:30; John 3:16, 36; 4:14, and many others.

"eternal covenant"[75] on the one hand, and "eternal fire"[76] and "eternal punishment"[77] on the other. Curiously, *aionion* is translated as "everlasting," when referring to destruction in 2 Thess 1:9, while the New Revised Standard Version is more consistent and gives "eternal" here, as in other places.

William Barclay helpfully explains the full meaning of *aionios*. It does *not* mean "forever and ever," but rather, "that which belongs to the world to come, or to God's world." Barclay cites the Greek myth of Tithonus, who lived forever without dying but grew older and older and more and more decrepit until life became an intolerable curse. Contrasted to this forever-and-ever existence, *eternal life* "is the life of God himself, and into that life we, too, may enter when we accept what Jesus Christ has done for us, and what he tells us about God."[78] But Barclay emphasizes that we need to be especially careful when interpreting the words about everlasting or eternal fire, punishment, judgment, and destruction:

> *Aionios* is the word of eternity as opposed to and contrasted with time. It is the word of deity as opposed to and contrasted with humanity. It is the word which can only really be applied to God . . . both the blessings which the faithful shall inherit and the punishment which the unfaithful shall receive . . . are such as befits God's nature and character to bestow and to inflict—and beyond that we . . . cannot go, except to remember that that nature and character are holy love.[79]

Condemnation and Judgment in the New Testament

In both Testaments, the Bible clearly says that that all men and women fall short of God's standards, and that all will be judged. (See the previous chapter.)

The statement that "man is destined to die once, and after that to face judgment"[80] is often used to support the view that there will be no "second chance" after death. However, if we look at the context, we will

75. Heb 13:20.
76. Matt 18:8; 25:41.
77. Matt 25:46.
78. Barclay, *New Testament Words*, 41.
79. Ibid., 36–37.
80. Heb 9:27.

see that the point of this comment is to compare the finality of death and judgment, which happens for each person only *once* with the finality of the *once for all* sacrificial death of Christ—which is not continually repeated like the animal sacrifices of the Old Testament:

> Now he has appeared once for all at the end of the ages to do away with sin by the sacrifice of himself. Just as man is destined to die once, and after that to face judgment, so Christ was sacrificed once to take away the sins of many people.[81]

It is precisely because we are all guilty before God and will all face judgment that Christ's death was so necessary. But the merciful savior is also the awesome judge: "'It is mine to avenge, I will repay,' says the Lord."[82] He bears the judgment and the condemnation in the body of Christ on the cross, but it is sobering to remember that despite the fact of Christ's atoning death for us, there will still be a final judgment, and this will result in punishment for some. This should be one of the factors that motivates us to seek to do God's will and keep his laws as we live out our lives in his sight.

But what does God's punishment, his vengeance, look like?

Of course we cannot know for certain, but as we have seen (p. 154–55), Gregory of Nyssa and other fathers of the early church believed that God's punishment is always disciplinary and remedial, and is thus part of the process of redemption. In support of this, William Barclay points out that there are two different Greek words that can be translated into English as "punishment" but have important differences in meaning in Greek:

a. *Kolasis*, used in Matt 25:46 and 2 Pet 2:9, is always used for *disciplinary punishment that is for the sake of the one who has done wrong* and is remedial in purpose.

b. A different word, *timoria*, is used for *vengeful punishment*. For example, in Acts 22:5 and 26:11, when Paul is persecuting the infant church.

Barclay explains:

> The word for punishment is *kolasis*. The word was originally a gardening word, and its original meaning was *pruning trees*. In

---

81. Heb 9:27–28.

82. Deut 32:35, quoted in Rom 12:19.

Greek there are two words for punishment, *timoria* and *kolasis,* and there is a quite definite distinction between them. Aristotle defines the difference; *kolasis* is for the sake of the one who suffers it; *timoria* is for the sake of the one who inflicts it (*Rhetoric* 1.10). Plato says that no one punishes (*kolazei*) a wrong-doer simply because he has done wrong—that would be to take unreasonable vengeance (*timoreitai*). We punish (*kolazei*) a wrong-doer in order that he may not do wrong again (*Protagoras* 323 E). Clement of Alexandria (*Stromateis* 4.24; 7.16) defines *kolasis* as pure *discipline,* and *timoria* as the return of evil for evil. Aulus Gellius says that *kolasis* is given that a man may be corrected; *timoria* is given that dignity and authority may be vindicated (*The Attic Nights* 7.14). The difference is quite clear in Greek and it is always observed. *Timoria* is retributive punishment; *kolasis* is remedial discipline. *Kolasis* is always given to amend and to cure.[83]

Gregory, as well as his Greek-speaking contemporaries, would of course have been familiar with this distinction, which is masked in our English translations. It throws new light on the devastating conclusion to Jesus' famous parable of the judgment in Matt 25:31–46.

Jesus compares the judgment to a farmer separating the sheep from the goats. Those who are condemned—not for doing anything bad, but for failing to act with compassion—are thrown into the fire prepared for the devil and his angels, and their final fate is to "go away to eternal punishment."[84] This sounds like a very traditional picture of hell, but in view of the meaning of *aionios,* "eternal," and *kolasis,* "disciplinary punishment," Barclay comments that the "eternal punishment" of Matt 25:46 describes "a disciplinary, curative punishment, and it certainly describes the punishment which only God can inflict."[85] This interpretation is more just, kinder, and more in keeping with the God of Love we serve than a more traditional and literal interpretation might be.

With this understanding, I now feel more nearly able to support the statement of faith (p. xiv) that triggered this exploration some forty years ago and motivated me to write this book!

In the UK criminal justice system, there has been a move in recent years to increase the use of "restorative justice processes" with the aim of making offenders realize the impact of the offence that they have committed on others: "Restorative processes give victims the chance to tell

83. Barclay, *Apostle's Creed,* 189.

84. Matt 25:41, 46.

85. Barclay, *Apostles' Creed,* 190.

offenders the real impact of their crime, to get answers to their questions, and an apology. Restorative justice holds offenders to account for what they have done, helps them understand the real impact of what they've done, to take responsibility and make amends."[86]

I would expect that any punishment that the Savior-Judge inflicts will be a kind of divine "restorative justice," and that God's restorative justice will be much more effective than our earthly justice services are ever able to be, for he will have all eternity in which to work his restoration.

Though we are often aware of this process at work during earthly life, it is manifestly not completed here, and it seems logical to expect that this purifying process will be completed (or even begun and completed) after death.

Is There Biblical Evidence of the Possibility of Forgiveness or Cleansing in the Age to Come?

Jesus said, "Anyone who speaks a word against the Son of Man will be forgiven, but anyone who speaks against the Holy Spirit will not be forgiven, either in this age or in the age to come,"[87] which seems to imply that it may be possible for some sins to be forgiven in the age to come. Similarly, when referring to those who will be "in danger of the fire of hell," he comments, "I tell you the truth, you will not get out until you have paid the last penny,"[88] which implies that escape from hell is at least a possibility.

Jesus' Parable of the Rich Man and Lazarus,[89] with its image of a gulf fixed between the Lazarus in Abraham's bosom and the rich man in Hades, is often taken as proof that there will be no second chance after death, but the rich man is beginning to understand the results of his self-centered lifestyle on earth and is beginning to think of others (his own family). This could, perhaps, represent the start of a postmortem repentance.

In John 5:25, Jesus says that "the dead will hear the voice of the Son of God, and those who hear will live." This is often taken to refer to those who are spiritually dead, but the straightforward meaning, once we

86. Restorative Justice Council, "What Is Restorative Justice?" http://www.restorativejustice.org.uk/what_is_restorative_justice/.

87. Matt 12:32.

88. Matt 5:26.

89. Luke 16:19–31.

allow ourselves to think in this way, is that those who are actually dead will have the opportunity to hear the voice of the Son of God, and if they hear (that is, if they respond to that voice), they will live. Jesus' raising of Lazarus[90] could perhaps be considered to be a sign that Jesus' voice, heard by Lazarus, will also be heard by others who have died. Certainly, John carefully chooses the miracles he records, calling them "signs" because they point beyond the miracle itself to something more, which he leaves his readers to discover.[91]

I wonder whether the refrain that Paul quotes in his letter to the Ephesians—probably from an Easter or baptismal hymn—could perhaps imply a belief that Christ would truly shine not only into the lives of those who believe in Christ, but also on the actually dead:

> Wake up, O sleeper,
> rise from the dead,
> and Christ will shine on you.[92]

Christ's Descent into Hell and the Final Defeat of Death and Hell

Peter glimpses Christ preaching in hell: "For Christ . . . was put to death in the body but made alive by the Spirit, through whom also he went and preached to the spirits in prison who disobeyed long ago."[93] And later, using similar imagery: "For this is the reason the gospel was preached even to those who are now dead, so that they might be judged according to men in regard to the body, but live according to God in regard to the spirit."[94]

Theologians debate the meaning of these verses. They have been taken as simply a way of showing that the holy men in Jewish history were not excluded from the salvation brought by Jesus, but knowing as we do that Christ's aim was to seek and save the lost,[95] it seems reasonable to accept the view that Christ, who had just suffered the worst that the world could throw at him in order to save that crucifying world,

90. John 11:38–43.
91. See John 2:11.
92. Eph 5:14.
93. 1 Pet 3:18–19.
94. 1 Pet 4:6.
95. Luke 19:10.

would be offering salvation. Certainly he is portrayed as *acting* in some way in hell.[96] The descent into hell was affirmed by most of the early church fathers, and is included in the Apostles' Creed.[97] Calvin affirmed:

> We must not omit the descent to hell, which was of not little importance to the accomplishment of redemption . . . there is nothing strange in its being said that he descended to hell, seeing he endured the death which is inflicted on the wicked by an angry God . . . he bore in his soul the tortures of condemned and ruined man.[98]

One might ask why it is only Peter who mentions Jesus preaching to those who had died. Could it be because Jesus shared what happened with his friend when he met him after his resurrection? Peter needed to be reassured that there was yet hope—even for him, the weak one, the one who had denied the master he loved.

The apocryphal books the *Gospel of Nicodemus* and the *Shepherd of Hermes* elaborate the descent into hell into the theme of the "Harrowing of Hell," which forms the basis of the Eastern Orthodox Church's Easter liturgy, in which Hades itself is given a voice:

> Today doth Hades groaning cry, "My might is sacrificed. The Shepherd is crucified and Adam raised. Them that I ruled I have lost. Them I devoured in my power I have disgorged them all. The Crucified hath opened the graves, and the power of death hath no avail.[99]

The cry of victory reaches an ecstatic crescendo in the chant that is repeated over and over again: "Christ is risen from the dead, trampling down death by death and upon those in the tombs bestowing life."

There is little doubt that the myth of the harrowing of hell has been elaborated in the apocryphal legends, and some Christians view the idea with suspicion, but it evokes a profound understanding of Christ's victory over sin, death, and hell, which is one of the earliest and most

96. In Acts 2:27, Peter quotes Ps 16:10, "you will not abandon me to the grave, nor let your Holy One see decay." Rom 10:6–7 and Eph 4:8–10 (quoting Ps 68:18) are also used to support the concept that Christ descended to hell or Hades.

97. "Its first appearance in a credal statement is in the Symbol of Sirmium in A.D. 359–60, and its first appearance in the Apostles' Creed is in AD 570" (Barclay, *Apostles' Creed*, 98).

98. Calvin, *Calvin's Institutes*, bk. 2, ch. 16, 266–67.

99. Norwich Cathedral, "Visitors' Trail 15: Reliquary Niche and Icon of the Resurrection," http://www.cathedral.org.uk/visitorinfo/map-info.aspx?m=1&l=15&p=394.

powerful views of the cross, and was a dominant theme in the theology of Martin Luther.

Jesus has authority over demons and has tied up the "strong man," [100] and Paul expresses Christ's victory in rich language and vivid metaphor:

> God made you alive with Christ. He forgave all our sins, having cancelled the written code, with its regulation that was against us and that stood opposed to us; he took it away, nailing it to the cross. And having disarmed the powers and authorities, he made a public spectacle of them triumphing over them by the cross. [101]

And again: "For he must reign until he has put all his enemies under his feet. The last enemy to be destroyed is death . . . so that God may be all in all." [102] Similarly, in Revelation John hears the triumphant Christ say, "I am the living One; I was dead, and behold I am alive for ever and ever! And I hold the keys of death and Hades." [103] Surely the Christ who died for the sins of the world will use those keys to open Hades and let its victims out rather than to lock them in! But we must be cautious here. In the next chapter (p.194–8), we see that some *are* excluded from heaven—at least until they are cleaned up.

Towards the end of Revelation, the devil is thrown into the lake of burning sulfur; then the dead are judged; "then death and Hades were thrown into the lake of fire." [104] The ultimate victory over hell is its destruction—a victory reflected in early hymns and liturgies such as the Homily of Melito of Sardis:

> I am he who put down death,
> and triumphed over the enemy,
> and trod upon Hades,
> and bound the Strong One
> and brought man safely home to the heights of the heavens. [105]

---

100. Mark 3:27 and parallels; "the strong man" is Satan.

101. Col 2:13–15.

102. 1 Cor 15:25–28.

103. Rev 1:17.

104. Rev 20:14.

105. This second-century hymn is quoted in Bernstein, *Formation of Hell*, 273. See chapter 1, (p. 25) but it is also relevant here.

The New Testament portrays Christ descending into hell as an *event* in time and space, but it can be seen as encompassing the whole of time. C.S. Lewis imagines a conversation where George MacDonald says:

> "It was not [just] once long ago that He did it [descended to hell]. Time does not work that way when once ye have left the Earth. All moments that have been or shall be were, or are, present in the moment of His descending. There is no spirit in prison to whom He did not preach."
>
> "And some hear him?"
>
> "Aye."[106]

The New Testament scholar John A. T. Robinson (1919–1983) sees hell as overcome. He writes: "The world *has been* redeemed. Hell has been harrowed, and none can finally make it their home. The shadow of the Cross has fallen aslant it: the halls of death are condemned property."[107]

On Easter Saturday 2008, Archbishop of York John Sentamu wrote a charming article in the *Daily Telegraph* about a young boy who was asked where he thought Jesus had gone after he died on Good Friday. The boy replied, "Jesus went to the darkest places of Hell." Then he paused and added, "He was looking for his friend, Judas."[108]

Maybe that boy, in all his simplicity, understood what the theologian Karl Barth discusses in a long section on "the rejected." He focuses on Judas as the model of one truly elected (because he was a chosen disciple) but also rejected (because of his betrayal and ultimate rejection of Jesus). He argues:

> It is a serious matter to be threatened by hell, sentenced to hell, worthy of hell, and already on the road to hell. On the other hand . . . we actually know of only one certain triumph of hell— the handing over of Jesus—and that this triumph of hell took place in order that it would never again be able to triumph over anyone . . . Scripture speaks of countless men, as it does of Judas, in such a way that we must assume that they have lived and died without even the possibility, let alone the fulfillment,

---

106. Lewis, *Great Divorce*, 114.

107. Robinson, *In the End God*, 132–33.

108. John Sentamu, "Easter Story Can Help Us Overcome Politics of Fear, Says Archbishop of York John Sentamu," *The Telegraph*, March 22, 2008, http://www.telegraph.co.uk/news/uknews/1582447/Easter-story-can-help-us-overcome-politics-of-fear-says-Archbishop-of-York-John-Sentamu.html.

of any saving repentance ... Whatever God may inflict on them, He certainly does not inflict what He inflicted on Himself by delivering up Jesus Christ, for He has done it for them in order that they should not suffer the judgment which accompanies the cleansing of the world's sin . . . in view of the efficacy of this event, we must not lose sight of the hope of the future deliverance of the rejected at the very frontier of perdition.[109]

Conclusion

The historic creeds simply state that Jesus will "judge the quick and the dead," and to leave the outcome to him—as indeed we must. The Judge is the Savior, and he will do what is right.

But if, as we have considered over the course of this chapter, *sheol* or Gehenna (Hades or hell) is remedial and cleansing, a place of purging with a chance to repent, a place of limited and just punishment graced with the continuing possibility of redemption (neither destruction nor everlasting punishment with no end and no escape), then those passages which speak of the final redemption of *all* mankind will be fulfilled, as well as the passages that undoubtedly suggest that there will be some, even many, who will go to hell. Such an interpretation makes sense of much that otherwise seems not to make sense, and it reconciles Scriptures that otherwise seem to be irreconcilable.

We have free will, and it is possible to reject God, so hell exists because hell is due to the rejection of God, but we have wondered whether it will be possible to continue to reject him forever, in full view of the holiness and pure *love* of God in the face of Jesus Christ.

We cannot say that all *must* be saved, for this is to deny free will, but I think that it is legitimate to hope that all *may* be saved. We must not despair of anyone's salvation but instead must long and pray expectantly for the reconciliation of all without exception.

There is no place for some terrible concentration camp or prison called hell, forever lurking in a remote corner out of sight of the land of the free. Hell will finally be destroyed—and the gates of heaven forever kept open. If, perhaps, there are some who resist God's love for eternity and eternally refuse to be cleansed, they will finally be destroyed with the hell that they have chosen.

109. Barth, *Doctrine of God*, 496–97. The whole section on "the determination of the rejected" in ibid., 449–506, is relevant.

7

God Will Be All in All

For Thine Is the Kingdom, the Power,
and the Glory Forever and Ever

I cannot tell how he will win the nations,
how he will claim his earthly heritage,
how satisfy the needs and aspirations
of east and west, of sinner and of sage.
But this I know, all flesh shall see his glory,
and he shall reap the harvest he has sown,
and some glad day his sun will shine in splendour
when he the saviour, saviour of the world is known.
—W. Y. FULLERTON (1857–1932)

All shall be well, and all manner of things shall be well.
—JULIAN OF NORWICH

Christ is risen from the dead, trampling down death by death, and to those
in the tombs he has given life.
—ORTHODOX RESURRECTION HYMN

MANY ANCIENT SOCIETIES BURIED their dead with elaborate provision for an afterlife, especially for those who were rich, particularly for the rulers (who are usually, by fair means or foul, among the richest).

The pyramids of ancient Egypt are a well-known example. The Egyptians hoped to spend unending life with the sun god, Osiris. However, this hope would only be fulfilled if the person passed a strenuous judgment and completed an arduous and complicated journey, which was provided for by the extravagant grave goods placed in the tomb.

Do the widespread, if varied, hopes for an afterlife of some kind simply demonstrate that most of us want to hang on to life for as long as we can, despite its pains and problems, and that we dread the finality of death for ourselves and those we care about?

Or do they point to an underlying reality? Are we "hardwired" to hope for some kind of continuity beyond the grave? Christians might hope that this is the case because we are made in the image of God and in some way have the stamp of immortality on our souls and spirits.

Whatever the reason, the widespread belief in an afterlife shows that human beings have always had theories about what lies beyond the grave.

Sheol

Interestingly, the Old Testament contains no traces of the complicated Egyptian ideas about the afterlife. Throughout most of the period, judgment was expected to work out during earthly life itself, and the dead (good and bad alike) were thought to "descend" into *sheol*[1]—literally descend, because *sheol* was thought to be the shadowy and uninviting abode of the dead located somewhere below the surface of the earth.[2] *Sheol* sometimes simply means "the grave" or "death" itself.[3] Because the differentiation of meanings is often difficult and highly subjective, some modern versions simply and wisely retain *sheol* without attempting to translate it.

1. Most of the ideas covered by the Hebrew *Sheol* are also found in the Assyro-Babylonian descriptions of the state of the dead in their various legends (*Jewish Encyclopaedia*, s.v. "sheol," accessed October 18, 2014, http://www.jewishencyclopedia.com/articles/13563-sheol).

2. The fact that *sheol* was below the earth could reflect the fact that the deceased were buried in subterranean tombs.

3. For example, Gen 37:35; Isa 38:10; Hos 13:14.

God was believed to continue to rule over *sheol* and to sometimes save his servants from its clutches.[4] Towards the end of the Old Testament period, a belief in resurrection and a more robust hope for life after death developed,[5] but Daniel 12:1–3 is the only passage in the Old Testament suggesting a postmortem judgment with the possibility of different destinations for the faithful and the wicked.

William Barclay explains this progression of ideas:

> God is not only the God of all the earth, but also the God of all the universe. Once that is seen, there can be no part of the universe which is separate from God, and therefore no room for a *Sheol* which is separate from God. So there emerges the idea that death cannot separate us from the God of Heaven and earth, and therefore that there is a life to come.[6]

Between the Old and New Testaments, the belief in an afterlife became more clearly articulated. Thus, the book of Enoch speaks of *sheol* giving back its dead,[7] and in the Psalms of Solomon we read: "They that fear the Lord shall rise unto eternal life; their life shall be in the light and it will never cease."[8]

The New Testament Picture of the Resurrection and Eternal Life

By the time of Christ, many but not all Jews believed that after the judgment there would be a resurrection of those who were deemed worthy.[9] God would raise all Israel, perhaps even all humans, from the dead and create a new world for them to live in. This hope was not the Greek idea of spiritual immortality, in which the body dies but the spirit continues in some ethereal way (which many people today still think of as "life after death"), but was instead a robust idea of a *bodily resurrection.*

---

4. For example, 1 Sam 2:6; Ps 139:8; Prov 15:11; Hos 13:14; Amos 9:2.

5. For example, Job 19:25–26; Isa 26:19.

6. Barclay, *Apostles' Creed*, 296–97.

7. En. 51:1–2.

8. *Pss. Sol.* 3:12.

9. Notably, the Pharisees believed in resurrection, but the Sadducees did not (Matt 22:23; Acts 4:2; 23:7–8).

Many Jews, and later Muslims, came to believe that the judgment would take place at the site of Mount Moriah,[10] where the Holy of Holies of Solomon's temple was situated, which is now the site of the Muslim shrine known as the Dome of the Rock ("the Rock" being Mount Moriah). Many Jews and Muslims therefore want to be buried as close to this holy site as possible, in a sort of grandstand seat with the best chance for a favorable judgment at the resurrection.[11]

The concept of resurrection was dramatically enhanced when it was claimed by Jesus' followers that he had risen from death. This was presented not as some inspiring myth, but as a sober *historical fact* that amazed those who saw him in his new but strange risen body.[12]

The central message of the apostles was the announcement that Jesus Christ had risen. So it was that Peter said, "God has raised this Jesus to life, and we are all witnesses of the fact . . . God has made this Jesus, whom you crucified, both Lord and Christ."[13] Paul summarized his message to the Athenians, who were steeped in Greek philosophy but totally ignorant of the Jewish roots of the emerging Christianity, by saying, "God . . . has set a day when he will judge the world with justice by the man he has appointed. He has given proof of this to all men by raising him from the dead."[14]

We may perhaps smile at some of the ideas of ancient peoples, and perhaps there were those who recognized that the elaborate preparations made for their dead were based on mythical stories and hopeful fantasies rather than historical facts, but the writers of the gospels are at pains to present their stories as *facts*. So it is that Paul emphasizes the importance of the historical basis for the gospel:

> We have testified about God that he raised Christ from the dead.
> But he did not raise him if in fact the dead are not raised. For if
> the dead are not raised, then Christ has not been raised either.
> And if Christ has not been raised, your faith is futile; you are still
> in your sins. Then those also who have fallen asleep in Christ

10. *Moriah* means "the Lord Provides"; it is believed to be the site of the mountain on which Abraham was about to offer his son Isaac when the Lord provided a ram which he was able to offer to God instead of Isaac (Gen 22:1–14).

11. This belief is one of the factors that have led to much rivalry—and many wars—for the possession of Jerusalem and jurisdiction over it.

12. See all four Gospels and nearly all the sermons in Acts and 1 Cor. 15:1–12.

13. Acts 2:32, 36.

14. Acts 17: 31.

are lost. If only for this life we have hope in Christ, we are to be pitied more than all men.

But Christ has indeed been raised from the dead, the first-fruits of those who have fallen asleep. For since death came through a man, the resurrection of the dead comes also through a man. For as in Adam all die, so in Christ all will be made alive.[15]

Paul looked forward to a final resurrection when the dead would rise in renewed and improved bodies—for who would want to rise in a worn-out body, crippled with fatal disease? "The body that is sown is perishable, it is raised imperishable; it is sown in weakness, it is raised in power; it is sown a natural body, it is raised a spiritual body."[16]

This has always been hard to believe. Paul knew when he wrote those words, just as we know now in the twenty-first century, that death is the end of life, is permanent, and (unless the body is rapidly embalmed or frozen) the stinking process of corruption soon sets in. Though the Jews and the gospel writers knew all these things just as well as we do, they claimed that Jesus' tomb was empty because he had risen from death and that he appeared to many people in a new strange body—a body that could appear and disappear, yet could eat and be touched. This was the anchor of their faith and the central plank of their preaching.

Theologian N. T. Wright aims to approach the Bible with the rigor of a historian. He has written widely in defense of the historicity of the resurrection, notably in his scholarly work *The Resurrection of the Son of God*, and also in *Surprised by Hope*, written under the more informal name of Tom Wright because it is geared towards the more general reader. He robustly argues that if Jesus had *not* risen from the dead, then he would have been, like many others around the first century BC and the first century AD, a *failed* messiah:

Crucifixion meant that the kingdom hadn't come, not that it had. Crucifixion of a would-be Messiah meant that he wasn't the Messiah, not that he was. When Jesus was crucified, every single disciple knew what it meant: we backed the wrong horse. The game is over . . . they were lucky to escape with their own lives . . . The early Christian future hope centred firmly on the resurrection.[17]

15. 1 Cor 15:15–22.

16. 1 Cor 15:42–44.

17. Wright, *Surprised by Hope*, 51–52.

In chapters 3 and 4 of *Surprised by Hope*, Wright marshals an array of arguments to support the claim that the resurrection was an event that *happened*, changing everything. Without the resurrection, there would certainly be no Christian church making its apparently preposterous claims that Jesus had risen—a faith that no persecution could shake.[18] Paul suffered a decade of conflict, persecution, shipwreck, floggings, and imprisonments, and he writes to the Philippians from house imprisonment in Rome with faith undimmed, but compared to the ringing proclamation of his first letter to the Corinthians quoted above, there is a hint of hesitation as he muses: "I want to know Christ and the power of his resurrection and the fellowship of sharing in his sufferings, becoming like him in his death, and so, somehow to attain to the resurrection from the dead."[19]

Our God is a God who suffers with us and redeems us. He is a God of resurrection, the living God who continually restores and recreates, and there are many glimpses in both the Old and New Testaments of a time when the world will be totally restored, renewed, and cleansed from sin, death, and corruption, when all humankind will worship God.

Before we move on to look at some of these biblical images, it is worth reminding ourselves that an important result of the concept of resurrection of the body—as contrasted with the Platonic idea of the immortality of the soul—is that there is a "sense of continuity as well as discontinuity between the present world . . . and the future, whatever it shall be, with the result that what we do in the present is seen to matter enormously."[20] The belief that there will be a resurrection followed by judgment should strongly motivate us to work to transform the earth and to work for the kingdom of God to come "on earth as it is in heaven." (See chapter 2).

A World Restored (the *Apokatastasis*)

After Jesus' resurrection, he appeared to the disciples over a period of about six weeks. As he prepared to leave them, the disciples asked, "Lord, are you at this time going to restore the kingdom to Israel?" The Messiah

18. There were people in the first century who claimed that Nero returned to life, and in the twentieth and twenty-first centuries there are those who believe that Elvis Presley has returned to life—but as far as I know, nobody has been prepared to die for these claims.

19. Phil 3:10–11.

20. Wright, *Surprised by Hope*, 37.

was expected to do just that, and Jesus replied, "It is not for you to know the times or dates the Father has set by his own authority. But you will receive power when the Holy Spirit comes upon you."[21] Soon after the promised Spirit had been given, Peter told the crowd that "Jesus . . . must remain in heaven until the time of *universal restoration* that God announced long ago through his holy prophets."[22] The Greek word that Peter used is a form of ἀποκατάστασις (*apokatastasis*) and is the only time the word is used in the New Testament; the concept draws on many Old Testament prophetic pictures and visions of a final restoration and renewal of all things, which we will explore below.

From about the sixth century, the word *apokatastasis* was sometimes used as a shorthand for the doctrine of universalism, which was widely debated in the early centuries of the church. For example, in the second century AD, Origen emphasized the *apokatastasis*, and he is widely quoted as teaching that even the devil would ultimately be saved, but he only wondered whether this might be a possibility and did not teach it as a dogma.[23]

However, these later debates were not what Peter had in mind; he was referring to the widespread Jewish hope that the Messiah would restore Jerusalem and the fortunes of the Jewish nation. The prophets had also expressed a wider hope that "the nations" that were then hostile to the Jewish people and to God would ultimately turn to belief in the God

---

21. Acts 1:6–8.

22. Acts 3:21.

23. "Origen's thinking was often quite speculative. He was often accused of teaching that the devil *would* be saved, but in his *Dialogue with Candidas* he had claimed only that that the devil *could* be saved [because of his free will, and God's eternal love], not that he *would* be saved" (Trigg, *Origen*, 139).

"Origen believed that because God is good, the process of redemption, which is not confined to this life on earth and does not only include the human race but angels also, will go on and on until God has won back all souls to himself, including even the devil [perhaps] . . . who retains freedom and rationality and must therefore have still the power to respond to the wonder of divine mercy. Because freedom is essential to the very constitution of rational beings, universal restoration cannot be asserted to be a predictable end in the sense that the cosmos is moving towards it by an irresistible evolution. But only a belief in total depravity so drastic as to make redemption an act of omnipotent power rather than gracious love can justify the denial of universalist hope. God never abandons anyone. The fire of his judgment is purifying and his punishment is always remedial, even if it may be extremely severe. And because freedom is eternal, even at the summit of the process when all have been restored [Origen speculates] that there may be another Fall, so that a series of unending cycles stretches out before the mind" (Chadwick, *History and Thought*, 192).

of the Jews and be redeemed. Clearly, none of this had happened during Jesus' lifetime, and his final words placed that hope in an unknown time in the future[24]—a time Christians are still waiting for, and a time that is largely encompassed by the ideas surrounding "the Day of the Lord" we looked at in chapter 5.

The Old Testament prophecies, though often very harsh, are also sprinkled with promises and visions of restoration, which Peter would have known. It will be helpful to look at some of them:

1. Psalm 22

This psalm, which amazingly foreshadows many of the traumas of the crucifixion, ends with a promise that:

> All the ends of the earth
> will remember and turn to the Lord,
> and all the families of the nations
> will bow down before him,
> for dominion belongs to the Lord
> And he rules over the nations.
> All the rich of the earth will feast and worship
> all who go down to the dust will kneel before him- . . .
> for he has done it.[25]

The psalmist proclaims, "for he has done it," but does not tell us what it is he has done. We are reminded of Jesus' cry from the cross: "it is finished,"[26] a transaction had been completed, and redemption had been accomplished. The resurrection revealed that the suffering of Christ on the cross was in fact a victory remembered by "all the ends of the earth," surprisingly foreseen in this psalm.

2. Isaiah

Isaiah prophesied that plenty of catastrophic and calamitous judgments would fall on both Israel and the nations, but like shafts of light, pictures

24. The earlier New Testament writers expected Christ to return very soon, but as this did not happen, their expectations became more distant.

25. Ps 22:27–31.

26. John 19:30.

of wonderful restoration break through. Faithless Israel is still God's servant and will be restored by the ideal servant—the "suffering servant," the
Messiah (fulfilled, Christians believe, by Jesus): "Here is my servant . . . he
will bring justice to the nations."[27]

Isaiah sees everyone on earth ultimately responding to the call of
the Lord and worshipping him:

> Turn to me and be saved,
> all you ends of the earth;
> for I am God and there is no other . . .
> Before me every knee will bow;
> by me every tongue will swear.
> they will say of me, "In the Lord alone
> are righteousness and strength."[28]

He portrays nature at peace within herself:

> The wolf will live with the lamb,
> the leopard will lie down with the goat,
> the calf and the lion and the yearling together;
> and a little child will lead them.
> The cow will feed with the bear,
> their young will lie down together,
> and the lion will eat straw like the ox.
> The infant will play near the hole of the cobra,
> and the young child put his hand into the viper's nest.
> They will neither harm nor destroy
> on all my holy mountain,
> for the earth will be full of the knowledge of the Lord
> as the waters cover the sea.[29]

In another picture, humanity is included in the vision of restoration:

> Behold, I will create
> new heavens and new earth.

---

27. Isa 42:1–4.

28. Isa 45:22–24.

29. Isa 11:6–9. Paul too speaks of the restoration of nature: "the creation itself will
be liberated from its bondage to decay and brought into the glorious freedom of the
children of God" (Rom 8:21).

The former things will not be remembered, nor will they come
to mind.

But be glad and rejoice for ever in what I will create,

for I will create Jerusalem to be a delight

and its people a joy . . .

The sound of weeping and of crying

will be heard in it no more.

Never again will there be in it

an infant who lives but a few days,

or an old man who does not live out his years;

He who dies at a hundred

will be thought a mere youth.[30]

Isaiah sees nations streaming to Jerusalem, and "from one New
Moon to another and from one Sabbath to another, all mankind will come
and bow down before me," says the Lord.[31] But Isaiah probably had no
concept of life after death, and his visions may have meant only that those
who had *survived* God's destructive punishment would be restored.[32]

3. Jeremiah

Jeremiah sees restoration after the calamity of exile:

"Only if the heavens above can be measured

and the foundation of the earth below be searched out

will I reject all the descendants of Israel

because of all they have done," declares the Lord. The days are
coming . . . when this city will be rebuilt for me . . . the whole valley where dead bodies and ashes are thrown . . . will be holy to
the Lord. The city will never again be uprooted or demolished.[33]

This prophecy is particularly poignant because the "valley where
dead bodies and ashes are thrown" was Gehenna, which became the
metaphor for hell. (See previous chapter, p. 150–51)

---

30. Isa 65:17-20.

31. Isa 66:23.

32. This is sometimes called "remnant theology."

33. Jer 31:37-40.

4. Ezekiel

Ezekiel paints wonderful word-pictures of restoration. Even Sodom, which was a byword for a city utterly destroyed because of sin, and Samaria, which was scorned because of its people were of mixed ancestry and worshipped at Mount Gerizim instead of Jerusalem, are both restored, along with Judah:

> I will restore the fortunes of Sodom and her daughters and of Samaria and her daughters, and your fortunes along with them ... Sodom with her daughters will return to what they were before, and you and your daughters will return to what you were before ... I will deal with you as you deserve, because you have despised my oath by breaking the covenant. Yet I will remember the covenant I made with you in the days of your youth, and I will establish an everlasting covenant with you.[34]

Ezekiel sees other lovely visions of restoration that are described towards the end of his book. In chapter 37 he sees a vision of a valley of dead, dry bones that come together into a great army into which the spirit of God breathes new life. The immediate meaning of this vision is that the people will return to their land after the exile in Babylon. A few chapters later in chapter 47, he sees a wonderful deep river flowing out from the temple and bringing life and refreshment even to the Dead Sea. Again, this is a promise of renewal and restoration for the people of Israel. Unlike the great prophecies of universal restoration in Isaiah, Ezekiel does not see restoration spreading to other nations; however, like many biblical prophecies, we can receive these visions ourselves as pictures of renewal and restoration in a wider sense.

5. Amos

Amos pronounces many severe judgments both on Israel and the surrounding nations, but his book draws to a close with a promise that "in that day I will restore David's fallen tent. I will repair its broken places, restore its ruins and build it as it used to be."[35] The book ends with a lovely vision of nature being so abundant that the reaper is overtaken by the ploughman and the planter by the one treading grapes, and with the exiled people returning and rebuilding the ruined cities.

34. Ezek 16:53, 55, 59–60.
35. Amos 9:11–15.

Some of the Old Testament prophecies of redemption refer to the rebuilding of Jerusalem, while others refer to return from exile (which in the minds of many Jews has never fully happened, because the prophecies have not been fully fulfilled). Isaiah's visions are expanded to include all the nations and nature herself.

Were these images a sort of mirage to keep the Jewish nation (and ourselves, now in the twenty-first century) going through the desert of real life on earth? Or can we think of them as glimpses of a future restoration of nature and all of humanity—indeed, of the whole cosmos?

The New Heaven and New Earth in the New Testament

Isaiah speaks of a new heaven and a new earth,[36] and the picture is taken up and expanded in Rev 21 and 22.

God said, "I am making everything new!" because "the first heaven and the first earth had passed away."[37] There will have been a sifting and sorting, a smelting and purging, a redemption and restoration, and what will be left is what cannot be shaken any further.[38] Purified and holy, it will be like a pure bride, so John sees "the Holy City, the new Jerusalem, coming down out of heaven from God, prepared as a bride beautifully dressed for her husband."[39]

The picture seems to be of a renewal of earth, as heaven "comes down" to join with earth and transform it. I will pick out a few points from John's visionary description:

36. Isa 65:17.

37. Rev 21:1, 5.

38. Heb 12:26– 28 speaks of the heavens being shaken as well as the earth, "for our God is a consuming fire" (p. 123 f.) and Hag 2:6–7 similarly speaks about God shaking the heavens and the earth, the sea and the dry land, and the nations, "and the desired of all nations will come."

39. Rev 21:2.

Heaven Will Be More Wonderful
Than We Can Imagine

I can get myself into stupid dead ends if I start thinking too literally about heaven (rather like the Sadducees in their cynical questions put to Jesus).[40] We must look behind the images to see what they are pointing to.

John describes the heavenly city, shaped like a massive cube about 1,400 miles long on every side, with 200 foot walls made of "pure gold, as pure as glass."[41] The cubic structure denotes symmetry and purity, and on the twelve gates are the names of the twelve tribes of Israel. This is a vision of God's people, Israel, restored, refined, and redeemed.

The city shines with the glory of God "like jasper, clear as crystal."[42] It is decorated with precious stones and streets of gold "like transparent glass."[43] All this sounds overpowering, almost tacky—like some churches I have seen that are so full of gilt paint that it is a restful relief to get out into wholesome sunshine, blue sky, and green grass. But of course John is using vivid figurative language: clues and pointers for things that are wonderful, clear, pure, and glorious beyond our earthbound imagination, accustomed as we are to dirt, grime, and things getting spoiled. The vision is trying to convey a pureness and perfection that is difficult for our earthbound souls to imagine:

> What will the resurrection be like? Indescribable, like heaven itself, but one can draw analogies: If death is like being stripped naked, the resurrection will be like being clothed in glory. If death is like returning to the soil, the resurrection will be like the quickening of the seed. If death mars creation, the resurrection will perfect it, restoring the image of God in man so that we may gaze "with open face" on the divine glory and be changed into its likeness (2 Cor 3:18). Immortality of the soul is not enough; soul and body together must be "swallowed up by life" (2 Cor 5:4).[44]

40. In Luke 20:27–33 and parallels, the Sadducees, trying to trick Jesus, pose a question about seven brothers who all married the same woman, though she failed to conceive by any of them: "now then, at the resurrection whose wife will she be, since the seven were married to her?"

41. Rev 21:15–21.

42. Rev 21:11.

43. Rev 21:21.

44. Zaleski and Zaleski, *Book of Heaven*, 373–74.

Sometimes on a lovely summer evening when everything is bathed in golden light, when the grass is greener than green, and everything glows golden in the low light of the sun, I have wondered: Is this a glimpse of the golden radiance of heaven?

In *The Great Divorce*, C. S. Lewis pictures everything in heaven to be *more real* than on earth. The people are more solid, the grass hard and sharp to tender, unaccustomed feet. A process of adaptation is needed, even by the redeemed, for "Heaven is reality itself, all that is fully real is Heavenly. For all that can be shaken will be shaken and only the unshakable remains."[45]

God's Glory Fills Everything; Sorrow and Pain Has Been Purged

John "heard a loud voice from the throne saying, 'Now the dwelling of God is with men, and he will live with them. They will be his people, and God himself will be with them and be their God. He will wipe every tear from their eyes. There will be no more death or mourning or crying or pain, for the old order of things has passed away.'"[46]

God's glory and love is revealed, unfettered by pain and evil, which is the reason everything is clear as crystal, letting the light through, transcendent in its beauty.

The thirsty can drink freely from the spring of the water of life, echoing the earlier promise that "never again will they hunger; never again will they thirst."[47] Physical and spiritual needs are fully satisfied. There will be no more longing after an apparently capricious, distant God, because he is no longer hidden. There is no need for a temple in the city "because the Lord God Almighty and the Lamb are its temple. The city does not need the sun or the moon to shine on it, for the glory of God gives it light, and the lamb is its lamp."[48]

45. Lewis, *Great Divorce*, 63.

46. Rev 21:3–4.

47. Rev 21:6, 7:16.

48. Rev 21:22–23.

There Is No Evil in the Cleansed City

"The cowardly, the unbelieving, the vile, the murderers, the sexually immoral, those who practice magic arts, the idolaters and all liars—their place will be in the fiery lake of burning sulfur," and so "nothing impure will ever enter it [the city], nor will anyone who does what is shameful or deceitful, but only those whose names are written in the Lamb's book of life."[49]

Now we see the reason for hell—to deal justly with evil, and thus keep heaven crystal-pure. If it were not for this "place," this "fiery lake" where evil is dealt with, heaven would rapidly become just as polluted and permeated with sin and evil as this life is, and so would cease to be heaven. (It is only possible to speak in earthly terms as we seek to deal with realities that we can only begin to understand in terms of metaphor.) God's "great double work of redemption and vengeance"[50] continues to keep heaven purged of sin. In chapter 5 we looked at the way fire is often used as a metaphor for God's wrath, his cleansing and purifying power, and the way he deals with evil, "for our 'God is a consuming fire,'"[51] and in chapter 6, I postulated that hell might be a place of cleansing.

Is it fanciful to see this lake of fire as a sort of cleansing anteroom to heaven, keeping it free from pollution? A very banal analogy comes to mind—the strong antiseptic footbaths visitors had to go through before entering a farmyard when foot-and-mouth disease was rife, as a precaution aimed at preventing the spread of the disease. Or one might adopt an analogy from computing; perhaps we can think of hell as a sort of "firewall," protecting the purity of heaven.

Is it possible to take the view that both "those who overcome" in Rev 21:7 and "the multitude who have come through the great tribulation" in 7:14 include those who have been through the fires of hell, and been cleansed by it?[52]

49. Rev 21:8, 27.

50. Motyer, *Isaiah: An Introduction*, 18.

51. Deut 4:24, quoted in Heb 12:29.

52. The more usual interpretation is that "the multitude who have come through the great tribulation" (Rev 7:14) are those who have been sanctified because of their faith in Christ at a time when the church was being persecuted. They are often thought to represent the same group as the 144,000 in Rev 7:4–8 (representing idealized Israel—widened into the multitude to include the idealized church). The multitude has sometimes been taken to be martyrs, but this is unlikely because they are such a vast crowd and because the martyrs had already been seen under the altar in Rev 6:9–11.

I am suggesting that Christ's sanctifying grace stretches beyond the grave, and

Whatever the merits or demerits of this interpretation, John see death and Hades finally destroyed.[53] If, perhaps, there are some who resist God's love for eternity, and forever refuse to be cleansed, then surely they will finally be destroyed with the hell that they have chosen. There is no room for an everlasting hell.

The Nations Will Walk by the Light of the Glory of God and Be Healed

For most of Revelation, the nations and their kings have been hostile. They have shared in the idolatry and economic violence of Babylon; they have oppressed and opposed God, his purposes and his people. But the earlier hints of God's wider redeeming purpose now come fully into play. The witness of the martyr-church in chapter 11 resulted in the nations, which had been raging against God, coming instead to give him glory (Rev 11:13). Now here they come in procession.[54]

In Revelation chapter 19, John had seen the nations being "struck down" by the rider on the white horse—who clearly represents Jesus—for he "is called Faithful and True," and "with justice he judges and makes war . . . and his name is the Word of God," and he "treads the winepress of the fury of the wrath of God Almighty."[55]

If we had finished reading Revelation at the end of chapter 19 with this devastating picture in mind, we might think that all the nations were doomed, but in the final picture of the new heaven and the new earth the vengeance is reversed, and we see the nations walking in the light of the glory of God and the Lamb and being healed by the leaves from the tree of life.[56]

"those who have come through the great tribulation," and "those who have overcome" includes those who have been redeemed through the cleansing fires of hell.

53. Rev 20:13. The Greek *Hades* is usually retained in modern versions, but is translated as "hell" in the Authorized Version.

54. Wright, *Revelation for Everyone*, 198–99.

55. Rev 19: 11–15.

56. Rev 21:23–24; 22:2. MacDonald outlines the final salvation of the nations in MacDonald, *The Evangelical Universalist*, 54–73, and interprets the book of Revelation from a universalist viewpoint in ibid., 106–32.

Once again, we see that vengeance is overcome by the redemptive power of God.

Only Those Whose Names Are Written in the Lamb's Book of Life Enter the City

We have seen that "nothing impure will ever enter the Holy City, nor will anyone who does what is shameful or deceitful, but only those whose names are written in the Lamb's book of life."[57] This is usually taken as a clear statement that there will be some who "make it" into the Holy City and some who are excluded, the assumption being that there are some whose names will *never* be written in the Book of Life. But I am warmed by Thomas Talbott's beguiling suggestion:

> Perhaps all the descendants of Adam . . . also go by a name that is not written in the Book of Life . . . Is "Abram" written there or "Abraham"? . . . People can receive a new name, and this is certainly consistent with the idea of a new birth or a new creation in Christ . . . Even though no new names are ever added, people can (as all Christians do) receive a new name, one that has always been written in the Book of Life from the foundation of the world.[58]

The Lamb was slain from the foundation of the world on behalf of the whole world, and I have been arguing that it is likely that God continues to seek and save the lost even beyond the grave. If this is the case, then that new name, which has always been written in the Book of Life from the foundation of the world, could be given even beyond the grave. Perhaps this is a case of special pleading, but we are of course using highly allegorical language—as John's language is throughout Revelation—and looking at the allegory through the lens of other Scriptures. This is very like the way that the New Testament writers sometimes treated the Old Testament.[59]

---

57. Rev 21:27.

58. Thomas Talbott, e-mail message to Gregory MacDonald, July 23, 2001, quoted in MacDonald, *Evangelical Universalist*, appendix 3.

59. For example, "our forefathers were all under the cloud and that they all passed through the sea. They were all baptized into Moses in the cloud and in the sea. They all ate the same spiritual food and drank the same spiritual drink for they drank from the spiritual rock that accompanied them, and that rock was Christ" (1 Cor. 10:1–4).

The Holy City Is Kept Pure, but
Its Gates Are Never Shut[60]

John declares that "Nothing impure will ever enter the city, nor will anyone who does what is shameful or deceitful," and "outside [the city] are
the dogs, those who practice magic arts, the sexually immoral, the murderers, the idolaters and everyone who loves and practices falsehood."[61]
At this point we may wonder whether anybody at all will ever enter
this Holy City. For who has not at some time been angry or had impure
thoughts (which Jesus said is as bad as murder or the act of adultery)?[62]
Who has never told a lie? Never put self or material gain on the throne
of his or her life? Of course we know from the rest of the New Testament
that indeed there will be no one pure enough to be saved by his or her
own merits, but only those who are redeemed by the grace of Christ—a
grace received through faith.

And we can also take heart because "on no day will its [the Holy
City's] gates ever be shut."[63] No one will be shut out of heaven forever
because God will forever be seeking and saving the lost. Moreover, it is
Jesus, the redeemer of the world, who holds the keys of death and Hades,
not the all too fallible Peter, who represents the church.[64] Surely, having
died for the salvation of every member of the human race, he will not
want to lock outside forever a single soul for whom he has died. Perhaps
he will look at some with eyes of blazing judgment and love, then send
them back for a time of purification in order keep the Holy City holy.

Paul, in some of his letters, sees that ultimately Jesus will "reconcile
to himself all things, whether things on earth or things in heaven, by making peace through his blood, shed on the cross," and "that at the name of
Jesus every knee should bow, in heaven and on earth and under the earth,
and every tongue confess that Jesus Christ is Lord."[65] Such passages give
us grounds to hope that in the end no one will be permanently excluded.

---

60. Rev 21:25.

61. Rev 21:27, 22:15.

62. Matt 5:22, 28.

63. Rev 21:25.

64. Rev 1:18.

65. Col 1:20; Phil 2:10–11, echoing Isa 45:23.

Heaven Will Not Be Boring!

It is said that Origen feared that people might fall from heaven because of a surfeit of glory, and I can understand that fear! If I get too literal-minded, I cringe at the thought of heaven being like an endless worship session. I can cope with perhaps twenty minutes of worship (and then only if the music is the kind I like), and perhaps that shows how unfitted I am for glory and why I have to remain a mysterian, unable to imagine the unimaginable (and I guess I am not alone in this).

Maybe heaven will be more like the garden of Eden, with redeemed mankind given the task of "tilling and keeping" the restored creation in order.[66] That resonates more readily with my earthbound soul and my love of nature and gardening than does the unearthly task of continuous ecstatic worship.

The "gardening metaphor" ties in with the appeal in the Lord's Prayer that "Your will be done on earth as in heaven," which was explored in chapter 2 when we looked at the importance of living and working for the kingdom of God in the here and now in quite practical ways. It also ties in with John's vision of the "new heaven and the new earth" being formed by the reuniting of heaven and earth as the holy city "*comes down to earth*," which Bishop James Jones nicely refers to as "the earthing of heaven."[67] (See p. 77).

There will be continuity between this world and the new creation in ways that we do not fully understand; perhaps it will be analogous to the continuity between Jesus' earthly body before death and that same body after the resurrection.

Tom Wright stresses that our understanding of the new creation shapes what we do now on earth:

> God's recreation of his wonderful world, which has begun with the resurrection of Jesus and continues mysteriously as God's people live in the risen Christ and by the Spirit in the present is not wasted. It will last all the way into God's new world. In fact it will be enhanced there . . . I have no idea what precisely this will mean in practice. I am putting up a signpost, not offering a photograph of what we will find when we get to where the signpost is pointing . . . In the new creation the ancient human mandate to look after the garden is dramatically reaffirmed . . .

66. Gen 1:28; 2:15.

67. Rev 21:2; Jones, *Jesus and the Earth*, 60ff.

The resurrection of Jesus is the reaffirmation of the goodness of creation . . . Creation is to be redeemed.[68]

This Hope of a New Heaven and Earth, with All Evil and Suffering Eliminated, Is Especially Precious to Those Who Suffer Now

Revelation was written at a time when the church was under intense persecution and is often treasured by those who are facing oppression. Of course, cynics often argue that this is the point: it is all delusion, wishful thinking, or a utopian dream of "pie in the sky when you die" to help people put up with trouble on earth. Or to use Marx's famous phrase, "Religion is the sigh of the oppressed creature, the heart of a heartless world, just as it is the spirit of a spiritless situation. It is the opium of the people." Marx has a point if Christians use their future hope as an excuse to do nothing now to mend the broken world, but as we have repeatedly seen, we should be motivated to try to mend the world in the here and now, with the future hope and the vision of how things could and should be to spur us on.

Our God offers a hope for the future that sustains those who are now being oppressed, as expressed in this lovely "Living Testimony" prayer from Burma, written by a persecuted Christian using the pen name "Pastor Simon":

> They call us displaced people
> But praise God: we are not misplaced.
> They say there is no hope for our future
> But praise God: our future is as bright as the promises of God.
> They say the life of our people is a misery
> But praise God: our life is a mystery.
> For what they say is what they see,
> And what they see is temporal.
> But ours is the eternal—
> All because we put ourselves
> In the hands of the God we trust.[69]

68. Wright, *Surprised by Hope*, 221–22.
69. Pastor Simon, "Living Testimony," in Cox and Rogers, *Stones Cry Out*, 11.

The Christian's hope points beyond this life. We have glimpses and premonitions, "signposts in the mist,"[70] pictures and metaphors to inspire and encourage us, but in the end we live in faith and *hope*: "Now faith is the assurance of things hoped for, the conviction of things not seen."[71]

If the great Christian doctrines of hope and salvation are true—hope in a God whose most profound and enduring attribute is love, hope of resurrection and the final restoration of all things, and hope of the ultimate triumph of good over evil—if these doctrines are true, then surely we can live in hope that in the end, when God's will is finally done, all people and all things will be redeemed, and God will be all in all.

---

70. Wright uses this evocative phrase several times in *Surprised by Hope*.

71. Heb 11:1.

Appendix

A Brief Look at the Possible Relevance of "Near-death Experiences"

A FRIEND OF MINE ended up intensive care, unconscious and in an extremely critical condition, due to complications following a routine operation. While she was in this state, she had a "near-death experience" that changed her life.

Up to that time she had been what one might call a "nominal Christian"—not an atheist or agnostic, you understand; if you had asked her, she would have said she believed in both God and Jesus, but this belief made no difference to her life. She did not go to church, read her Bible, pray, or try to serve God, but this "encounter with Jesus" (for that was what she believed it was) transformed her life. She became a passionate Christian, serving Jesus with unswerving loyalty and deep faith until her death over twenty years later.

Her experience was not unique.

There is much current interest in "near-death experiences" (NDEs), and many have been recorded in recent years, but there are also more ancient accounts.

Bede, in his *Ecclesiastical History* (completed in AD 731), recounts what would now be called an NDE, told to him by a monk called Drythelm:

> A man already dead returned to bodily life and related many
> notable things that he had seen . . . He fell ill and grew steadily
> worse until the crisis came, and in the early hours of one night
> he died. But at daybreak he returned to life . . . [He reassured

his wife,] "Do not be frightened; for I have truly risen from the grasp of death, and I am allowed to live among men again. But henceforward I must not live as I used to, and must adopt a very different way of life". . . Thus he related what he had seen: "He that led me had a shining countenance and a bright garment, and we went on silently, as I thought, toward the north-east. Walking on, we came to a vale of great breadth and depth, but of infinite length; on the left it appeared full of dreadful flames, the other side was no less horrid for violent hail and cold snow flying in all directions; both places were full of men's souls, which seemed by turns to be tossed from one side to the other, as it were by a violent storm . . . I began to think that this perhaps might be hell, of whose intolerable flames I had often heard tell. My guide, who went before me, answered to my thought, saying, 'Do not believe so, for this is not the hell you imagine.'"[1]

It turned out that Drythelm was in purgatory. Later he came to an even darker place, with masses of flames "rising as though from a great pit," "leaping up and falling back again into the depths of the chasm," "and as the tongues of flame rose, they were filled with the souls of men."

He saw souls dragged down howling by wicked spirits. Some of the dark spirits threatened to seize Drythelm and drag him down, but they "did not dare touch me." He saw what seemed to be a bright star shining in the gloom, and his guide reappeared. Then the evil spirits "scattered and took to flight." He was led out of the darkness into a beautiful, fragrant meadow filled with bright light, and the scent of flowers completely dispelled the stench of the previous darkness. He was led still farther on:

Farther on, I discovered before me a much more beautiful light, and therein heard sweet voices of persons singing, and so wonderful a fragrance proceeded from the place, that the other which I had before thought most delicious, then seemed to me but very indifferent; even as that extraordinary brightness of the flowery field, compared with this appeared mean and inconsiderable. When I began to hope we should enter that delightful place, my guide on a sudden stood still; and then turning back, led me back by the way we came.[2]

Perhaps this account bears the stamp of medieval beliefs, including fears of a very literal and almost physical purgatory and hell, but it is also

1. Bede, *Ecclesiastical History*, bk. 5, ch. 12, 284–85.
2. Ibid., 287.

remarkably similar to many modern NDEs. I have read or heard several modern accounts of a horrendously unpleasant hell-like experience, usually followed by a pleasant and beautiful "heavenly" experience.

Melvin Morse and Paul Perry's book *Transformed by the Light* is based on interviews with hundreds of children and adults who have experienced a near-death episode. Morse and Perry list nine traits of NDEs, though most people experience only one or two of these traits.

The following is a summary of their list, citing a typical example in each case:

1. *A sense of being dead*: but still being "totally and completely me" after a cardiac arrest.

2. *Peace and painlessness*: "I no longer felt fear, nor did I feel my body," as a housewife who "died" after an auto wreck explained.

3. *Out-of-body experience*: such as "looking down on myself in my hospital bed, [with] doctors and nurses moving busily around me" after a near-fatal reaction to medication.

4. *Tunnel experience*: "I felt myself being sucked up this tunnel . . . I had a sense of moving forward very rapidly," as one patient reported after being struck by lightning.

5. *People of light*: "I was met at the end of the tunnel by a bunch of people . . . all glowing from the inside like lanterns. The whole place was glowing in the same way, like everything in it was filled with light. I didn't know any of the people . . . but they all seemed to love me very much," in the words of a ten-year-old boy who experienced a cardiac arrest.

6. *A being of light*: or an experience of overwhelming love, or both. As one middle-aged woman described a childhood NDE, "It was warm and light in this garden, and it was beautiful. I looked around the garden and there was this Being. The garden was extraordinarily beautiful, but everything paled in his presence. I felt completely loved and completely nourished by him. It was the most delightful feeling I've ever known. Although it was several years ago, I can still feel that feeling."

7. *Life review*: a rapid review of good and bad things done or experienced. As an Ohio woman who had a NDE explained of her

experience, "I was the very people I hurt and I was the very people that I helped to feel good."

8. *Reluctance to return to earth and normal life*: "He [the being of light] told me I had to go back, that there was more work to be done. I was then sucked back into my body. There was no other way to describe it . . . For a moment I was angry at being brought back to life," in the words of a cardiologist who was resuscitated by one of his peers.

9. *Personality transformation after the event*: "The first thing I saw when I awoke . . . was a flower, and I cried. Believe it or not, I had never really seen a flower until I came back from death. One thing I learnt when I died was that we are all part of one big living universe. If we think we can hurt another person or another living being without hurting ourselves, we are sadly mistaken," as one sixty-two-year-old businessman said after surviving a cardiac arrest.

Such a transformation in personality is one of the most universal effects of an NDE, and it is the reason for Morse and Perry's choice of title: "They had nearly all died in very different ways. After talking with them I realized they had one important thing in common. *They were transformed . . .* Low death anxiety and a zest for life were common traits."[3]

In 1944, Dr. Carl Jung, the founder of analytical psychology, broke his foot. He writes that "this misadventure was followed by a heart attack. In a state of unconsciousness I experienced deliriums and visions which must have begun when I hung on the edge of death."[4] Jung describes a vision of the earth as if seen from space (interestingly, about two decades before photographs taken by astronauts became universally available). Jung continues to describe his experience, which might now be classified as an NDE:

> An entrance led into a small antechamber. To the right of the entrance, a black Hindu sat silently in a lotus posture upon a stone bench. He wore a white gown, and I knew he expected me . . . As I approached the steps leading up to the entrance into the rock, a strange thing happened: I had the feeling that everything was being sloughed away; everything I aimed at or wished for or thought, the whole phantasmagoria of earthly

3. Morse and Perry, *Transformed by the Light*, vii–x, 9. The rest of the book is an exploration of many case histories that illustrate the transformation of personality after NDE.

4. Jung, *Memories, Dreams, Reflections*, 320.

existence, fell away or was stripped from me—an extremely painful process. Nevertheless, something remained; it was as if I now carried along with me everything I had ever experienced or done, everything that had happened around me. I might also say: it was with me, and I was it . . . and I felt with great certainty: this is what I am. "I am this bundle of what has been, and what has been accomplished" . . . Everything seemed to be past; what remained was a 'fait accompli,' without any reference back to what had been. There was no longer any regret that something had dropped away or been taken away. On the contrary: I had everything that I was, and that was everything.[5]

This and other experiences left a profound mark on Jung, who became increasingly interested in dreams and symbols. He believed the human psyche exists in three parts: the ego (the conscious mind), the personal unconscious, and the collective unconscious, the latter being a sort of reservoir of all the experience and knowledge of the human species. To be psychologically healthy, Jung believed, a person's conscious and unconscious minds should be completely integrated so that the individual becomes his or her "true self." Analytical psychology aims to facilitate this process of integration.

In an article in *Triple Helix*, the magazine of the Christian Medical Fellowship, Dr. Alexander Bunn confirms that NDEs are common and are not simply hallucinations caused by the effects of drugs, but he advises caution in relying on NDEs as a source of revelation, warning us that we should not build doctrines around such experiences:

Near death experiences are surprisingly common, have standardised features, and are difficult to explain on the basis of drugs, endogenous endorphins, hypoxia, hallucinations or in terms of upbringing or culture. Recent research has led support to the belief that consciousness out-survives the brain, prompting speculation about the existence of an afterlife. But, even if NDEs do provide knowledge about the supernatural . . . the Bible warns of the dangers of relying on this form of revelation; spirits need to be tested.[6]

I agree with Bunn that we should be cautious in interpreting such accounts, but it seems valid to say that the growing literature about NDEs

5. Ibid., 321–22.
6. Bunn, "Near Death Experiences," 16.

seems to lend support to the possibility of some kind of life after earthly death, though it would be extremely foolish to build a doctrine on such subjective evidence. Many scientists believe that these experiences are simply due to the occipital lobe of the brain being deprived of oxygen— but in that case, why the life-changing effect that is so often described following an NDE?

The experience is usually a rapturously beautiful one that transforms the individual, who "returns to ordinary life" afterwards. As we have seen, this beautiful experience is sometimes preceded by one that is horrific and hell-like, but (at least in the accounts that I have come across) the beautiful experience that usually follows leaves its transforming mark on the person who has nearly died. This tends to offer support to my thesis that hell is a place of cleansing rather than of everlasting punishment.

Bibliography

Amos, Clare. *The Book of Genesis*. Epworth Commentaries. Peterborough, UK: Epworth, 2004.

Anderson, Ray Sherman. *Theology, Death and Dying*. Signposts in Theology. Oxford: Blackwell, 1986.

Atkinson, B. F. C. *Life and Immortality*. Taunton, UK: Goodman, 1968.

Augustine, Saint. "Sermons on Selected Lessons of the New Testament." In *The Early Church Fathers and Other Works*, edited by Philip Schaff. Edinburgh: Eerdmans, 1867. Reprint, Dallas, TX: The Electronic Bible and Eternal Word Television Network, 1996. http://www.theworkofgod.org/Library/Sermons/Agustine.htm.

Baker, John Austin. *The Foolishness of God*. London: Darton, Longman, & Todd, 1970.

Bainton, Roland Herbert. *Here I Stand: A Life of Martin Luther*. Mentor Book MT310. New York: Mentor, 1955.

Barclay, William. *The Apostles' Creed*. Louisville: Westminster John Knox, 2005.

———. *New Testament Words*. London: SCM, 1964.

———. *The Mind of St. Paul*. Pavenham, UK: St. Mark's, 2010.

Barr, James. *Holy Scripture: Canon, Authority, Criticism: The Sprunt Lectures Delivered at Union Theological Seminary, Richmond, Virginia, February 1982*. Oxford: Clarendon, 1983.

Barth, Karl. *The Doctrine of God: Part II*. Vol. 2 of *Church Dogmatics*. Edinburgh: T. & T. Clark, 1957.

———. *The Doctrine of Reconciliation*. Vol. 4 of *Church Dogmatics*. Edinburgh: T. & T. Clark, 1956–1969.

Baughen, Michael A., and Jubilate Hymns. *Hymns for Today's Church*. 2nd ed. London: Hodder & Stoughton, 1988.

Bede, the Venerable. *Ecclesiastical History of the English People: With Bede's Letter to Egbert*. Translated by Leo Sherley-Price and revised by R. E. Latham. Rev. ed. New York: Penguin, 1990.

Bell, Rob. *Love Wins: A Book about Heaven, Hell, and the Fate of Every Person Who Ever Lived*. New York: HarperOne, 2011.

Bernstein, Alan E. *The Formation of Hell: Death and Retribution in the Ancient and Early Christian Worlds*. London: University College London Press, 1993.

Blue, Lionel. *To Heaven with the Scribes and Pharisees: The Lord of Hosts in Suburbia; The Jewish Path to God*. London: Darton, Longman, & Todd, 1975.

Booth, Mark, and A. N. Wilson. *The Christian Testament Since the Bible: Part III.* Harmondsworth, UK: Penguin, 1985.

Bunn, Alexander. "Near Death Experiences." *Triple Helix Magazine*, 2001, 16.

Calvin, Jean. *Calvin's Institutes*. Grand Rapids: Associated Publishers and Authors, 1971.

Cassidy, Sheila. *Sharing the Darkness: The Spirituality of Caring.* London: Darton, Longman, & Todd, 1988.

Castle, Tony. *A Treasury of Prayer: Christian Prayer for All Occasions.* London: Hodder & Stoughton, 1993.

Cecil, Jessica. "The Destruction of Sodom and Gomorrah." *BBC History*, February 17, 2011. http://www.bbc.co.uk/history/ancient/cultures/sodom_gomorrah_01.shtml.

Chadwick, Henry. *History and Thought of the Early Church.* Collected Studies 164. London: Variorum Reprints, 1982.

Church of England. *Common Worship: Services and Prayers for the Church of England.* London: Church House, 2000.

Copan, Paul. *Is God a Moral Monster? Making Sense of the Old Testament God.* Grand Rapids: Baker, 2011.

Cox, Caroline, and Benedict Rogers. *The Very Stones Cry Out: The Persecuted Church: Pain, Passion and Praise.* New York: Continuum, 2011.

Dodd, C. H. *The Epistle of Paul to the Romans.* London: Fontana, 1959.

Dowsett, Dick, and Overseas Missionary Fellowship. *God, That's Not Fair! Understanding Eternal Punishment and the Christian's Urgent Mission.* Milton Keynes, UK: Authentic Media, 2006. (Reprint)

Edwards, David L., and John R. W. Stott. *Essentials.* London: Hodder & Stoughton, 1988.

Faulkner, Neil. *Apocalypse: The Great Jewish Revolt against Rome, AD 66–73.* Stroud, UK: Tempos, 2002.

Froom, Le Roy Edwin. *The Conditionalist Faith of Our Fathers.* Washington, D.C.: Review & Herald, 1966.

Fudge, Edward. *The Fire That Consumes: A Biblical and Historical Study of Final Punishment.* Houston: Providential, 1982.

Garner, Rod. *Like a Bottle in the Smoke: Meditations on Mystery.* Peterborough, UK: Inspire, 2006.

———. *On Being Saved: The Roots of Redemption.* London: Darton, Longman, & Todd, 2011.

Greene, Graham. *Brighton Rock: An Entertainment.* Vintage Classics. New York: Viking, 1938.

Guillebaud, Harold E. *The Righteous Judge: A Study of the Biblical Doctrine of Everlasting Punishment.Taunton, UK: Phoenix, 1964.

Gulley, Philip, and Mulholland, James. *If Grace Is True: Why God Will Save Every Person.* New York: HarperOne, 2003.

Hick, John. *Evil and the God of Love.* Basingstoke, UK: Palgrave Macmillan, 1966, 1977, 1985.

Humphries, Colin J. *The Miracles of Exodus: A Scientist's Discovery of the Extraordinary Natural Causes of the Biblical Stories.* London: Continuum, 2003.

Irenaeus. *Against Heresies.* From vol. 1 of *Ante-Nicene Fathers*, edited by Alexander Roberts, James Donaldson, and A. Cleveland Coxe, and translated by Alexander

Roberts and William Rambaut. Buffalo, NY: Christian Literature, 1885. Revised and edited for *New Advent* by Kevin Knight, 2009. http://www.newadvent.org/fathers/0103303.htm.

Jones, James. *Jesus and the Earth.* London: SPCK, 2003.

———. *Why Do People Suffer? The Scandal of Pain in God's World.* Oxford: Lion, 1993.

Josephus, Flavius. *Antiquities of the Jews.* In *The Works of Flavius Josephus: The Jewish Historian,* translated by William Whiston. London: Bowyer, 1737. http://www.sacred-texts.com/jud/josephus/ant-10.htm.

Jung, C. G. *Memories, Dreams, Reflections.* Edited by Anelia Jaffé and translated by Richard Winston and Clara Winston. London: Fontana, 1995.

Kendall, R. T., and David Rosen. *The Christian and the Pharisee: Two Outspoken Religious Leaders Debate the Road to Heaven.* London: Hodder & Stoughton, 2006.

King, Martin Luther, Jr. *Strength to Love.* Philadelphia: Fortress, 1963.

Kivengere, Festo. *Revolutionary Love.* Eastbourne, UK: Kingsway, 1985.

Kuhrt, Stephen. *Tom Wright for Everyone: Putting the Theology of N. T. Wright into Practice in the Local Church.* London: SPCK, 2011.

Lewis, C. S. *The Great Divorce: A Dream.* Glasgow: Fontana, 1946.

———. *A Grief Observed.* London: Faber & Faber, 1961.

———. *Mere Christianity.* London: Bles, 1952. Reprint, London: Fount Paperbacks, 1977.

———. *The Problem of Pain.* Publisher: New York: HarperOne, 2001.

MacCulloch, Diarmaid. *A History of Christianity: The First Three Thousand Years.* London: Lane, 2009.

MacDonald, Gregory. *The Evangelical Universalist.* London: SPCK, 2008.

Macgregor, G. H. C. *The New Testament Basis of Pacifism.* London: Clarke, 1936.

McGrath, Alister E. *Dawkins' God: Genes, Memes, and the Meaning of Life.* Malden, MA: Blackwell, 2007.

———. *Historical Theology: An Introduction to the History of Christian Thought.* Malden, MA: Blackwell, 1998.

Milne A. A. *Now We Are Six.* 3rd ed. London: Methuen, 1927.

Morgan, Alison. *The Wild Gospel: Bringing Truth to Life.* Oxford: Monarch, 2004.

Morse, Melvin, and Paul Perry. *Transformed by the Light: The Powerful Effect of Near-death Experiences on People's Lives.* Book Club Associates, 1992.

Motyer, J. Alec. *The Prophecy of Isaiah: An Introduction and Commentary.* Leicester, UK: InterVarsity, 1993.

———. *Isaiah: An Introduction and Commentary.* Tyndale Old Testament Commentaries 18. Downers' Grove: InterVarsity, 1999.

Murphy-O'Connor, Jerome. *Paul: A Critical Life.* New York: Oxford University Press, 1996.

National Council of the Churches of Christ in the United States of America and the Inclusive Language Lectionary Committee. *An Inclusive Language Lectionary: Readings for Year A.* Philadelphia: Pilgrim, 1983.

O'Grady, Selina. *And Man Created God: A History of the World at the Time of Jesus.* London: Atlantic, 2012.

Parker, Mike. "God Gave Them Strength to Forgive." *Inspire* 90 (2014) 18–19.

Pawson, David J. *Unlocking the Bible.* London: HarperCollins, 2007.

Polkinghorne, John C. *Science and Providence: God's Interaction with the World.* London: SPCK, 1989.

Ratcliffe, Susan. *Oxford Dictionary of Quotations by Subject.* 2nd ed. New York: Oxford
    University Press, 2010.

Restorative Justice Council. "What Is Restorative Justice?" August 18, 2014. http://
    www.restorativejustice.org.uk/what_is_restorative_justice/.

Richardson, Don. *Peace Child.* Glendale, CA: Regal, 1974.

Robinson, John A. T. *In the End, God: A Study of the Christian Doctrine of the Last
    Things.* Fontana Books, 1968.

Sanders, E. P. *Paul.* Oxford: Oxford University Press, 1991.

Sayers, Dorothy L. *Christian Letters to a Post-Christian World: A Selection of Essays.*
    Grand Rapids: Eerdmans, 1969.

Shillito, Edward. "Jesus of the Scars." In *The Message of the New Testament: Promises
    Kept*, by Mark Dever, 199. Wheaton, IL: Crossway, 2005.

Stott, John R. W. *The Living Church.* Inter Varsity Press, 2007.

Tacitus. *The Annals.* Translated by Alfred John Church and William Jackson Brodribb.
    Internet Classics Archive, edited by Daniel C. Stevenson, Web Atomics. http://
    classics.mit.edu/Tacitus/annals.mb.txt.

Tertullian. *Concerning Spectacles, Pseudepigrapha, Apocrypha and Sacred Writings.*
    http://www.pseudepigrapha.com/LostBooks/tertullian_spectacles.htm.

Tournier, Paul. *Guilt and Grace: A Psychological Study.* Translated by Arthur W.
    Heathcote et al. London: Hodder & Stoughton, 1962.

Trigg, Joseph Wilson. *Origen: The Bible and Philosophy in the Third-century Church.*
    Atlanta: John Knox, 1983.

Tutu, Desmond M., and Mpho A. Tutu. *The Book of Forgiving: The Fourfold Path for
    Healing Ourselves and Our World.* New York: HaperCollins, 2014.

Wenham, John W. "The Case for Conditional Immortality: Paper 6." In *Universalism
    and the Doctrine of Hell: Papers Presented at the Fourth Edinburgh Conference in
    Christian Dogmatics, 1991*, edited by Nigel M. de S. Cameron, 151–61. Grand
    Rapids: Baker, 1992.

———. *The Enigma of Evil: Can We Believe in the Goodness of God?* Grand Rapids:
    InterVarsity, 1985.

Wiesel, Elie. *Night.* Translated by Stella Rodway. New York: Hill & Wang, 1960.

Wright, N. T. *Evil and the Justice of God.* London: SPCK, 2006.

———. *Hebrews for Everyone.* London: SPCK, 2003.

———. *Jesus and the Victory of God.* London: SPCK, 1996.

———. *Matthew for Everyone: Part I.* London: SPCK, 2002.

———. "New Perspectives on Paul." Presentation at the 10th Edinburgh Dogmatics
    Conference, Rutherford House, Edinburgh, August 25–28, 2003.

———. *The New Testament and the People of God.* London: SPCK, 1992.

———. *The Radical Evangelical: Seeking a Place to Stand.* London: SPCK, 1996.

———. *The Resurrection of the Son of God.* London: SPCK, 2003.

———. *Revelation for Everyone.* London: SPCK, 2011.

———. *Surprised by Hope.* London: SPCK, 2007.

Zaleski, Carol, and Philip Zaleski, eds. *The Book of Heaven: An Anthology of Writings
    from Ancient to Modern Times.* New York: Oxford University Press, 2000.

Author Index

Subject Index

Scripture Index

Galatians
1:4	22
1:15–16	85
1:22	130
Chap 2, 3, 5,	130
2:20	22
3:27	130
4:6	56n203

Ephesians
1:1	75m
1:4	4
1:3–11, 18	137
1:10–11, 22	6n23, 141
3:18–19	v
4:4	65
4:8–10	176n96
4:18–19	158n30
4:22	35
4:32	97
5:2, 25	22
5:6	49n171, 50

Philippians
1:1	75
2:7–8	29
2:10–11	2n3 and 4, 6, 71, 141n95 and 96, 143, 159, 185, 197
3:4–6	7n25
3:10–11	185
3:19	145, 146

Colossians
1:2	75
1:15–20	6
1:20	2n3 and 4, 141, 197
1:25–27	95
2:13	50
2:13–15	24, 177
3:5–16	130
3:6	49, 50
3:9	35
3:10	33

1 Thessalonians
1:4–6	137
1:10	50
2:16	49, 50
5:9	50

2 Thessalonians
1:6–10	170 n72
1:9	2n2, 171
2:13	4

1 Timothy
1:13	158
2:3–6	2, 21, 36, 112, 141
2:6	22, 29
4:10	141

2 Timothy
1:10	4, 144
2:25	130

Titus
2:14	22
3:5–7	130

Hebrews
2:14–17	18
5:8–9	14
9	24n83
9:5	132
12:7–10	57
12:17	130
12:28–29	124
12:29	194

James
1:3	45n158
1:15	145
1:18	130
2	130
3:6	151
3:9	33
5:20	145

Lightning Source UK Ltd.
Milton Keynes UK
UKOW06f0157080315

247470UK00002B/37/P